A NIGHT SKY LACED
WITH FLAMING BULLETS

A call—"Stand up and hook up!"—rang through the C-47 cabin. It took an effort to stand. The paratroopers felt huge and bloated with their burdensome combat gear as they staggered into position, one behind the other. Hearts beat faster—and skipped beats. Stomachs churned. Palms sweated. It would only be seconds now.

Suddenly the green light—Go!—flashed on and troopers began leaping into the dark unknown. Clearing the C-47, Martin saw the enormous rectangle of black sky and felt the angry hurricane blasts ripping at his body. Then there was the white flash of exultation—his parachute popped open.

Moments later the darkness burst into flaming iridescence. Streams of angry white tracers from the ground laced the sky around Martin and the other troopers as they floated earthward under their billowing white canopies. Bullets hissed past the helpless Martin and ripped through his parachute. There was no question about it: He and his comrades were dropping onto a lethal hornets' nest.

THEY JUMPED AT MIDNIGHT

THE "CRASH" PARACHUTE MISSIONS THAT TURNED THE TIDE AT SALERNO

WILLIAM B. BREUER

JOVE BOOKS, NEW YORK

THEY JUMPED AT MIDNIGHT

A Jove Book / published by arrangement with
the author

PRINTING HISTORY
Zeus Publishers edition published 1983
Jove edition / October 1990

ISBN: 0-515-10425-6

Jove Books are published by The Berkley Publishing Group,
200 Madison Avenue, New York, New York 10016.
The name ''JOVE'' and the ''J'' logo
are trademarks belonging to Jove Publications, Inc.

PRINTED IN THE UNITED STATES OF AMERICA

10 9 8 7 6 5 4 3 2 1

Dedicated to
WILLIAM PELHAM YARBOROUGH
Lieutenant General (Ret.)

*Gallant warrior from the sky,
innovator, visionary, leader
of fighting men, patriot*

Acknowledgments

CREATING THIS BOOK would have been impossible without the invaluable assistance of scores of former warriors who participated in the parachute missions at Salerno–Avellino which tipped the scales toward the Anglo-Americans when victory or disaster hung in the balance on the flaming beachhead. They probed memories of that pivotal return of Allied armies to continental Europe in World War II and relayed them to the author in personal, telephonic and written communications. They dug up old combat diaries, letters and official reports and made these available.

The author also was blessed with the dedicated and active assistance of four of the most knowledgeable authorities on the death struggle at Salerno beachhead. All of these personalities found time from heavy commitments to read and critique chapter drafts, answer key questions, and contribute insights to the critical military operation on the Italian mainland.

Long retired but keen, active and possessors of computer-like memories, these four officers were General Mark Wayne

Clark, who as Fifth Army commander at Salerno bore the ultimate responsibility; Lieutenant General James M. Gavin, who bailed out at the head of his parachute regiment; Lieutenant General William P. Yarborough, airborne advisor to General Clark, who conceived and recommended the crucial "crash" paratrooper missions; and Colonel Warren R. Williams, who jumped with his battalion and led it in the savage fight to seize and hold Hill 424, where the Germans made their last desperate effort to break through to the sea.

The author expresses his deep appreciation to the retired distinguished Military Editor of the *London Times*, Hugh Pond, a wartime major of the British 6th Airborne Division (the famed Red Devils), for making available his extensive recollections and data on the German army activities and civilians at Salerno.

Lou Varrone, a former American paratrooper, was most helpful with names, details and anecdotes with regard to civilians around Avellino, deep behind German lines. These Avellino civilians were and are his relatives and friends.

Colonel Donald P. Shaw, director, and his superb staff at the United States Army History Institute provided research assistance and background documents from its archives. Laurence Maxton, an amateur airborne historian, furnished the author with significant research material.

Times of airborne task force takeoffs and mass parachute jumps were dug out of United States Air Force records. The German viewpoint and actions at the higher levels of command were drawn from numerous authoritative sources, including the memoirs of Field Marshal Albert Kesselring, Field Marshal Wilhelm Keitel, and Lieutenant General Fridolin von Senger und Etterlin.

WILLIAM B. BREUER
Chicago
April 1983

Contents

Introduction

MOMENTOUS EVENTS WERE unfolding in the Mediterranean region in mid-1943. Spearheaded by parachute elements of the U.S. 82nd Airborne Division and glidermen of the British 1st Airborne Division, a massive Anglo-American force invaded Sicily on July 9 and overran that key outpost of Adolph Hitler's Fortress Europe in a lightning 38-day campaign.

The major disaster in Sicily broke the back of an already demoralized Italian military establishment and civilian population. On July 25 mild little King Victor Emmanuel III summarily dismissed Hitler's good friend, Benito Mussolini, as Italian premier, a post the squat, bombastic dictator had held for 21 years. The monarch then had Mussolini arrested and locked up at an undisclosed locale.

Hoping to continue the momentum from the Sicilian victory, the American-British Combined Chiefs of Staff, meeting in a stormy session in Quebec, on August 18 ordered General Dwight D. Eisenhower, a self-styled Kansas farm boy and Allied Supreme Commander in the Mediterranean, to invade Italy.

The assault on Hitler's *Festung Europa* (Fortress Europe) would consist of two coordinated amphibious operations. General Bernard L. Montgomery's British Eighth Army would "leapfrog" from Sicily across the narrow Strait of Messina onto the toe of mainland Italy under cover of darkness on September 3. The maneuver was code-named *Operation Baytown*.

Montgomery's mission was to draw off enemy forces from in front of U.S. Lieutenant General Mark W. Clark's Fifth Army, which would storm ashore six days later, on September 9, at the Gulf of Salerno, far up the western coast of mountainous Italy. Code-named *Operation Avalanche*, the Fifth Army assault had as its primary objective the capture of the large port of Naples, on D-Day + 13. *Avalanche* would be the Allies' Sunday punch.

To thwart powerful German forces around Rome from rushing southward into Fifth Army assault troops coming ashore, the 82nd Airborne Division was assigned a key mission: Land along the east-west flowing Volturno River, 40 miles north of Salerno City, in an operation code-named *Giant 1*.

Late in August, electrifying events were in motion behind the scenes. King Victor Emmanuel and his new premier, aging Marshal Pietro Badaglio, through an emissary, gained an armistice with the United States and Great Britain, after which Italy would join the war against Germany. Frightened by the specter of bloody German retaliation, the Italians requested that an entire Allied airborne division be dropped on Rome to secure the capital. Eisenhower agreed.

As a result, *Giant 1* was cancelled. Highly distressed that the elite 82nd Airborne Division (known as the All Americans) was taken from him just before the Salerno invasion to jump on Rome, General Clark was soothed by the Supreme Commander in fatherly tones: "Now, keep your shirt on."

Announcing the Italian armistice had to be delicately timed. Eisenhower would read the surrender terms over Radio Algiers on the evening of September 8, and Marshal Badoglio would follow suit over Radio Rome, only hours before the Fifth Army assault at Salerno. On hearing General Eisenhower broadcast the surrender, Major General Matthew B. Ridgway's 82nd Airborne Division would take off from Sicilian airfields to drop around Rome.

1
Suicide Mission: Jump on Rome

GENERAL MATT RIDGWAY, the brusque, no-nonsense commander of the 82nd Airborne Division, strode briskly into the quonset hut that housed the operations center of Fifteenth Army Group at Cassibile, Sicily. It was late in the evening of September 2, and a tired Mediterranean sun was lazily drifting into the depths of the western horizon.

Earlier in the day at his headquarters near Kairouan, in North Africa, Ridgway had received an urgent message from Allied Force Headquarters, Algiers: Report at once to Fifteenth Army Group. There was no mention of the reason for the order.

Winging his way across the clear blue Mediterranean Sea, Ridgway had mixed feelings about the pressing summons. On the one hand he was elated over the possibility his airborne command might receive a new mission after having been informed earlier in the day that *Giant 1*, the drop along the Volturno River, had been cancelled. On the other hand, he and his 82nd Airborne commanders were always apprehensive on learning that a new mission was in the works. Too many of these airborne missions, the men who would carry them out knew, were wild-eyed schemes concocted at the higher levels by officers totally unfamiliar with the capabilities and limitations of parachute and glider forces.

Now at the operations center in Cassibile, a British colonel got right to the point. There was no time for idle chit-chat. Such an approach suited Ridgway fine. It was his customary style for conducting business on urgent matters.

"You will land the strongest airborne force possible on three airfields just north of Rome the night of September 8–9 and seize control of the city," the operations officer explained. "The mission will be code-named *Giant 2*."

Ridgway was shocked that an airborne operation of that complexity and peril would be laid on by the Allied high command without prior consultation with the commanding general of the division scheduled to accomplish the mission. He listened in silence as the briefing continued.

The British colonel went on to explain that other key facets of the plan to seize Rome from the Germans called for the extensive cooperation of Italian troops and an amphibious landing near the mouth of the historic Tiber River where it emptied into the Tyrrhenian Sea.

Dedicated soldier that he was, General Ridgway offered no immediate protest to the Rome airborne operation. It called for dropping a few thousand lightly armed paratroopers, without artillery support, antitank guns, tanks, tactical air cover, or a reasonably certain method for resupply into the midst of heavy German troop concentrations in and around a sprawling city of 3 million people, 200 miles from the nearest armed Allied soldier.

Giant 2 had all the ingredients of a suicide mission.

Ridgway, tormented in mind and spirit, slept fitfully that night. Foremost in his thoughts was the specter of swarms of German panzers around Rome descending upon his isolated paratroopers. His parachutists would have only the woefully ineffective 2.36-inch rocket launchers (bazookas) to ward off enemy tanks. And the bazooka rockets in Sicily bounced off the front of German Tigers much as a mosquito would bounce off the hide of a charging rhinoceros.

Giant 2 was an ambitious plan. It called for the entire 82nd Airborne Division to be delivered in and around Rome on two successive nights. Colonel Reuben H. Tucker's 504th Parachute Infantry Regiment would drop the first night on Fubara airport, just north of the Tiber River, near the Tyrrhenian Sea. Tucker and his parachutists would take off from scattered airfields in Sicily at 6:30 P.M. the evening of September 8. Their cue to liftoff for Rome would be hearing the voice of Supreme Commander Dwight Eisenhower reading Italian armistice terms over Radio Algiers.

Colonel James M. Gavin's 505th Parachute Infantry Regiment would bail out the next night over Glidonia, Littoria and Centrocella airfields, all located about 25 miles northeast of Rome. After Gavin's men had seized the three airfields, the 325th Glider Infantry Regiment of Colonel Harry Lewis, headquarters, signal, medical and light artillery components would land in C-47s.

Meanwhile, at his office on the top floor of the St. George Hotel in Algiers, General Eisenhower was conferring with two civilians. They were Robert Murphy, a high-level member of the United States diplomatic corps who had been sent to the Mediterranean a year before to take charge of American non-military interests, and Harold Macmillan, a prominent British diplomat.

Visualizing the civilian chaos once the 82nd Airborne had seized Rome, General Ridgway had insisted that the experienced Murphy and Macmillan accompany the paratroopers and glidermen into Rome and bring order out of anarchy in the civil sector.

It was a hazardous task General Ridgway was proposing for the two diplomats—but a vital one. Murphy and Macmillan leaped to accept the assignment. But Eisenhower was skeptical, even deeply concerned, as to the safety of the diplomats.

Now, seated before the Supreme Commander, Murphy and Macmillan were, in effect, pleading their case. Eisenhower listened in silence, brow furrowed, chewing idly on the tips of his horn-rimmed reading glasses. As the diplomats awaited a verdict, Eisenhower stared at each man for a moment. Then

he remarked dryly: "Well, all right, you can go. As far as I
know there's nothing in army regulations which says diplomats are not expendable."

On the evening of September 5, Lieutenant General Mark W.
Clark, his three stars glistening in the setting Mediterranean sun, boarded the command ship, USS *Ancon*, in Algiers
harbor. Clark, who two days before had been admonished by
his boss, Dwight Eisenhower, to "keep your shirt on," was
beset by inner torment. His concerns were more than the
customary ones of a general going into major combat action
for the first time. Clark could not shake off the haunting vision of German forces rushing south over the Volturno River
to smash into his vulnerable seaborne invaders. There would
be no battle-tested 82nd Airborne Division at the Volturno to
halt or slow down these enemy reinforcements.

The first evening aboard the *Ancon*, the tall general decided to retire early. He had spent a long, exhausting day and
knew he needed all the strength he could muster for the crucial days and nights that lay ahead. Before turning off the
light, Clark, as long had been his custom each day, read from
a little book he carried entitled *Daily Word*, a Unity publi-
cation.

Flipping the pages to the prayer for September 5, 1943,
the Fifth Army commander was startled to note that the prayer
for this particular day seemed to have been prepared precisely
for the current circumstances. It read, in part:

Father, in Thy name I pray, let me know Thy will today. With Thee I am unafraid, for on Thee my mind is
stayed. Though a thousand foes surround, safe in Thee
I shall be found.

I have faith that Thou will be, always guarding and
directing me. In the air, on sea, on land, Thy sure
protection is at hand. Momently Thy love I share, Thy
grace, and Thy protecting care.

Mark Clark flipped off the light. He slept well that night.
Shortly after dawn, the *Ancon* edged out of Algiers harbor

to join a convoy of nearly 70 vessels escorted by the United States cruisers *Philadelphia*, *Boise* and *Savannah* and 14 destroyers. Clark's convoy would rendezvous with others sailing from North African and Sicilian ports.

As the *Ancon* was moving out to sea, it passed a tiny native vessel. The Algerian civilians on board waved vigorously at the Allied soldiers lining the deck. One called out, "Have a good time in Naples!"

Men on the *Ancon* were startled. If these Algerian civilians knew the target of the Allied assault, did the Germans know it also?

Since 46-year-old Matt Ridgway of the 82nd Airborne Division had received orders for the parachute drops on Rome a few days before, he and his two young paratroop colonels, James Gavin and Reuben Tucker, had become increasingly concerned over what promised to be the almost certain destruction of the elite unit. As a result of their growing alarm, a difficult decision was reached: General Ridgway would seek to get *Giant 2* cancelled.

The 82nd Airborne commander met hurriedly with General Harold R.L.G. Alexander, leader of Fifteenth Army Group, and Major General Walter B. "Beetle" Smith, Eisenhower's Chief of Staff and alter ego. Alexander and Smith listened without comment to General Ridgway's presentation of the military factors which indicated disaster for the paratroopers and glidermen. His pleadings were in vain: The drop on Rome stood as planned.

The die was cast.

As a result, on September 4 and 5, the 82nd Airborne Division was flown from its tent encampment in Tunisia to Sicily in order to depart for Rome from airfields closer to the Italian capital.

On the afternoon of September 6, the 82nd Airborne's two parachute colonels, Reuben Tucker and James Gavin, were given sealed envelopes at the division's encampment outside Licata, Sicily. Inside were secret orders detailing *Giant 2*, the airborne strike to take control of Rome. Taking his envelope to a deserted olive grove near the operations center, 31-year-old Rube Tucker went over the plan. He let out a low whistle as if to say: "This is the hottest job of the war!"

That night in his barracks, Colonel Tucker was briefing his commanders on the parachute operation, now less than 48 hours away. Despite security precautions to prevent un- authorized personnel from overhearing his remarks, Tucker became increasingly enthused and his words behind closed doors echoed down the hall where several war correspondents were lounging.

Tucker's booming voice warned his confidants in the bar- racks room: "Now you fellows know and I know what I'm talking about. But if anybody so much as mentions the name of that goddamned *town*, I'll have him court-martialed and shot."

"That town" was Rome.

Elsewhere a rumor swept the 82nd Airborne camp: Guards had received orders to shoot anyone trying to leave the grounds without official permission.

"Do you think that rumor is true?" a trooper asked a comrade.

"I'll be goddamned if I know!" was the reply. "But I'm sure not going to be the first one to find out—the hard way!"

The shoot-to-kill rumor sparked the wildest speculation among troopers as to the target of the impending parachute mission. "We're jumping out over Berlin," one trooper con- fided to his comrades. "A real suicide mission. We're sup- posed to kill Hitler."

Earlier that morning three figures dressed in paratrooper uniforms were seated at the foot of an olive tree at a secluded portion of the 82nd Airborne encampment. They were deeply involved in conversation. Colonel George Lynch, a staff of- ficer in the All American division, was relating the latest details on *Giant 2* to Cy Korman, a correspondent of the *Chicago Tribune*, and Richard Tregaskis, a syndicated re- porter and noted author. The two war correspondents would accompany the 82nd Airborne and had already been briefed on plans for the Rome operation.

"According to the latest poop we've obtained," Colonel Lynch began in a secretive tone, even though there was not another human for a hundred yards, "the Italians will light the way into the airfields for us. They will also turn on beacons which will light the way for our C-47 pilots to locate the airfields."

Tregaskis and Korman listened in silence. In their minds was the big question: "How do we *know* the Italians are going to do all these things—and what if they don't?"

Lynch continued: "The Italians are even going to make a diversion for us with their own airplanes, shooting down any *Luftwaffe* fighter planes that may try to interfere with our operation."

The correspondents were dubious. They thought: The Italian air force was almost totally reluctant to fight the Anglo-Americans in Sicily two months before, so why would Italianpilots suddenly battle the *Luftwaffe* in the skies above Rome?

"There are strong *Wehrmacht* forces in Italy, including a battle-tested panzer division in the immediate Rome area," Colonel Lynch continued. "But if we move quickly and deploy our forces skillfully, we may be able to influence the fate of the entire Italian campaign."

The three men got to their feet, and with a wide grin Lynch added, "Hell, if everything goes all right we will even have our own fighter planes installed at the Italian airfields around Rome by nightfall. And the Italian planes and pilots will be at our disposal."

Colonel Lynch knew, as did Korman and Tregaskis, that this rosy litany of high-level Allied hopes was replete with "ifs," "buts," and "maybes." Lynch was simply projecting the point of view of General Eisenhower and his top aides.

Despite his early enthusiasm for the Rome airborne mission, Eisenhower became increasingly concerned that *Giant 2* could result in a momentous disaster. The Supreme Commander was particularly worried over the true intentions of the Italian government. Italian assistance was crucial to the success of the airborne operation.

Eisenhower, with the hours ticking away and time for the parachute drops edging closer, made a crucial decision: He would send two American officers on a perilous trek into enemy-held Rome to determine first-hand if the Italians could

PROPOSED AND ACTUAL MISSIONS
IN THE
INVASION OF ITALY
LEGEND

produce all that General Giuseppe Castellano, the armistice emissary, assured the Allies that they could.

Selected for the clandestine mission were Brigadier General Maxwell D. Taylor, the 43-year-old artillery commander of the 82nd Airborne Division, and Colonel William Tudor Gardiner, commander of a Troop Carrier squadron stationed in Sicily. Each man was chosen because of his demonstrated resourcefulness and ability to speak and understand Italian.

General Taylor taught languages at West Point from 1927 to 1932, and spoke five languages fluently. The burly Gardiner, a lawyer and former governor of Maine, had excelled as college oarsman. He learned to fly at age 45. At the time he appeared before General Eisenhower to receive instructions Gardiner was 53.

Taylor, the senior officer of the two-man team, was told that he had total authority to radio back from Rome any changes in the parachute operation that he felt were vital. He was also empowered to cancel the 82nd Airborne drop if he determined conditions in Rome might result in disaster for the invading force from the sky.

If Taylor's decision was to cancel the mass drop, he had to radio a single word—"Innocuous."

Boarding a British PT boat for the first leg of their crucial mission, General Taylor and Colonel Gardiner left the harbor in Palermo, Sicily, at 2 A.M. on September 7. It would be only 41 hours until Colonel Rube Tucker and his 504th Parachute Infantry Regiment lifted off to bail out over Rome. The dark waters of the Tyrrhenian Sea were rough and menacing, but at 6:45 A.M. the fast motor-torpedo boat reached its first destination—Ustica island, due north of Palermo.

Minutes after reaching Ustica, Taylor and Gardiner sighted an Italian corvette racing toward them from the open sea. It was a tense moment. Was this a friendly Italian crew aboard or the German *Kriegsmarine* manning an Italian vessel sent to scuttle the Rome-bound delegation—literally?

The corvette *Ibis* edged alongside the PT boat as Taylor and Gardiner breathed sighs of relief. It was a "friendly" Italian crew.

Sailors on the *Ibis* had difficulty in mooring the vessels

together in order to transfer the two Americans. Heavy winds had whipped the sea into angry high waves. So the PT boat and the corvette stood off as the Italian ship lowered a smaller boat in which to transfer Taylor and Gardiner. The two craft, bobbing and swaying in the heavy swells, were about 30 yards apart.

The Americans looked on as two Italian sailors and a navy officer climbed into the tiny transfer boat. Then an Italian army officer got into the boat. Then another army officer leaped in, followed by several others. Finally three Italian navy men and 10 army officers had shoe-horned their way into the little craft.

Expecting the transfer boat to capsize in the tossing waves at any moment, Taylor and Gardiner were relieved to see the tiny vessel edge alongside the PT boat. The two Americans somehow squeezed on board and the return trip to the *Ibis* was negotiated without capsizing—much to the astonishment of Gardiner and Taylor. An immaculately uniformed Italian admiral greeted the Americans on the *Ibis*, and the small warship set a course for the bustling port of Gaeta, 75 miles south of Rome. The ship arrived there at 5:30 P.M.

Shortly before reaching the dock at Gaeta, the Italian admiral said to the Americans, "I would strongly suggest that you remove your insignia and hide your decorations before we go ashore. You must look disconsolate, as though you are American pilots who had been shot down and are now prisoners."

Both Americans removed their insignia and Gardiner took off the rows of ribbons for his Silver Star, Legion of Merit, Air Medal and other decorations. Inwardly he felt foolish for wearing the "fruit salad" on a clandestine operation deep into enemy territory. As an afterthought, Gardiner tossed a British cape over his uniform.

The two Americans and the admiral walked to a waiting Italian navy staff car and climbed into the back seat. With a clashing of gears, the driver moved off through the narrow streets of Gaeta, crowded with humanity, donkey carts, bicycles, farm wagons and an occasional civilian automobile, property of a local high-ranking Fascist. Presently the navy staff car reduced speed. In front were two truckloads of German soldiers moving along slowly in the same direction. The alarmed driver felt it unwise to pass the *Wehrmacht* vehicle and possibly attract the suspicions of the occupants if the Germans would spot the two Americans.

On the outskirts of Gaeta, General Taylor and Colonel Gardiner were transferred to an ambulance for the 75-mile run up the twisting coastal road to Rome. The pair of Americans and the Italian admiral, who spent much time talking about his ship's pre-war visit to southern and western ports in the United States, and an Italian in civilian clothes scrambled into the back of the medical vehicle, its several red crosses gleaming in the sunlight. The driver sped northward with his "patients."

Taylor and Gardiner regularly peeked out of the three slots in the back of the ambulance to view German soldiers in the villages through which the vehicle passed. On occasion the ambulance had to slow to pick its way through marching companies of *Wehrmacht* infantry.

Suddenly, an electric wave of apprehension flooded the ambulance. It had rounded a sharp curve in the road and came upon a checkpoint manned by several Germans. A stern-faced *Wehrmacht* soldier, a Schmeisser machine pistol gripped in one hand, stood in the center of the road, lifted a hand and shouted: *"Halten Sie!"* (Halt!)

The driver pumped the brakes and the ancient Italian medical vehicle lurched to a stop 10 feet in front of the German sentry, a tall, blond man with a stern face. His coal-bucket shaped helmet was clamped tightly on his head and his jackboots were polished to a high gloss. There was a little slot at the front of the ambulance compartment through which Taylor and Gardiner could see the sentry. Other German soldiers were in a nearby guardhouse.

The two Americans felt their hearts skip a beat as the German soldier walked up to the driver's side and barked, "Let me see your papers!" The driver instantly produced his authorization for the trip (transferring wounded American prisoners to a hospital in Rome) and the German scanned the document intensely. Without another word or change of expression, the sentry handed the paper back to the driver, then peered into the slot in the front of the patient compartment.

The stoic German, still without a word or change of expression, jumped down from the ambulance and waved the vehicle onward. With a raucous shifting of gears, the medical vehicle and its high-ranking American officers churned off along the coastal road once again. It had been a close call.

Slowed in the motor journey by numerous road blocks, the two Americans arrived at the Palazzo Caprara, in Rome, at 8:30 P.M., just as night was drawing its ominous cloak about the Eternal City on the seven hills. The large old stone building was part of the Italian war office.

General Taylor and Colonel Gardiner made prompt inquiries as to the whereabouts of General Giuseppe Castellano, the diminutive young officer who had been Premier Pietro Badoglio's emissary in armistice negotiations with the Allies in Madrid, Lisbon and later Sicily. They were told that Castellano was "unavailable," and could not be seen until morning. Taylor and Gardiner shot quick glances at each other. They did not like the way matters were shaping up. Why would Castellano not be on hand to greet them?

A number of Italian officers appeared at the Palazzo Caprara and identified themselves as aides to *Generale di Corpo d'Armata* Giacomo Carboni, who had been chief of the Italian army intelligence since August 18 and who, only a few days previously, had been issued an ambiguous verbal order by Marshal Badoglio to "protect Rome" without advising Carboni against whom or what he was to protect it.

The two Americans had dinner with the pleasant Italian staff officers who, at the conclusion of the meal, told Taylor and Gardiner, "We know you must be quite tired. We should leave you alone for the night and you can talk with General Carboni in the morning."

Taylor and Gardiner now were convinced the Italians were stalling. Quite obviously, the pair of Americans did not make the lengthy, dangerous trek into hostile Rome to promptly go to bed.

"I insist that you send for General Carboni, immediately," Taylor told the staff officers. Realizing General Taylor was firm in his position, one of the Italians slipped out of the room and returned a few minutes later. "The general is on his way and will be here shortly," he told the Americans.

At 10:15 P.M., General Carboni and several aides arrived. With him he had a large map which showed the disposition of his four divisions around Rome.

"But the Germans have greatly increased their forces in the vicinity," Carboni explained with a trace of concern. "There had been 8,000 Germans to the south of Rome and 3,000 to the north. But they have reinforced the area and now there are 125 heavy tanks and 150 light tanks and 24,000 men south of Rome, and 12,000 north of Rome."

Carboni paused only briefly to allow the Americans to digest his gloomy presentation, then resumed: "In addition, the Germans have about 12,000 men on both sides of the Tiber in the Rome vicinity with 100 artillery pieces. Most of those are .88s, which, as you know, are deadly against low-flying airplanes."

The Italian general had more adverse news on the situation around Rome only 24 hours before Rube Tucker's 504th Parachute Infantry Regiment was to bail out over nearby airfields and move quickly in the direction of Rome.

"Kesselring has become increasingly suspicious of our intentions," Carboni stated. "They have cut off the gasoline supply to our Italian forces in the area and some of our ammunition." *Feldmarschall* Albert Kesselring was commander-in-chief of all *Wehrmacht* forces in the Mediterranean region.

Carboni told the Americans that he was convinced that Anglo-American forces were far too small for both the landing at Salerno and the parachute mission on Rome. "If an armistice were publicly announced over Radio Rome, the Germans would promptly march on the city, take control of it, and restore a Fascist government to power."

"What would you suggest be done?" General Taylor asked.

"Land north of Rome with at least 15 divisions," was the reply. "The Gulf of Salerno is too far away from Rome."

Taylor and Gardiner tried not to reveal their inner aston-

ishment. The Italians were not supposed to know that the
Allies would strike at Salerno.

Had the wily General Carboni tossed in the Gulf of Salerno as an educated guess to see what would be the facial
reactions to the disclosure that he apparently knew the precise
landing beaches? Or was the Salerno target a matter of common knowledge among Italian and German military leaders?
At that very moment a massive convoy of 500 Allied vessels
was steaming toward the white beaches of Salerno.

"What about your emissary General Castellano's repeated
promises of assistance from the Italian military for the parachute drop?" the grim-faced General Taylor inquired.

Carboni shrugged his shoulders. "Castellano did not have
the facts when he was talking with your leaders and did not
know the Germans had taken gasoline and ammunition from
our units," Carboni explained. "Nor did he know that the
Germans had rushed in reinforcements around Rome."

Taylor, thoughtfully, told Carboni that in light of the considerable changes in the situation around Rome he would have
to meet with Marshal Badoglio at once. It was then nearing
midnight.

Covering their insignia but still in full uniform, General
Taylor and Colonel Gardiner, accompanied by the nervous
General Carboni, were driven through the darkened, eerie
streets of Rome to the residence occupied by 74-year-old
Marshal Badoglio, the head of the Italian government. Badoglio lived in a sumptuous mansion of much marble and
tile, surrounded by a large garden alive with flowers, shrubbery and trees.

The household servants were up as there had been an air
raid on the outskirts of Rome. One of them awakened the old
marshal and 15 minutes later the head of the Italian state
received his American visitors in his study. Badoglio greeted
Taylor and Gardiner cordially and without waste of time the
conference began. It was a tense moment. The stakes were
high—the possible destruction of the U.S. 82nd Airborne Division. The elite parachute fighting unit would be taking off
for Rome from airfields in Sicily in 17 hours.

Badoglio spent several minutes explaining his great desire

to cooperate with the Allies. "But if I declare an armistice now, the Germans will take Rome and put in a government unfriendly to us," he explained with an apologetic tone.

General Taylor by now was fast losing his patience with the vacillating attitude of the Italian leaders. He glanced at his watch; every minute of indecision that ticked by brought the All American division that much closer to being irretrievably committed.

"Marshal, you should know that this current situation is most serious and I must warn you of the consequences to your government, the Italian people and the nation because of your change in attitude," the American airborne officer stated firmly.

"I am helpless to do anything," the aging marshal responded resignedly.

Frustrated, deeply concerned, anxious, Taylor and Gardiner knew they had reached an impasse with the reluctant Italian leaders. The parting was amicable, with profuse expressions of regret, respect and enduring friendship from both sides.

As the Americans started for the door, Marshal Badoglio and General Carboni stood at attention and clicked their booted heels together in precise European military fashion. In response, feeling awkward and foolish to a degree, Taylor and Gardiner did likewise. They were unschooled in the heel-clicking practice.

With tears in his eyes over the dilemma in which he had become entwined while endeavoring to avoid bloodshed and destruction for his tormented and warweary Italy, Badoglio said softy, "I have been a soldier for nearly 50 years." It was as though he longed to add, "And now look at the mess I'm in—at odds with both sides."

Before leaving Badoglio's mansion at 1:10 A.M. on September 8, General Taylor arranged to wire his own estimate of the Rome situation to General Eisenhower in Algiers. The drop on Rome was only 23 hours away. The clock was ticking.

A few hours later, a glorious dawn broke over the Mediterranean. In their stifling hot tent encampment around Li-

cata, Sicily, members of Colonel Rube Tucker's 504th
Parachute Infantry Regiment began to stir. An aura of anxiety
and excitement hovered over the landscape. Before another
daybreak arrived, these men knew they would be fighting for
control of the fabled city of Rome. At least, those who survived would be fighting.

Shortly after a breakfast of powdered eggs, the Five-O-
Fours, grim-faced and with idle conversation at a minimum,
began drawing ammunition and rations. Then began one of
the most nerve-wracking parts of any parachute drop behind
enemy lines—waiting for the mission to commence.

An ancient Sicilian schoolhouse was serving as headquarters of the Troop Carrier Command whose lumbering C-47s
would transport the paratroopers to the designated airfields
around Rome. Conversation among the young pilots was at a
minimum, and the usual nervous stomachs and taut nerves
were commonplace. They knew that Rome was ringed with
German and Italian antiaircraft guns, particularly along the
historic Tiber River astride which they would fly.

The operations room in the schoolhouse was a particular
beehive of activity. It was crammed with perspiring, cursing,
wildly gesticulating Air Corps officers winding up final details for the transportation phase of *Giant 2*.

At 8:10 A.M. that morning, the eighth, the decoded messages from Maxwell Taylor and Badoglio were handed to a
tense General Eisenhower in his office atop the St. George
Hotel in Algiers. Putting on his reading glasses, the Supreme
Commander anxiously perused the radiograms. General Taylor's message declared that the airborne landings around Rome
would probably meet with disaster, due to the failure of the
Italians to declare an armistice and to safeguard the airfields,
furnish transportation for the American parachutists, and
carry out operations to assist the invaders.

Taylor's message concluded that he was awaiting instructions on how to proceed.

Badoglio, in his radiogram, merely outlined the set of circumstances as to why he could not fulfill the agreements he had
previously approved—the public announcement of the armistice
and rendering assistance to the 82nd Airborne Division.

Eisenhower was both furious and deeply disturbed. He hastily called a staff conference and a radiogram was hurriedly composed and fired off to Marshal Badoglio. The Supreme Commander sternly warned Badoglio that postponing the armistice announcement was unacceptable:

"I intend to broadcast the existence of the armistice at the hour originally planned (6:30 P.M. that same day, September 8). If you or any part of your armed forces fail to cooperate, as previously agreed, I will publish to the world the full report of this affair."

In Rome, the aging head of state read the strongly worded Eisenhower radiogram. It was obvious that the Supreme Commander was thoroughly angry. Confused, alarmed, caught in the center of a situation from which there appeared to be no solution, Badoglio agreed to read the armistice terms over Radio Rome as planned, one-half hour after Eisenhower broadcast the terms over Radio Algiers.

After a few hours of fitful sleep, General Taylor and Colonel Gardiner arose shortly after dawn in Rome. At 8:45 A.M., Italian Major Gino Marchesi appeared and told the two Americans that the messages to Eisenhower's headquarters had gone out at 1:55 A.M. and moments later another staff officer arrived to report the messages had been received at Algiers.

As the morning progressed, Taylor and Gardiner became increasingly nervous as no reply was forthcoming from AFHQ (Allied Force Headquarters) to their request for "further instructions." By 11 A.M., despite the best glares the two Americans could send at the radio receiving set, the instrument remained silent. What to do now? The moment of decision was at hand for Taylor.

Acting with the authority given to him by the Supreme Commander, at 11:55 A.M., only 12 hours before Colonel Tucker's Five-O-Fours were to bail out over the airfields near Rome, Taylor fired off a two-word message to the Supreme Commander in Algiers—"Situation Innocuous."

Giant 2, the ambitious airborne operation which had been opposed as disastrous in concept by combat commanders in the 82nd Airborne Division, was summarily cancelled.

Eisenhower issued the cancellation order in Algiers. But the paratroopers were located several hundred miles across the Mediterranean Sea, in Sicily. The plan called for Colonel Reuben Tucker and his Five-O-Fours to be loaded into their C-47s at Sicilian airfields when General Eisenhower read armistice terms with Italy over Radio Algiers at 6:30 that evening. As soon as 82nd Airborne commanders heard the Supreme Commander's voice, the paratroop-laden C-47s were to liftoff for Rome.

It was a primitive communications arrangement, one fraught with the danger of misunderstanding.

Eisenhower was worried that Colonel Tucker might not receive the message that the Rome mission had been cancelled. Or that the message might be garbled or misinterpreted. So he ordered Brigadier General Lyman L. Lemnitzer, an American and Deputy Chief of Staff of Fifteenth Army Group, to fly immediately to Sicily and personally hand the cancellation of *Giant 2* order to General Ridgway, commander of the 82nd Airborne.

Lemnitzer and his pilot promptly took off from Bizerte, in North Africa, and set a course for Licata, Sicily. The U.S. Air Corps pilot became disoriented and instead of knifing over the southern coast of Sicily near Licata he nearly missed the large island entirely.

The general with the crucial order became increasingly nervous as the minutes ticked by and the pilot could not orient himself. Finally, in the northeast portion of the triangular-shaped island, Lemnitzer and the pilot spotted a landmark—towering Mount Etna. The aircraft reversed its course and headed for its destination.

As time for General Eisenhower's armistice broadcast neared, General Ridgway and his aides drove to the Troop Carrier Command headquarters near Licata. There, gathered around a radio, the airborne officers awaited the announcement over Radio Algiers. At 6:25 P.M., five minutes before Eisenhower was to take to the airwaves, the radio began to cackle, hum and roar. Then it fell silent.

The frantic officers cursed the set and hammered on it with their fists. It refused to operate. Colonel Ralph P. Eaton,

Ridgway's Chief of Staff, dashed down the hall in search of another radio. Eaton located a small commercial receiver, snatched it off a table and bolted back into the room where the officers were gathered. The set was flipped on—just in time to hear General Eisenhower's concluding sentence.

The signal to launch the parachute strike on Rome had been given.

General Ridgway and his aides dashed out of Troop Carrier Command and back to the 82nd Airborne headquarters. Colonel Tucker was immediately signaled to take off. At several airfields motors revved and the bulky C-47s began moving onto the runways.

With several of the squat, low-winged transport planes already in the air, General Limnitzer landed at Licata airfield, rushed to General Ridgway and breathlessly advised him of the cancellation order. Frantic messages were sent recalling C-47s already in the air.

In Rome, the aging and frightened Marshal Pietro Badoglio hesitated in following Eisenhower's Algiers broadcast with one of his own. The minutes ticked by. At Allied Force Headquarters anxious officers paced the floor. Would Badoglio make the announcement over Radio Rome?

More time elapsed. Only Italian music came over Radio Rome. At 7:59 P.M. the music ceased. There were several moments of silence. With trembling voice, Marshal Badoglio began reading the terms of the armistice to a startled Italian homefront and armed forces.

There were other listeners—the German *Wehrmacht*.

Within minutes of Badoglio's aircast, the energetic *Feldmarschall* Albert Kesselring began firing out orders from his headquarters just south of Rome. Kesselring's first concern was to gain firm control of the Eternal City, the major communications center for all of southern Italy, so that *General der Panzer Truppen* Heinrich von Vietinghoff's Tenth Army would not be isolated. Tenth Army was defending the Gulf of Salerno, where the mammoth Allied blow was anticipated, and fighting a rear-guard action against the British Eighth Army in the toe and heel of the Italian boot.

Under urgent orders from Kesselring, the battle-tested 3rd

Panzer Grenadier Division, located just north of Rome between Viterbo and Lake Bolsena, promptly brushed aside elements of two Italian divisions. It sped along two parallel highways, *Via Claudia* and *Via Cassia*, and was into Rome in strength shortly after midnight.

At the same time the 3rd Panzer was racing for Rome from the north, the veteran 2nd Parachute Division, positioned some 10 miles south of the capital, was hurrying to the Eternal City over three principal highways. The tough German paratroopers had rapidly overcome token resistance from the Italian *Piacenza* Division and by dawn the 2nd Parachute Division was in the heart of Rome.

Had not *Giant 2* been cancelled by General Eisenhower at the final minute, Colonel Rube Tucker and his 1,700 lightly armed paratroopers—or what remained of them—would have been confronted by the 26,000 battle-tested troops of two experienced German divisions, supported by tanks, artillery and the *Luftwaffe*.

2
A Grim Wehrmacht
Lies in Wait

A BRILLIANT MEDITERRANEAN sun was peeking timidly over the towering limestone and marble Apennine mountain range of southern Italy as a tall, blond German officer of classic Nordic features emerged from a farmhouse a stone's throw from the sandy shoreline of the Tyrrhenian Sea, along the breathlessly beautiful Gulf of Salerno.

Major Herbert Duppenbecker, commanding officer of the 1st Panzer Grenadier Battalion of the battle-tested and fully-equipped 16th Panzer Division, paused briefly to gaze upward at the splendor of the cloudless blue skies and to breathe deeply of the invigorating early morning sea breezes which wafted gently over his farmhouse command post. It was September 8, 1943.

The young battalion commander had slept fitfully during the night. All up and down the vast sweep of the Gulf of Salerno during the hours of darkness continuous explosions had caused the ground under his farmhouse to tremble. England's Royal Air Force heavy bombers had been out in great strength, striking at key communications centers, bridges, road junctions and suspected *Wehrmacht* headquarters along the Gulf. Allied bombers had been pounding installations along the shoreline and just inland since July 1, more than 10 weeks previously. Few towns had escaped the nocturnal fury of the high-flying RAF Wellingtons and Sterlings: Eboli, Battipaglia, Salerno, Agropoli, Paestum—all these and more had been bombed in recent weeks. Curiously, the dock installations at Salerno had been spared the destruction heaped on the other sections of the town.

Major Duppenbecker was in command of 624 *Wehrmacht* soldiers, many of whom had been involved in savage fighting in Russia, France and elsewhere. His grenadier (infantry) battalion consisted of three companies of riflemen and machine gunners, a heavy support company, and an antiaircraft company. Despite the recent Axis loss of adjacent Sicily and the devastating *Wehrmacht* reversals on the Russian front, the morale in Duppenbecker's battalion was high. The men had great confidence in themselves and their officers, and the officers, in turn, had extreme faith in the tenacity and fighting spirit of the men.

Despite the confidence Major Duppenbecker held in his fighting men, his mission was a source of gnawing concern. *Wehrmacht* doctrine had always been that a battalion should cover a defensive front not to exceed 1,200 yards. Yet his grenadier battalion was scattered along the Gulf of Salerno from the ancient town of Paestum northward to the mouth of the Sele River, a distance of nine miles.

It did little to ease the German major's mind to know that the commander of the 16th Panzer Division, *Generalmajor* Rudolf Sickenhius, had assured his combat leaders that the division's mission was not to halt the Allied seaborne smash but to slow it down until inland reserves could be rushed in for a coordinated counterattack to drive the Anglo-Americans into the sea.

Keeping his concerns well hidden, Major Duppenbecker swung a long leg into the sidecar of a waiting motorcycle and pulled his lanky body in after it. The corporal driver, goggles in place and rifle strapped over his back, revved the motor and in a cloud of dust raced off down the narrow road. The major was bound for his regular morning inspection of battalion positions along nine miles of the Gulf of Salerno. Time was short. The Allies were coiled and ready to strike, he knew.

A few miles inland, at his headquarters in a large old mansion tucked away in the foothills, General Sickenhius was beset with the same worries as Major Duppenbacker, only on a much broader scale. He had 17,000 troops and 100 tanks at his disposal. But his men were spread out along the Gulf for 31 miles, from Agropoli northward to the tip of the mountainous Sorrento Peninsula which jutted out into the Tyrrhenian Sea and guarded the plains leading into the port of Naples.

Due to the long defensive sector, a continuous line was impossible. Instead, General Sickenhius had built eight strong points and manned each with infantry companies supported by automatic weapons, mortars, artillery and tanks. In order to provide information on Allied moves on the beachhead, Sickenhius had established observation posts and signal units at gaps between strong points.

The 16th Panzer Division had performed with distinction for many months on the flaming Russian battlegrounds, only to be cut to pieces and nearly destroyed in the brutal fighting at Stalingrad, 10 months previously. The remnants of Sickenhius' battered division were shifted to occupation duty in France, where the division was reconstituted and soon pronounced battle-worthy.

With a massive Allied invasion looming, the 16th Panzer was rushed to central Italy and assigned a sector along the Gulf of Salerno.

General Sickenhius knew that the Allies soon would smash into his thinly-spread division with all the military and industrial might the Anglo-Americans could muster. Experienced commander as he was, General Sickenhius knew his division was about to be cut to pieces for a second time. But he was a German soldier, sworn to fight to the death if need be for the Führer and the Fatherland. He would do his duty—come what may.

Twenty miles north of the port of Salerno and far back from the threatened beaches along the Tyrrhenian Sea, *Signora* Margherita Ciccone and her hard-working daughter Anna were toiling through the normal heavy chores at their modest little home in the farming village of Sirico, a few miles from the important traffic center of Avellino.

The sparse population in the Avellino region survived by laboring from dawn to dark to scratch out an existence on the sloping, boulder-strewn, barren fields, with the aid of donkeys and mules. A standing joke had been the question of whether the donkeys and mules were helping out the humans or vice versa.

Avellino, for centuries quiet and unpretentious, sat in the mountains just north of the intersection of three principal highways, 7, 88 and 90. The only rail line between Rome, a hundred miles to the north, and Salerno ran through Avellino. The devout, hard-working natives of the region knew nothing about military maps. But had they known, they would have instantly recognized that the traffic center of Avellino would be a key target for attention from both sides should violence erupt along the Gulf of Salerno.

Signora Ciccone and teenaged Anna, a beauty with silky black hair and the flashing eyes of the classic Italian lady, were chopping firewood and discussing the alarming events of recent days and nights. Only the night before, Allied bombers had flown over and dropped several bombs, one of which fell in the center of normally tranquil Avellino, killing two civilians and demolishing a building.

"Mamma, do you think the American and British soldiers will come to Avellino like everyone says they will?" Anna asked her industrious mother.

"Goodness, no, my dear," *Signora* Ciccone replied. "If the Americans and British come to Italy what on earth would they want around a place like this?"

The mother's assurance did little to calm Anna's inner fears of the Avellino region becoming a battleground.

Along the Gulf of Salerno that morning of September 8, steady streams of refugees were pouring out of towns and villages for the relative safety of the hills farther inland. Like

hunted animals of equatorial jungles, Italian civilians had a
sixth sense that warned them danger was fast approaching and
to flee while they were still able.

Out of Battipaglia and Agropoli and Paestum and Salerno,
all up and down the Gulf, pitiful little caravans of Italian
natives plodded along in a direction away from the white
sandy beaches, fleeing the holocaust they knew was about to
descend upon the region. Baby buggies, donkey carts, rickety
farm wagons, battered old bicycles, here and there an ancient
relic of an automobile pulled by a mule, any conveyance that
would roll, clogged the roads. Piled aboard were elderly or
crippled men and women, small children and mothers with
tiny babies suckling at breasts, tattered mattresses, flimsy
suitcases bulging with extra clothing, blankets, tables, chairs
and sanctified crosses hurriedly removed from walls. Even
pet animals, sheep and hogs were brought along.

Always the refugees, wide-eyed with fear, asked of each
other: "When are they coming?" All knew who "they" were:
American and British soldiers whose appearance along the
Gulf of Salerno would touch off a violent and lethal confrontation with the waiting *Wehrmacht*, bringing widespread death
and destruction to the region.

Three weeks previously after adjacent Sicily had fallen to
the Anglo-American armies in a lightning campaign lasting
38 days, leaving a powerful Allied war machine coiled to
spring only two miles from mainland Italy across the Strait
of Messina, a high level conference had convened at *Ober-
befehlshaber, Sued* (Commander in Chief, South), at Frascati, 10 miles south of Rome. Purpose of the meeting: To
analyze where the Allies would strike next now that Sicily
had been lost.

Generalfeldmarschall Albert Kesselring, the capable commander of all German forces in the Mediterranean, told his
aides that he was convinced the Allies would not risk landings
outside the range of tactical air cover based in Sicily. That
left only three beaches where the Anglo-Americans could
mount an assault, Kesselring declared. Two of those beaches
had distinct disadvantages to an amphibious landing. Pointing

to a wall map of Italy, the field marshal told his avid listeners that by deduction that left only one locale for the invaders to strike—along the Gulf of Salerno.

Feldmarschall Kesselring had arrived at the same military conclusion in pin-pointing the site of the Allied landing as had General Dwight Eisenhower and his planners in selecting the Salerno beaches.

Now on September 8, Major Herbert Duppenbecker was continuing his inspection of his grenadier battalion's positions along nine miles of coastline. He and his motorcycle driver rolled along over dusty roads through an abundance of olive groves, vineyards and tomato fields, which dotted a lush landscape made green by the several rivers that meandered lazily through the countryside before emptying into the Tyrrhenian Sea.

Off in the distance was 3556-foot Monte Soprano, which dominated much of the coastline and from where German observers, unseen but already in place on its flat crown, could view the shore and plains for many miles in each direction. Near the towering peak was the perfect cone of Monte Sortane, rising majestically 2710 feet into the cloudless Mediterranean sky.

Near the water's edge at Paestum could be seen two nearly perfect Greek temples and a few columns of a third, all framed with a backdrop of green vegetation. Together with a surrounding wall of Cyclopean masonry, these were the visible remains of a Roman presence centuries before.

Now the beauty and tranquility of the ancient Roman temples had been marred by the accouterments of war. A German signal unit had set up operations there and ugly communications wires had been strung around the columns and radiated out in several directions. It was one of the observation posts which would notify General Sickenhius of Alled activities once the battle was joined.

Along the water line German soldiers, most stripped to the waist to absorb the warm rays of the Mediterranean sun, were idly lounging on white sand dunes and gazing out over the glistening, calm blue water of the Tyrrhenian Sea. Here and there along the Gulf, little knots of bronzed German soldiers—totally naked—were splashing about joyfully in the gentle swells of the surf.

It was not all relaxation for these grenadiers of the 16th Panzer Division. Just south of the Sele River where it emptied into the Tyrrhenian, junior officers and noncoms were directing their perspiring men in feverishly strengthening their positions. Some of the Germans were hacking at underbrush to clear fields of fire. About 50 yards from the shoreline two machine-gun posts, each weapon's field of fire interlocked with the other's, were positioned to rake the beach with streams of bullets. At various points menacing .88-millimeter guns poked barrels at the beach.

Soldiers, either those hard at work or others who had already performed their duties and were cooling off in the clear blue waters of the sea, were all careful not to wander into the mine fields that saturated the shoreline.

Had these generally carefree young German fighting men possessed supernatural powers which permitted them to see 100 miles over the horizon, the view would have shocked them. A mighty Allied convoy of nearly 500 ships, each crammed with assault troops, guns and other sinews of war, was cutting through the water bound for the Gulf of Salerno. So large was the onrushing armada that it covered nearly 1,000 square miles of sea.

On board the *Samuel Chase*, a command and communications vessel, American Captain Fred Stallings was busily involved perfecting the radio procedure he would use after the landing. High on his left sleeve Stallings wore an insignia depicting an arrowhead with a large letter T superimposed on it. Stallings and his comrades were proud of that T. It stood for Texas and he and nearly all of his 36th Infantry Division comrades were from the Lone Star State.

While Captain Stallings was idly testing the dial on his radio, he picked up an English-language broadcast from Zurich. Stallings and other officers in the cabin of the *Samuel Chase* were startled to hear the voice announce:

> A large convoy of American and British vessels has left ports in North Africa and is now at sea. An Allied landing in the Naples–Salerno area is expected.

Stallings and the others stared at each other in silence. Now, it appeared, the entire world was aware that the Anglo-Americans were going to strike at Salerno—within hours.

At Frascati, south of Rome, *Feldmarschall* Albert Kesselring was finalizing a message to be relayed immediately to all *Wehrmacht* units in southern Italy. Only an hour later, Colonel William Dornemann, whose 16th Reconnaissance Section was responsible for defending the coastline north and northwest of the post of Salerno, was reading Kesselring's exhortation:

> The invading enemy in the area Naples–Salerno must be completely annihilated and, in addition, driven in the sea. I require ruthless employment of all the might of the Army units.

At 3:15 P.M., German commanders along the Gulf of Salerno received an urgent message from Tenth Army: "Powerful fleet of 100 ships 50 kilometers from the coast."

Luftwaffe reconnaissance pilots apparently had spotted the advance ships in the much larger Allied armada.

Only 30 minutes later *Wehrmacht* units throughout Italy leaped into action on receiving one word from Kesselring's headquarters at Frascati—*Orkan!* (hurricane).

That was the code word to advise German commanders that a major Anglo-American assault was imminent.

Along many miles of sun-bleached white beaches, from the ancient Roman temples at Paestum northward past Salerno and the rugged Sorrento Peninsula and beyond the port of Naples, a beehive of activity erupted. Armored cars rushed about, tanks clanked into firing positions, and trucks crammed with heavily armed grenadiers sped through the villages toward the shoreline.

Grenadiers dashed for their foxholes and mortarmen once again checked the sights on their weapons to assure that their first rounds would fall right on the beaches. Machine gunners at sand-bagged positions near the water fired test bursts out to sea. Officers rushed to and fro shouting orders, motorcycle couriers raced through the rubble strewn streets of Battipaglia, Salerno, Paestum and other towns and across bridges over the Sele River.

Platoons of grenadiers, hob-nailed boots echoing off the hard-surface roads, double-timed to assigned defensive positions. Some distance to the rear German artillerymen checked over their guns and muscled additional shells into place by the weapons.

It was organized chaos. Each German soldier knew where he was to be positioned and each weapon was in its precise place and ready to be fired at the invading enemy. By 4:50 P.M. the 16th Panzer Division was ready for impending action, fully alert, and tensely awaiting the appearance of the Allied war machine.

As grim *Wehrmacht* soldiers in lone foxholes and at strongpoints along the Gulf of Salerno anxiously peered out to sea, nervous tension hung over them like a cloud. The agony of waiting for certain violence to strike was often the worst lot for a combat soldier.

Minutes ticked away. Minutes faded into hours. Soon an ominous cloak of darkness was drawn over the Gulf of Salerno. Where were the Americans and British? Why didn't they come? An eerie hush had fallen over the landscape. The ghostly silence was gently broken on occasion by the muffled cough of a sentry, the click of a rifle bolt as a nervous grenadier checked his weapon, or the soft cackle of a field radio.

At farmhouse command posts German officers and enlisted men alike were hurriedly scrawling last-minute letters to loved ones back in the Fatherland. These might be the last messages they would ever write home.

German *Wehrmacht* along the tranquil Gulf of Salerno watched and waited.

Earlier that day many miles out to sea, the massive Allied armada steamed onward through the calm waters. The weather was perfect—a beautiful September day. American and British fighting men dozed on deck under the benevolent rays of the warm Mediterranean sun. Here and there crap games erupted. There were notes being written home. On some ships Catholic priests were hearing confessions. To many, the trek into battle was more in the order of a passenger cruise after weeks of arduous training on the glazing deserts of North Africa.

Those who stood along the railings and looked into the distance could see nothing but ships—and more ships. Some vessels had barrage balloons floating above them, secured by long steel cables, designed to discourage ambitious *Luftwaffe* pilots from bombing and strafing at low levels. Despite the evident trappings of war, in the warm sun and gentle Mediterranean breezes war to many seemed far away.

At 6:25 P.M., only nine hours before American and British assault forces were to storm ashore on continental Europe, the men aboard the *Samuel Chase* were snapping fingers and tapping toes to the melodic strains of Glenn Miller's orchestra blaring out the popular tune, "In the Mood," over the ship's loudspeaker. In the middle of the song the music was cut off. The amplifier fell silent. Curses rang out.

Minutes later a solemn voice intoned over the loudspeaker: "Stand by for an important announcement." A curtain of silence dropped over the decks. Another voice followed moments later:

"This is General Dwight D. Eisenhower, Commander in Chief of the Allied forces. The Italian government has surrendered its armed forces unconditionally . . ."

Cheers erupted from the throats of the American fighting men, drowning out the remainder of the two-minute statement. Men slapped each other on the back. Faces were wreathed in smiles. Hands were clasped. Soldiers embraced. Men rolled on the decks in glee.

The wild scene was duplicated on scores of other troop ships. Joy was unrestrained. Shouts rang out: "We'll land on the dock in Naples! . . . Home for Christmas! . . . The war's over!" The revelry was unbounded. A holiday mood prevailed. There would be no bloody encounter on the beaches of the Gulf of Salerno.

A few senior army officers were appalled by the development. In their frenzy of excitement, the Texans had overlooked one key factor: Instead of demoralized Italian troops defending the beaches, the Anglo-American assault waves would run up against tenacious, battle-tested German troops.

A 36th Division colonel grabbed a loudspeaker, mounted a pile of boxes, and shouted at the wildly cheering troops: "Men, the landing in the morning will be tough—real tough. We'll be up against some of the Germans' best troops. They'll fight. And they'll fight hard!"

The ominous warning fell on deaf ears. As soon as the colonel concluded his brief remarks, the cheering broke out once more. "A dock landing in Naples! . . . Booze and broads! . . . Home for Christmas!"

Among the British soldiers, the reaction was identical. Loud cheers and shouts of joy, men clasping hands and dancing wildly on deck. Officers hurrying to their cabins for their rations of whiskey and gin. Toasts to the King and the Empire and to Providence for the last-minute reprieve. "It's all over but the shouting! . . . Good Old Winnie (Churchill)! . . . Naples saloons tonight!"

In his cabin on the *Ancon*, General Mark Clark, commander of Fifth Army, had one more worry to add to his burden due to the festive conduct of his fighting men following Eisenhower's bombshell announcement. The fighting edge of the assault troops had been dulled. Any kind of resistance on the beaches would now, because it would be unexpected, seem even worse to the troops going ashore.

Clark figuratively shrugged his shoulders, hoped for the best, braced for the worst. With only hours until the run into the German-held beaches, there was little, if anything, the army commander could do about the mental outlook of his men.

At 10:10 P.M., *Generalfeldmarschall* Albert Kesselring, imperturbable as always, was placing a series of telephone calls to *Wehrmacht* commanders in Italy. It had been only two hours since Marshal Pietro Badoglio had read the Italian armistice terms over Radio Rome. Now Kesselring was making certain all was ready to rapidly implement Operation *Achse*, the German plan for disarming the defecting Italian armed forces.

Minutes after Kesselring had concluded his telephone conversations, at 10:28 P.M., the code phrase *Ernte Einbringen* (bring in the harvest) was flashed to German command posts. Its meaning: Launch *Asche* with all possible speed.

Kesselring then fired off a telegram to Heinrich von Vietinghoff, commander of Tenth Army. The *Wehrmacht* field marshal was indignant. Earlier that evening he had told his aides that the Italians had ''committed the basest treachery . . . behind our backs.'' Until Badoglio's broadcast on Radio Rome earlier that night Kesselring had been fond of his Italian partners. Now Von Vietinghoff became aware, by the tone of the telegram, that Kesselring had totally reversed his personal feelings for the Italians:

> If we retain our fighting spirit and remain dead calm,
> I am confident that we will continue to perform the
> tasks entrusted to us by the Führer. (Italian troops) must
> be ruthlessly disarmed. No mercy must be shown the
> traitors. Long live the Führer. Kesselring.

With typical Teutonic efficiency, the *Wehrmacht* began disarming the Italians. A mixture of diplomacy, ingenuity and violence, depending upon what the individual situation called for, was employed. Many Italian units were surrounded and disarmed before they could take any kind of action. Thousands of Italian soldiers simply slipped out of army barracks into the night and surfaced a day or two later at their homes, civilians once again.

In most cases as Italian soldiers laid down their weapons, they could hardly disguise their elation. Demoralized, confused, poorly led, war weary and forced to fight for a vague cause in which they never believed, Italian soldiers returned home cheerfully. Few chose to join the German *Wehrmacht* to continue the fight.

Some artillery and machine gun units destroyed key mechanisms in their weapons before the Germans confiscated them. Depending upon the views of the local Italian commander, some formations turned over their artillery, mortars and automatic weapons intact, together with large stocks of ammunition.

At 1 A.M. on September 9 at the *Oberkommando der Wehrmacht* in Berlin, Adolf Hitler and his two confidants, *Feldmarschall* Wilhelm Keitel and *Generaloberst* Alfred Jodl, were anxiously awaiting reports from Italy on Operation *Achse*. The Führer and his aides grew increasingly elated. Reports indicated the disarming of the Italians had progressed with greater ease and rapidity than had been expected. Now the German leaders could focus full attention on an even greater threat: The approach of a massive Allied invasion fleet near Salerno.

Earlier that night, as the unseen Anglo-American sea armada edged closer to its anchorage 10 miles off the shoreline along the Gulf, an eerie hush had fallen over the beaches. Here and there along the dark coastline German searchlights burst into iridescent brilliance, scoured the seascape, then flickered off.

At 9 P.M. the ominous silence along the shoreline was broken when German soldiers in foxholes near the water and on the massive heights overlooking the vast sweep of the Gulf of Salerno detected a purring noise off in the distance and high in the Mediterranean sky. Veterans promptly recognized the sound: A mighty Allied bomber fleet was approaching.

The first faint hum grew increasingly more intense and soon developed into an ear-piercing roar. Royal Air Force Wellington and Halifax bombers were now directly over the beaches. In an instant the blackness of night was swept away as scores of brilliant white parachute flares bathed the landscape for miles around with their ghostly iridescence.

Minutes later German soldiers along the shoreline and Italian civilians huddled in fear heard the eerie whine and whistle of clusters of bombs plunging madly through space on their trek to earth. Gigantic explosions rocked the terrain and turned wooden structures into splinters and stone buildings into crumbling piles of masonry.

The heaviest Allied bomber assault in the 10-week aerial bombardment along the Gulf of Salerno was under way.

Towns and villages felt the fury of the might of Allied

bombers: Salerno, Battipaglia, Gaeta, Eboli, Fornia, Paestum, Pontenza, Altavilla. Bridges up and down the coastline were pounded, as were road junctions, supply dumps, railroad tracks, radar sites, artillery positions and German command posts.

German antiaircraft guns, rushed into the region two days before, blasted away at the tormentors high in the Mediterranean sky. The Hotel Montestella in Salerno, which had been a key *Wehrmacht* headquarters, was flattened. Its German occupants had departed the day before. Much of residential Salerno was destroyed, but the docks were spared. They would be needed to bring in Allied supplies.

The explosions grew less frequent and the roar of powerful bomber engines evaporated into the distance. It was 10:35 P.M. An eerie hush once more blanketed the white sands of the Gulf of Salerno. Here and there could be heard the muffled scraping of shovels as *Wehrmacht* riflemen and machine gunners along the shoreline began digging their foxholes even deeper.

Tension grew as the tranquil minutes ticked away. At his foxhole near the water line an hour later, a young German corporal was peering intently into the blackness out to sea. Suddenly, his nerves, already taut, jangled and his body stiffened. A short distance to his front, perhaps a half-mile from shore, he detected the brief muted glow of a blue light. He nervously cranked his field telephone and reported his sighting to his company commander.

The German captain told the corporal to remain alert and report any more suspicious sightings.

As the company commander and his noncom were discussing the situation in hushed tones, at points less than a mile offshore Allied midget submarines had surfaced. These tiny undersea craft, jammed with crews of three to five men, had silently slipped into position several nights before and had the perilous task of scouting the landing beaches with their periscopes.

Now, with Allied H-Hour fast approaching, the miniature submarines had surfaced for one final look at the landing beaches along the Gulf of Salerno where American and British assault troops would storm ashore. The skippers of the submarines were busily engaged in flashing blue-light coded signals to unseen troop ships hovering in the darkness out to sea.

German forces along the Gulf of Salerno were now in a high state of readiness. Tension, already heavy, grew in intensity. A *Kriegsmarine* (navy) station near Salerno City flashed a warning: "Picking up ship engines a short distance from shore."

It was 10 minutes past midnight on September 9.

Ten to twelve miles off the coastline of the Gulf of Salerno, the ghostly hulks of hundreds of Allied ships were rolling gently in the calm waters of the Tyrrhenian Sea. Under the protective blanket of night, the armada had stealthily edged into position shortly before 11 P.M.

Hazily outlined were the sleek configurations of cruisers and destroyers. Command ships bristled with a maze of antennae jabbing slender fingers into the dark sky. Smaller vessels carrying messages darted to and fro between the larger ships, much like waterbugs scurrying about in a farmer's pond.

Pouring out over the seascape was the sound of windlasses whirling as booms on the ships swung out amphibious craft and lowered them gingerly to the dark, calm water. Muted loudspeakers rasped out an occasional message. Ears were cocked for the ominous sounds foretelling the arrival of the *Luftwaffe*. Even the most myopic German bombardier could hardly have missed, so vast was the armada.

Presently loudspeakers on troop ships called out: "Lower landing boats!"

Like a well-oiled machine navy men sprang into action. Chains rattled in the davits and grating noises erupted as the sailors expertly inched the tiny assault craft into the water.

Below deck in the cramped, dingy holds of the transport ships, assault troops waited, nervous and tense. Gone was the euphoria that had gripped most of them a few hours before with General Eisenhower's announcement of the Italian armistice.

Soon intercom systems in the holds called out a chilling message: "Assault troops to your boarding stations!"

Allied infantrymen scrambled up steel ladders and onto the decks, then to their assigned positions along the railings just above the assault boats, which could be heard down below gently banging into the steel sides of the transport ships.

The infantrymen, burdened with heavy combat gear, were nervous and tense. Stomachs knotted and churned. Perspiration dotted foreheads. Palms were sweaty. Old friends grimly shook hands. There were whispers of "Good Luck!" and "See you on the beach!" Some men vomited.

On transports carrying assault troops of the green 36th Infantry Division, loudspeakers exhorted the men: "Get in there, Texans, and give 'em hell!"

Miles to the north in ships lying off the mountainous Sorrento Peninsula, British Commandos under youthful Brigadier Robert Laycock were likewise being urged over loudspeakers to "Remember Coventry! Remember Dunkirk!" To the British, these battlecries carried deep emotional significance.

As American and British fighting men stood silently along railings, loudspeakers blared out: "Now hear this. Board your landing boats!"

It was the dreaded order most did not want to hear. Yet each knew it had to come.

With a heavy rustle of equipment, assault troops climbed over railings and began the hazardous descent down slippery rope ladders and into landing craft. Curses rang out as men lost their footing in the tangled web of rope or were struck heavy blows in the face by rifle barrels of struggling comrades climbing down alongside.

As each assault boat was filled, it circled the mother ship until all landing craft were crammed with fighting men and their weapons. A final order echoed over the seascape: "Away all boats!" The 10-mile run to the shoreline, Round One in the death struggle for a slender slice of Adolph Hitler's *Festung Europa* (Fortress Europe), had commenced.

3
Paratroopers Seize
a Radar Island

As THE MASSIVE Allied fleet, a hydra-headed monster breathing steel and explosives, lurked in the inky darkness some 10 miles off the shoreline along the Gulf of Salerno, diversionary actions were unfolding to confuse the German command and to draw enemy troops away from the beachhead.

Just north of Anglo-American landing beaches at midnight, 16 PT boats, fast motorized launches armed with torpedos and automatic weapons, dashed boldly into the inky blackness of the harbor in German-held Naples. Under Lieutenant Commander Stanley M. Barnes, the small PT boats, designed for darting raids, proceeded to shoot up the Naples docks and military installations.

As German telephones and radios at command posts in Naples sent out a flood of messages to higher levels concerning the Allied naval attack on Naples, General Mark Clark's assault troops were preparing to storm ashore 20 miles to the south.

At the same time Commander Barnes' PT boats were shooting up Naples harbor, 20 miles to the north, near the

mouth of the Volturno River, another small Allied flotilla had
edged into the Gulf of Gaeta under the protective cover of
night. Commanded by Captain Charles L. Andrews, Jr., this
naval force consisted of a destroyer, two Dutch gunboats, six
motor launches, four sub-chasers and five motor boats. Some
of the vessels were equipped with deception devices.

At 12:35 A.M. Navy Captain Andrews' vessels opened fire
at preselected targets along and behind the beaches. Officers
in Andrews' diversionary force were not too concerned if
their guns hit designated targets; the primary function of the
handful of craft was to "raise as much hell as possible and
draw off enemy troops from Salerno."

About one hour before Captain Andrews' hodge-podge
collection of vessels had slipped into the Gulf of Gaeta, one
of its British PT boats had peeled off from the others and
plowed through the calm, dark waters in the direction of the
tiny, undistinguished little island of Ventotene, several miles
offshore from the coastal city of Gaeta. On board were 46
American paratroopers.

The airborne men, commanded by Lieutenant Charles C. W.
Howland, belonged to the veteran 509th Parachute Infantry
Battalion, the first United States airborne unit to go overseas
and the first to make a combat jump. During the invasion of
North Africa by Anglo-American troops the previous Novem-
ber, the 509th battalion had spearheaded the assault by jump-
ing inland near Oran and occupying the key LaSenia and
Tafaraoui airfields.

Ventotene island was the location of a German radar in-
stallation. The mission of the paratroopers was to knock out
the enemy facility. The radar site was relatively small, well
camouflaged and its precise location was not known to Allied
intelligence. These factors ruled out bombing from the air,
so a small raiding force was handed the job.

At the time the Ventotene raid was conceived six days
previously, the mission was considered crucial. Guarded by
an unknown number of Germans, the radar could pick up and
report on activities of the 82nd Airborne Division which was
to drop Colonel Reuben Tucker's 504th Parachute Infantry
Regiment near Rome on the same night as the Ventotene raid.

Now, unknown to Lieutenant Howland's band of paratroopers, the mission to knock out the enemy radar had lost some of its crucial significance, as the Rome airborne mission had been cancelled a few hours previously.

The Ventontene mission was assigned to the 509th Parachute Infantry Battalion and its commander, Lieutenant Colonel Doyle R. Yardley, picked Lieutenant Howland to lead the assault. Howland, 25 years of age, had performed with distinction during the North African campaign.

Secrecy surrounded planning for the Ventotene mission. The 45 paratroopers who would carry out the raid under Howland were told only that the operation was to knock out a key Axis facility. The precise target—Ventotene—was never mentioned.

"It will sure as hell be a hairy mission," was all that Lieutenant Howland could reveal in early planning stages.

Wily German intelligence officers, skilled and experienced, could have pieced together bits and pieces of evidence, had they learned of the impending Ventotene raid, to rightly conclude the Allies were about to launch a large airborne operation in the area. The logical target would be: Rome.

For the raid on Ventotene, Lieutenant Howland divided his force into two platoons. One was commanded by Lieutenant Kenneth R. Shaker, a former soldier of fortune who had fought in the Spanish Civil War as an infantry private, and leading the other platoon was Lieutenant Wilber B. McClintock. Senior noncom in the raiding party was 1st Sergeant Mike O'Brien.

Lieutenant Howland and his 45 paratroopers shoe-horned their way into a British PT boat in Bizerte, North Africa, the previous morning, September 7. Barely 60 feet long, the motor torpedo boat was aswarm with wiggling humanity; in addition to the navy crew and the parachutists, there was a wide assortment of machine guns, land mines, bazookas, explosives and other paraphernalia of war piled about.

As part of Navy Captain Charles Andrews' naval task force, which the following night would shoot up the beaches along the Gulf of Gaeta, the gray-painted PT boat with its 46

airborne passengers edged out of Bizerte harbor and set a
course for Palermo, Sicily, across the azure Mediterranean
Sea. Arriving at Palermo, the leader of the paratrooper raiding party, Lieutenant Howland, scrambled up onto the docks
and went into the city to pick up last-minute intelligence on
Ventotene. He returned to the PT boat two hours after departing.

In the meantime, Howland's paratroopers were becoming
increasingly irritable with their cramped situation on the small
boat, and now as they stomped about on the docks awaiting
the lieutenant's return they filled the sky with picturesque
language, damning the United States Army for "yet another
hurry up and wait" operation.

"Hop aboard, we're moving out," Howland called out,
and the parachutists began climbing into the PT boat.

"Now we know how goddamned sardines in a can feel!"
a trooper loudly observed.

Along with the other vessels in Captain Andrews' flotilla,
the British PT boat and its paratroopers moved out to sea on
the next leg of the journey. Other than Lieutenant Howland,
none of the airborne men knew that the next destination was
an exotic Italian isle fabled in song and verse—Capri.

As the little convoy steadily burrowed on through the water and the minutes and hours ticked away, Private Dolphus
R. Walker, a 20-year-old scout of the paratroopers, reflected
on a factor he considered strange: Hundreds of Allied vessels
were supposed to be steaming toward the Gulf of Salerno at
that precise moment, but neither he nor his comrades had
sighted another ship besides those in his little group.

"Do you think the big Allied convoy is lost, or are we
lost?" Walker mused to a fellow trooper, only half in jest.

Docking amidst the lush greenery of Capri, the paratrooper raiding party once again bided its time as Lieutenant
Howland went in search of his latest instructions and, hopefully, up-to-date intelligence on the situation at Ventotene.
Returning to the PT boat an hour later, Howland and his
parachutists squeezed into the 60-foot-long craft once again
and shortly the flotilla edged out to sea on its final leg of the

journey that would take the vessels to the Gulf of Gaeta and the nearby German-held island of Ventotene.

Eventually the Mediterranean sun made its daily plunge into the western horizon and an eerie cloak of darkness was tossed over the region. It was a clear night. The stars were out and a gentle breeze was blowing. The paratroopers on the PT boat could feel the craft slowing. Looming ominously to their front was the dim silhouette of a heavily-wooded piece of land—Ventotene.

The engines were shut down as far as possible so as not to alert German sentries. The only sound was the gentle rustling of birds fluttering through the trees along the shoreline and the soft hum of the boat motor. Paratroopers gripped their weapons tightly as the PT boat edged closer to the rickety dock, barely visible in the darkness.

A soft thud was heard as the motor boat brushed against the dock, which appeared to be deserted. The troopers exhaled a collective sigh of relief: German gunners hidden along the shoreline would have cut the parachutists to ribbons and blasted the PT boat out of the water.

The airborne men, as noiselessly as possible, began slipping out of the PT boat, one by one, and took up firing positions along the dark beach. Despite efforts to the contrary, there was much rattling of weapons and rustling of equipment.

"For Chrissake, quit making all that goddamned racket," a voice called out in the darkness in a stage whisper.

Howland kept his men in position along the shoreline for several minutes while straining to hear or see some indication of an enemy presence. There was only the muted sound of crickets chirping joyfully.

The lieutenant, peering intently to his front, could discern the silhouette of a large hill which appeared to be about 300 yards to his front. Speaking in hushed tones, Howland said, "I need a volunteer to go up that hill and look around for anything unusual."

Private Dolphus Walker, the scout who had been concerned over not sighting the massive Allied convoy earlier that day, volunteered for the job. Considerable peril was in-

volved. If the Germans were on the island in force, they would
certainly have a position on the dominating elevation.

"Now be sure to keep your eyes open," Howland told
Walker.

"What kind of unusual am I looking for?" Walker inquired.

"Anything that's unusual," Howland responded. "Krauts
mainly."

Walker, known to his comrades as "Doc," gripped his
rifle tightly and walked off into the night. Despite the inky
blackness, Walker detected the faint outlines of the hill he
was to reconnoiter. As he got closer to the elevation, he could
see that it was more of a mountain than a hill, tall, steep and
heavily wooded. Before starting up the incline, he paused
briefly to listen for any sound of enemy activity. He heard
nothing but the gentle rustle of trees swaying in the breeze
that swept in from the sea.

Seeking a way up the mountain, Walker happened across
a trail and started his climb to the top. The trail was steep
and twisting and took him in a wide circle around to the far
side of the mountain. It was a strenuous climb that left him
gasping for breath, so he stopped periodically to rest and to
listen for any indication of an enemy nearby.

Walker had just finished a short rest and was moving up
the path again when he froze in his tracks: His ears detected
the something "unusual" Lieutenant Howland had told him
to listen and watch for—the sound of heavy snoring out in
the darkness to his front. Walker stepped off the trail and
listened intently. Cautiously he inched forward, rifle at the
ready, as the snoring continued. Suddenly the trooper halted.
There alongside the path was the crumpled form of a man
deep in slumber.

Walker slowly edged up to the snoring figure. In the darkness he could see the large belt buckle, the hob-nailed boots,
a coal bucket shaped helmet and a bolt-action rifle beside
him on the ground. It was a German soldier who was either
drunk or had fallen asleep on sentry duty.

The American stood over the sleeping figure and pondered
what to do about him. A shot through the head would arouse

the entire island. Walker thought of knifing him but, somehow, that seemed unsportsmanlike.

A trace of a devious smile flickered across Walker's face.
He thought, "Here's one Kraut I'll teach a lesson to he'll
never forget." If the "lesson" was effective, the German
would not have much time left in which to forget.

As did most paratroopers, Walker carried with him in
combat a two-foot length of piano wire—ideal for silently
strangling sentries. He attached the thin wire to the safety
ring of a hand grenade, and pulled the pin halfway out. When
the pin was removed all the way, the grenade would explode.
The trooper stooped and gingerly attached the other end
of the piano wire to the snoring German's foot, and placed
the grenade between the man's legs. Walker then stole off
into the darkness, moving on up the path for about a hundred
yards.

The parachutist found a hole and crawled into it to await
the explosion back down the trail which would signal that the
German had, in effect, just committed suicide by waking up
and stirring, thereby pulling the grenade pin all the way out.

Walker remained in the hole along side the path for nearly
an hour, watching and listening for any indication of enemy
activity. He was surprised that the grenade attached to the
sleeping German sentry's leg had not exploded by now. But,
he thought, the soldier might still be sleeping.

As Walker maintained his lonely one-man listening post,
he heard a rustling sound back down the path. Someone was
moving up the trail toward him. He tensed and moved his
rifle into firing position. It was probably the German who had
been asleep returning to his bivouac area. How had the German kept from blowing himself up? Walker asked himself.

The rustling sound got louder and seconds later the paratrooper could discern the faint silhouette of a man coming up
the trail toward him. As the figure came closer, Walker peered
intently through the darkness at the man's helmet. Did it have
the distinctive coalbucket shape of those worn by the German
Wehrmacht?

When the approaching figure was less than 20 yards away,
Walker could see that the helmet was American in configu-

ration. He challenged the approaching figure in a stage whisper and received the correct countersign. Private Amos Dunlap moved on toward Walker.

"I've come to relieve you," Dunlap stated. "Had a hell of a time finding you. Lieutenant Howland sent me up. He and the others went on inland to find the Kraut radar."

"Did you pass the Kraut?" Doc Walker asked.

"What Kraut?"

"The one laying asleep and snoring so damned loud along the path down there a little way. I booby-trapped the bastard."

"I didn't see any Kraut back there. He must have woke up and moved on."

Disappointed and puzzled as to how the German sentry had escaped from blowing himself up, Walker shouldered his Garand rifle and moved back down the mountain.

As Walker was attaching his makeshift booby-trap to the sleeping German sentry, down at the foot of the mountain Lieutenant Howland had formed his men into single file and marched inland in search of the radar site. The troopers passed through a tiny, sleeping village without awakening the residents and later halted before the shadowy contours of a high hill that loomed before them.

Howland and his officers held a hurried, whispered conversation. They concluded that the radar facility might be located on the elevation, but there was no sign of enemy activity there.

As the Americans paused briefly, a shadowy figure suddenly emerged from the darkness. He was wearing civilian clothes and identified himself in broken English as a professor who had been banished from the mainland because he was opposed to the Fascist government. Howland and the others eyed the elderly man suspiciously, and became even more leery of the stranger when he volunteered that he was a friend of the German major who commanded the radar station.

"Yes," the pleasant professor replied to Howland's question, "the radar is located at the top of the hill." The Italian also said that an undetermined number of German troops guarded the key facility.

Saying that he wished to avoid bloodshed and to assist the Americans, the professor agreed to lead the paratroopers up a path to the radar site and to act as an intermediary to try to arrange a German surrender to the Americans.

Still suspicious of the Italian and his motives, Howland ordered Lieutenant Shaker to take his platoon up the hill behind the professor. "Watch the son of a bitch!" was Howland's parting admonition to his platoon leader.

With the professor in the lead, the file of paratroopers moved on up the hill. When the column was about 75 yards from the top of the elevation, the Italian raised his hand and the column halted.

"I suggest that you remain here with your men," the professor said to Shaker. "I'll go on to the top and into the radar site. They know me and will let me in. I'll talk to the German major and see what can be done."

Shaker, concerned that the Italian was more bent on warning his "friend" that the radar site was about to be attacked than he was on securing a peaceful surrender, hurriedly turned the suggestion over in his mind. "Okay, you can go ahead," the platoon leader finally agreed. "But you'd better be goddamned careful or we're coming after you as well as the Krauts." Shaker patted his Tommy gun for emphasis.

"I understand," the professor replied courteously, displaying no outward emotion to Shaker's implied threat of what would happen to him if he were intent on treachery. The Italian moved on up the path and soon disappeared into the darkness. Shaker, meanwhile, deployed his men in a defensive position around the narrow path.

Five minutes went by. Then 10 minutes. The clock ticked on and a suspicious Shaker became increasingly concerned. Twenty minutes elapsed, then 25. There was no sign of the courteous, elderly professor who had taken it upon himself to arrange a bloodless surrender of the *Wehrmacht* force on Ventotene.

A half-hour went by and Shaker passed the word among his troopers, "Get ready to assault the radar station!"

The sound of rifle bolts clicking as the Americans tested their weapons drifted through the night air. There was a rustling of equipment as the men moved out into the path. It would be a charge fraught with peril as the number of Germans they would encounter on top of the hill was unknown, and neither Shaker nor any of his men had any idea what a radar station looked like. In the dark, they might have a difficult time seizing and destroying it, provided they were able to dispose of the *Wehrmacht* force guarding the facility.

Shaker was about to move his men forward into the attack when a shadowy figure was seen moving back down the hill toward the Americans. It was the Italian professor.

"What the hell took you so long?" the lieutenant demanded.

Unruffled by Shaker's sharp remark, the Italian responded, "The major didn't know what to do, and was greatly concerned with his honor. I told him what you said, that you had an entire regiment of paratroopers surrounding the hill and an Allied fleet offshore. That unless he surrendered his men promptly, they would be decimated."

Shaker winced inwardly at the hoax he had perpetrated. The "regiment" consisted of 46 paratroopers and the "Allied fleet" was one British PT boat.

"He thought about what I had to say for quite awhile," the professor continued. "Then finally he agreed that the only sensible course was to surrender his men and the radar station."

Pausing only momentarily, the Italian said, "But the major will surrender only to an officer of his rank or above."

The fast-thinking Shaker gruffly told the professor, "Well, I'm a full colonel and I've got an entire regiment behind me. Tell the son of a bitch if he doesn't surrender immediately we're going to kick hell out of him and his men and blast his goddamned radar clear off that hill!"

Shaker was aware the professor could see his silver bar insignia of a first lieutenant, but was counting on the fact that the Italian probably did not know one American insignia from another. In this, Shaker was correct. The Italian turned to head back up the hill and soon was enveloped by the darkness.

Some 10 minutes later a huge explosion at the top of the hill rocked the ground, accompanied by spurts of orange flame shooting high into the black sky. The troopers huddled a short distance down the hill felt like cheering—the Germans had done the Americans' job for them by blowing up the radar station themselves.

Then, out of the darkness, Lieutenant Shaker and his 23 troopers saw a line of shadowy figures, hands on their heads, marching down the path toward them. The German major and his 114-man force were surrendering.

When the elderly professor politely introduced the German major to ''Colonel'' Shaker, the *Wehrmacht* officer stared intently at the silver bar of a first lieutenant on the American's shirt collar and knew that he had been hoodwinked.

''Where is the rest of your regiment?'' the German demanded.

''Oh, they're back down the hill,'' Ken Shaker replied breezily.

The ''rest of the regiment'' indeed was back down the hill—Lieutenant Howland, Lieutenant McClintock and their 21 paratroopers who were serving as a backup force if Shaker and his men ran into trouble.

Now the proud *Wehrmacht* officer realized he was undergoing the humiliation of having to surrender to an American of much lower rank. But nothing could be done to reverse the situation. The Germans had destroyed or thrown away their personal weapons before filing down the hill, and had blown up the radar station.

The German-held island of Ventotene had fallen without a shot being fired.

Word was promptly sent back down the hill to the awaiting commander of the raiding force, Lieutenant Howland, of the capture of the German garrison. Elated that the mission had been achieved without bloodshed, Howland and Lieutenant McClintock, the platoon leader, headed back through the darkness to the PT boat.

The two officers, dim silhouettes in the darkness of night

and the overhanging trees, walked unknowingly within 20 yards of a paratroop sentry, Private First Class Stanley Gerk. Shortly after the raiding party had landed earlier that night Lieutenant Howland had told Gerk, "Stan, take your BAR (Browning automatic rifle) and go down the shoreline about 50 yards and guard our flank. Shoot anyone who doesn't reply to your challenge."

Now the alert Gerk had spotted the two dim figures strolling past his position. "Halt!" Gerk called out Howland and McClintock, busily engaged in antimated conversation, kept walking. "Halt!" Gerk cried again. Still the two unidentified shadowy forms did not respond. Gerk summoned all his lung power and shouted for a final time, "Halt, or I'll blow your goddamned heads off!" The two figures froze in place.

Howland called out the password for the night. Gerk recognized his commander's voice and lowered his Browning automatic rifle.

As troopers on the hill near the radar site were searching the captured Germans, Sergeant Carl Salisbury learned that the Americans had "hooked some prized fish." Three of the prisoners were not military men but radar technicians. They would prove valuable to Allied intelligence, which was desperate to learn more about enemy radar.

The Germans were marched to a schoolhouse and placed inside under guard, then a radio appeal was sent out for a ship to take the captives off the island.

By 3 A.M., Ventotene was securely in Allied hands.

Along the Gulf of Salerno where the seaborne American assault would strike, U.S. Ensign George Anderson was aboard his tiny scout craft anchored in the inky blackness only 400 yards off a strip of white sand code-named Red Beach. Anderson hurriedly placed his hand over his mouth to stifle a cough. Strict silence on his part and those of his handful of sailors was a matter of life and death. It was 2:30 A.M. on September 9 and in one hour elements of the U.S. 36th Infantry Division would depend upon Ensign Anderson to guide them onto the designated beach just north of Paestum.

A ghostly hush hovered over the shoreline as Anderson

and his men squatted like sitting ducks within easy rifle distance of shore. The tiny scout craft was so near the enemy that the Americans could detect the shadowy silhouettes of German vehicles moving about on shore and hear the occasional shout of a *Wehrmacht* officer calling to his grenadiers. Despite strict orders to the contrary, Germans dug in along the water line nervously lighted cigarettes, and the quick flickers of illumination were seen by Ensign Anderson and his men.

Anderson and his men, to avoid detection from the shore, were wearing special rubber-soled shoes and all personal equipment which might rattle was securely taped to their outer clothing. Special pains were taken to see that all lights were extinguished below deck when it was necessary to open or close hatchways.

A short distance up the coast from where Ensign Anderson was going through his paces, also a mere 400 yards from enemy gunners on shore, was a similar scout boat commanded by a U.S. Coast Guard officer, Lieutenant (JG) Grady Holloway, who would guide infantry assault waves into Green beach with a flashing green light.

In order to be certain that he was in the correct location, Holloway took a fix on the ancient Roman watchtower at Paestum which loomed in shadowy outline off in the distance. Lieutenant Holloway felt relieved—he was precisely on mark.

Spaced at intervals in front of the proper beaches along the 31-mile length of the Gulf of Salerno were other scout boats commanded by American and British naval officers. Not only was their job one of peril, but a heavy burden of responsibility had been placed on these junior officers' young shoulders. If assault troops were directed to the wrong beaches, the entire invasion could be jeopardized.

In the darkness hours before, these tiny scout boats had sailed in close to shore to guide in the minesweepers, whose job it was to clear paths for the landing craft. Once the paths had been cleared of mines, the scout boats took up their positions just offshore. There these little boats remained for hours, always in danger of discovery and annihilation.

Now, one hour before landing craft with troops of the 36th

Infantry Division would storm ashore, Ensign Anderson began blinking his red light out to sea. If Germans on shore
were going to detect his boat, this would be the time when
they would do it. Anderson could not see the vast Allied
armada 10 miles out to sea. But he knew they were there and
that at the moment landing craft were preparing for the run
to the beaches.

The stretch of shoreline to be assaulted by the Texans of
the 36th Division was just north of ancient Paestum and was
divided into four sectors: Red, Green, Yellow and Blue
beaches. There was a scout craft lying 400 yards offshore for
each of these beaches, and the navy commander in each boat
had a light to flash out to sea which conformed in color to
the designated beach.

Suddenly the quietude over the Gulf of Salerno was angrily
shattered. At 2:35 A.M. four heavy coastal guns along the
northern sector where the British X Corps would land opened
fire on approaching assault craft carrying American Rangers
under Lieutenant Colonel William O. Darby and British
Commandos led by Brigadier Robert Laycock. These were
Italian guns, but manned by Germans. Only a few hours previously, after Italian Marshal Badoglio announced the armistice over Radio Rome, *Wehrmacht* troops seized the coastal
batteries from the Italians along the Gulf of Salerno.

Nearly one hour prior to the main Anglo-American assault, Darby's and Laycock's elite forces were heading toward
Vietri and Maiori, coastal towns along the rugged and mountainous Sorrento Peninsula, to seize the high ground overlooking the Allied landing beaches and deny the heights to
German artillery observers. Once the high ground was taken,
the Rangers and Commandos were to block the narrow
mountain passes leading from Naples through which the
Wehrmacht could rush reinforcements to the beachhead.

In early planning for *Avalanche*, seizing these mountain
passes on the Sorrento Peninsula was to have been the task
of parachute elements of the 82nd Airborne Division.

Despite their unfamiliarity with the Italian coastal guns,
the German crews were deadly accurate. One of the first high-
caliber shells slammed into an American LST (landing ship

tank) loaded with Darby's Rangers, killing and wounding
many of the infantrymen and navy crew and sending the craft
plunging to the bottom of the Tyrrhenian Sea.

Any lingering hope harbored by Allied commanders that
the Salerno amphibious assault would take the Germans by
surprise vanished into the crisp night air. British destroyers
HMS *Blankney* and *Brecon* and the USS *Biscayne* opened fire
on the coastal battery and in minutes the German-manned
guns fell silent.

Colonel Darby's little flotilla hit its designated beach at
3:10 A.M. As the Rangers scrambled out of their assault craft
and on to shore they were surprised to find no Germans dug
in along the beach. Not a shot was fired. Darby and his men
pushed on inland and occupied the high ground overlooking
the key Chiunzi Pass.

Twenty minutes after Darby's men touched shore, Brigadier Laycock's Commandos stormed onto the beach. Laycock's men had been delayed in their landing for a short
period of time as another Italian coastal battery manned by
Germans had poured fire into the approaching assault craft
before being knocked out by guns of the HMS *Blackmore*.

Laycock's Commandos had a short but bitter fight with
grenadiers of the 16th Panzer Division before pushing on to
LaMolina Pass where they dug in on high ground towering
over the road and railway leading through the defile to the
beachhead.

An hour before Brigadier Laycock's Commandos touched
shore, General Richard McCreery, commander of the assaulting British X Corps, was engaged in urgent discussion with
naval gunnery officers on his command ship lying off the
beaches. McCreey's 46th and 56th Divisions would within the
hour assault the beaches to the south of the Commandos.
McCreery and other Allied commanders on the scene had
been given the latitude in the final hours to call for a prelim-
inary bombardment or seek to gain a foothold on shore
through surprise.

McCreery chose the naval barrage. "The Germans know
we're here," he reasoned. "Besides, a heavy barrage will
raise the morale of our assault troops."

At 3 A.M. an ear-splitting roar erupted from a line of British and American warships offshore and the sky was aglow with the brilliant flashes of large-caliber guns sending death-dealing missiles into German positions along the beaches to be struck by men of the 46th and 56th Divisions. The torrential rain of explosives continued for 20 minutes. Shortly after it lifted British Tommies leaped from their beached assault craft and an intense firefight broke out. In customary fashion, the German defenders recovered rapidly from the effects of the mind-numbing barrage and resisted fiercely.

At the same time, 10 miles to the south of the British landing beaches, American Ensign George Anderson was furiously blinking his muted red light out to sea from the rear of his tiny scout boat swaying gently in the dark waters 400 yards from German defenders on the beach. Off in the distance, in the direction of the unseen Allied armada, Anderson detected the faint purr of engines. He felt his heart begin to pound with increasing intensity—this was the sound of scores of small landing craft crammed with Texans of the 36th Infantry Division and heading for Red, Green, Yellow and Blue beaches.

Many miles to the north, the dark sky was aglow with flashes from the guns of Allied warship pounding the British landing beaches. But along Red Beach in the American sector a strange stillness blanketed the coastline.

At German positions among the sand dunes of Red Beach, the enemy also could hear the hum of many engines and knew Allied assault craft were bearing down on them. Grenadiers in their foxholes squeezed rifle stocks and machine gunners hurriedly checked their weapons. Stomachs churned. Foreheads were damp with perspiration. The Germans watched. And waited. The full weight of the armed and industrial might of the Anglo-Americans was about to smash into them.

Now the hum of approaching boat engines grew louder . . . and louder. Ensign Anderson, blinking his red light held in slightly trembling hands, was perspiring profusely from the extreme tension. He expected the shoreline—and his scout boat—to be bathed in brilliant white light at any moment from flares launched into the dark sky by the foe on

land. Anderson knew he would be in the direct line of fire
when enemy gunners and riflemen on shore opened up against
the approaching assault craft. Yet only darkness and silence
prevailed.

The total absence of an Allied naval bombardment of
beaches to be assaulted by the 36th Division puzzled Ensign
Anderson. He did not know that, a short time previously,
General Fred Walker, commander of the Texas National
Guard outfit, had elected not to pound the beach with gunfire
from warships offshore.

"Our troops might be hit by short rounds from our own
ships," he had explained. "And there are no appropriate targets for naval gunfire. I see no reason to kill a lot of Italian
civilians and destroy their homes."

Soon the puttering of boat engines accelerated into a roar
as clusters of troop-filled assault craft reached the scout boat
and swept past on both sides. Anderson heaved a sigh of
relief. But his crucial task had not been completed. With hell
to break out any moment, Anderson had to remain at his post
400 yards offshore and guide in succeeding waves with his
flashing red light.

The first assault wave had reached a point 40 yards from
the white sands of the beach. Grating noises pierced the still
air as creaking ramps were lowered. One by one the Texans,
burdened by heavy combat gear, lowered themselves into the
dark, shallow waters and began laboriously wading toward
the shoreline.

"Just like the practice landings back in the States," many
of the wading men thought. Overhead the sky was spangled
with stars. A mild breeze was blowing. The only sounds to
be heard were the muted movements of the Texans wading
through the surf and the gentle lapping of waves on the white
sands just ahead. Otherwise there was a ghostlike stillness.

Suddenly . . . Swisssshh - CRACK! Swisssshh - CRACK!

Two loud explosions erupted among the American infantrymen in the surf. A pair of German high-velocity .88-
millimeter guns had opened fire at point-blank range against
the invaders. The flat-trajectory trek of the screaming missiles was faster than sound, so the swishing noise of the shell's

flight was heard an instant before the sharp crack of the muzzle blast.

Swisssshh - CRACK! Other .88s joined in. As if on cue, a cacophony of sound scourged the shoreline as German machine guns and rifles raked the wading and helpless Americans with deadly accuracy. Moments later the shoreline was bathed in the brilliance of high noon in the tropics as the defenders shot flares into the air.

Streams of white tracers created grotesque geometric patterns as thousands of bullets hissed past and into the Thirty-Sixers caught in the mammoth ambush. The machine gun slugs, sounding like swarms of angry bees, ricocheted off the water and caused fiery sparks where they struck the assault boats' steel hides.

Screams from the water's edge pierced the air where Americans were struck by some of the thousands of whistling bullets. In the brilliance of the German flares, faces of the Texans were ghostly and contorted with fear, a deep numbing fear.

Hearing shots fired in anger for the first time, the invaders' ordeal had only begun. There were loud explosions all along the surf and shoreline, coupled with blinding flashes that shot fingers of flame into the sky. German mortars, dug in a few hundred yards to the rear, began to pound the American landing beaches. Days previously, these mortars, manned by skilled veterans of the 16th Panzer division, had zeroed in on these beaches. Now it was only a matter of dropping shells into the mouths of the mortar barrels and waiting for the lethal explosions among the invaders only a few seconds later.

There were more piercing, agonizing screams from the surf as men's bodies were mutilated by jagged, white-hot mortar fragments. Cries of "Medic! Medic!" went unheeded. Medics were being cut down also.

Along the massive heights just inland, German artillery observers promptly went into action. These commanding elevations, particularly towering Monte Soprano and the high ground around the little towns of Altavilla and Albanella, offered the defenders a commanding view of the entire sweep of the American landing beaches.

Now from these heights, with the illumination furnished by the German flares that hovered over the sand dunes and had turned night into day, *Wehrmacht* officers could pick and choose their targets from among the huddled masses of brown-clad Americans seeking desperately to reach land and gain cover from the frightening holocaust.

Behind the chain of mountains white flashes lighted the sky. German artillery batteries had opened fire on the invaders and shortly the Americans heard the eerie scream of clusters of shells racing into their midst. Tremendous explosions all along the shore sent gushers of water and sand reaching into the sky. Sickening thuds told where shell fragments plowed into the bodies of soldiers with no place to hide.

One by one, the Texans stumbled up onto the sand, fell, picked themselves up, crawled a few yards forward, collapsed again. They inched along, exhausted and drained emotionally, seeking a sand dune or patch of weeds or clump of scrub brush, anything that could shield them against the ravages of the blistering automatic weapons fire and the mortar and artillery explosions which had instantly transformed the beautiful Gulf of Salerno into the lower bowels of Dante's Inferno.

In this moment of impending disaster, the steel will of the Texans, descendents of those who stood at the Alamo, came to the fore. Staff Sergeant Quillan H. McMichen was preparing to leap out of his assault boat when its ramp dropped. The ramp stuck and no amount of kicking or cursing by the soldiers in the craft could dislodge it. Sergeant McMichen was struck in the chest and shoulder by German machine gun slugs.

Panic set in as the men in the boat sought to get out to escape the torrent of fire being directed at the little craft. Ignoring his serious wounds, McMichen assumed the solo chore of kicking and pounding with his fists on the stuck ramp until, creaking and groaning, it slowly fell into the water.

"Follow me!" Sergeant McMichen shouted to the others in the boat as he led them through the curtain of fire and onto the beach. He was gasping for breath as the result of the bullet in his chest, and one arm was almost useless. His wool uniform was saturated with blood from the wounds. Despite his agony, McMichen positioned his men along the shoreline and ordered them to commence firing. Moments later the sergeant was struck by a machine gun bullet for the third time. He toppled over dead.

Sergeant Manuel S. Gonzales, along with several comrades, had taken cover behind a low sand dune. Spotting the little knot of Americans hovering behind the dune, an enemy machine gun only a short distance away began sending bursts of tracers at the Americans, clear targets in the light of the flares. "Stay here, I'll get the bastards!" Gonzales called to the others.

Cradling his Garand rifle across his arms, Gonzales began laboriously crawling through the sand toward the machine-gun nest. The *Wehrmacht* gunners spotted the Thirty-Sixer and turned their full attention toward him. A tracer bullet glanced off his back pack, setting it afire. Gonzales managed to shed the pack and continued to crawl toward his tormentors. A grenade was tossed at him and exploded nearby, sending white-hot jagged chunks of steel into his body.

Gonzales was dazed by the force of the grenade explosion and in extreme pain from the hot metal fragments that had ripped him open. Blood began to form in a pool underneath him. Bullets continued to zip just over his head. Summoning all his strength and inner spirit, the sergeant inched on forward until he was only 15 yards from the spitting enemy machine gun. Turning onto his side, he detached a grenade from his web belt and barely had the strength remaining to pull out the pin. With one final burst of determination, the sergeant tossed the grenade and heard an explosion and saw an orange flame erupt from the enemy machine-gun nest. Screams rang out above the din of the lethal melee swirling all around. The three enemy gunners crumpled into heaps—dead. His work done, Gonzales, bleeding profusely from his wounds, lapsed into unconsciousness.

In the mass confusion along the 36th Division beaches, Private J. C. Jones was pinned down with a group of frightened, disorganized and demoralized soldiers. Taking stock of the situation, Jones began issuing orders to the men, told them to follow him, and led them forward off the beach. The hodge-podge little group, under Private Jones' leadership, knocked out several German machine guns.

Sergeant Glen O. Hiller was seriously wounded when struck by a bullet while wading ashore. He refused to be evacuated and continued on to the shore at the head of his squad. Only after his men were organized and into position did the sergeant, weak from loss of blood, agree to return to a hospital ship offshore for treatment.

Lieutenant Colonel Samuel S. Graham was a battalion commander without a battalion. Due to a mixup in landing-boat schedules, Graham had reached shore ahead of his unit. Declining to merely take cover and wait for his battalion to catch up with him, Colonel Graham gathered together some 65 disorganized and leaderless soldiers from assorted units and began fighting inland from the beach. Along the way his collection of soldiers knocked out three machine-gun nests and a mortar position.

Despite the chaos rampant on the white sands of Salerno, the American invaders steadily pushed inland and when a horrified Mediterranean sun peeked over the towering Apennines that morning of D-Day it looked down on a scene of spectacular carnage. Bodies of young Texans, many grotesquely mutilated, floundered in the surf or lay crumpled among the sand dunes. Rocking gently along the shoreline were the twisted or burned hulks of scores of landing craft which had been struck by shells or had hit land mines which laced the shore in profusion.

Gaining a thin slice of real estate along the Gulf of Salerno had been an expensive one for the Americans and British. But Fifth Army was ashore, reinforcements and supplies were landing and assault troops were pushing inland against tenacious German defenders.

Furiously struck by the Anglo-Americans at several points along the 31-mile stretch of beach that was its to defend, the German 16th Panzer Division did not disintegrate under the sledgehammer blow. It had done its job—slowing down the invaders while *Wehrmacht* reinforcements were rushed into place to ring the beachhead with a noose of steel.

Due to the chaotic conditions along the fireswept Gulf of Salerno, battle information was slow in reaching the German Tenth Army commander, *General der Panzer Truppen* Heinrich von Vietinghoff, at his headquarters in the Apennine village of Sant Angelo di Lombardi. But by 8 A.M.—only four hours after the initial landings at Salerno—Von Vietinghoff had pieced together a clear picture of the situation.

The wily Tenth Army commander was convinced that this was the Allies' *grosslandung* (main landing), as, he concluded, the British and Americans did not have the military resources to launch another major effort farther north in the vicinity of Rome.

Now Von Vietinghoff was confronted with a perplexing question. He had heard nothing from his boss, *Feldmarschall* Kesselring, who was busy in Rome disarming Italian forces and securing the city against possible Allied parachute assaults. Was Von Vietinghoff to withdraw to Rome or attempt to repel the Salerno invasion?

General von Vietinghoff, an aggressive commander, sensed an opportunity to inflict a major disaster on the Allies in their effort to establish a large force on continental Europe. Without waiting on word from Kesselring, the Tenth Army commander made up his mind. He would oppose the Anglo-American landing with all the resources at his disposal. He picked up his field telephone. Within the hour *Wehrmacht* forces from throughout central Italy were racing for the Salerno beaches.

4
"Be Ruthless!
Annihilate Them!"

THAT MORNING OF September 9, *Feldmarschall* Kesselring at his headquarters at Frascati was breathing deep sighs of relief. Operation *Achse*, the disarming of Italian forces, had progressed much more rapidly and smoothly than anticipated. Two veteran *Wehrmacht* divisions had raced into Rome during the night and had the Eternal City under control. One hundred and thirty miles south of Rome the Allies had landed during the night, but Kesselring was convinced that the invasion could be contained and the Anglo-Americans driven back into the sea.

At 9:15 A.M. Kesselring told his aides that the Salerno effort was undoubtedly the Allied *grosslandung*, that Eisenhower was too cautious to attack outside the range of tactical air cover based in Sicily, and that the Germans might have been in "real trouble" had the Allies landed near Rome. Such an assault near the Italian capital would have cut off all German forces in southern Italy, Kesselring believed.

Early that morning of Allied D-Day at Salerno, Romans were arousing from a fitful night of sleep in which they sought to gather strength to face yet another bleak day in the 2,683rd year of the Eternal City's existence. Before retiring citizens had been shocked to hear over Radio Rome that Italy was no longer a war partner of the Third Reich. Now, on awakening, war weary Romans were in for a jolt: During the night the German *Wehrmacht* had disarmed Italian army units in the region and seized control of Rome.

On this beautiful morning in the Mediterranean, the civilian population of Rome came down with an infectious new disease—a nervous twitch of the head. People sitting in sidewalk cafes along the fashionable *Via Vittorio Veneto* and the *Vicolo del Cinque* (Little Street of the Five) in the thieves' quarter of the capital, those idly lounging on street corners or bustling about toward some presumably important appointment, all periodically cast their eyes upward into the clear blue sky. Then they promptly lowered their gazes to the ground, as though fearful of being caught in the act.

All of the Romans were looking skyward for one reason: The hoped for sight of Allied parachutes floating toward the ground, paratroopers on the way to rescue the Romans from the clutches of their former German partners. Word had swept through Rome like a brush fire across a dry prairie in recent days that the Allies were planning to parachute a large force into the Eternal City.

Along the *Via del Babuino* (Street of the Baboon) a Roman who had not heard of the coming of Allied paratroopers but had noticed the head-twitching by civilians stopped a passerby who was staring into the sky. "Pardon me, sir," he began. "But what is it everyone is looking up for?"

Alarmed that he might be "caught," the Roman rushed off without a word in reply.

On the terrace of a cafe near the 1850-year-old crumbling ruins of the Colosseum, a man was standing near the railing, scanning the blue sky with his binoculars as several companions sat anxiously nearby. He lowered the binoculars, put them back into the case, and muttered, "Something must have gone wrong." Everyone on the terrace slowly got to his or her feet and drifted away.

What had "gone wrong" was that General Maxwell Tay-

lor and Colonel William Gardiner, the two American officers
who had been in Rome clandestinely only the day before, had
called off the 82nd Airborne jump on the outskirts of the
capital when it became obvious that the parachute mission
would meet with disaster.

Unknown to the confused millions of Romans that morning of the ninth, the legally constituted government of Italy
had fled during the chaotic nighttime hours. King Victor Emmanuel, old, pathetic, physically infirm, nervous, had piled
into an old Italian car at his palace shortly after Marshal Badoglio read the armistice terms over Radio Rome. The marshal, also elderly and shaky, had climbed into another vehicle.
Other government officials and the chiefs of the army, navy
and air force entered cars and, with lights extinguished, the
little convoy began weaving its way out of Rome.

The governmental party traveled on the *Via Tiburtina*, one
of the few exit roads not blocked by German forces. Leaving
the shadowy silhouette of the Eternal City in the background,
the king and his entourage drove eastward toward the Adriatic
coast, arriving at the harbor at Pescara while it was still covered in darkness. There the party boarded an Italian navy ship
and sailed southward to the coastal town of Brindisi, in the
heel of the Italian boot, where King Victor Emmanuel established the government of Italy.

While General Mark Clark's Fifth Army troops on the Salerno beachhead continued to consolidate their positions and
push on inland on the ninth—D-Day—several Allied warships
were steaming into the harbor at Taranto, an Italian pilot
aboard each ship. *Operation Slapstick*, a diversionary landing
in the Italian heel, was underway. The convoy was carrying
assorted troops of Bernard Montgomery's Eighth Army which
had made its main landing in the Italian toe six days previously.

The pilot in one of the cruisers, the USS *Boise*, suggested
a mooring site in the harbor which the ship's captain declined
in favor of a berth at the mole. The HMS *Abdiel*, carrying
members of the elite British 1st Parachute Division, edged
into the berth declined by the skipper of the *Boise*. A few
hours later, as the *Abdiel* was discharging its complement of

Red Devils, a contact mine exploded under her. Within a few minutes the *Abdiel* sank out of sight. Forty-eight members of the crew and 101 British airborne men were killed by the explosion or drowned.

It was the only human loss. The Germans had pulled out of Taranto several hours before the arrival of the Allied task force.

On the Salerno beachhead, *Avalanche* was progressing according to plan, and by nightfall elements of the U.S. 36th Division had driven inland for five miles. The British on the northern sector also moved steadily ahead against sporadic but fierce resistance. General Rudolph Sickenius' panzers and grenadiers were precisely following the role laid out for them: Fight and fall back, then fight again and withdraw only under heavy pressure.

At Frascati, *Feldmarschall* Kesselring had belatedly concurred with Von Vietinghoff's independently reached decision to rush reinforcements to Salerno instead of withdrawing Tenth Army northward toward Rome and conceding a foothold on continental Europe to the Allies. Kesselring had chosen to make Salerno the supreme test of German armed might. It was along this 31-mile stretch of Italian coastline that he would demonstrate to the world, once and for all, the invincibility of the *Wehrmacht*.

Even as Vietinghoff was congregating his Tenth Army around the Allied beachhead, Kesselring was rushing troops, guns and panzers to the Salerno area from northern Italy and from as far away as France and the Balkans. The Great Buildup Race was on.

The classic question was: Could the Anglo-Americans bring in troops, armor and supplies over water, from bases several hundred miles away in Sicily and North Africa, at a faster pace than could the German *Wehrmacht* by land from points throughout southern Europe and the Balkans?

Even as fighting men of the Allies were pushing inland, for miles around the once insignificant little town of Salerno the earth heaved and shuddered under the thrashings of tens of thousands of German grenadiers, hundreds of vehicles, swarms of panzers and artillery pieces, all rushing toward

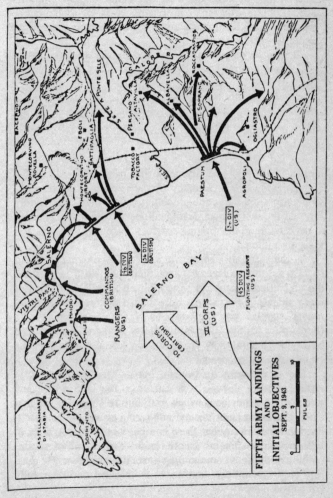

FIFTH ARMY LANDINGS
AND
INITIAL OBJECTIVES
SEPT. 9, 1943

MILES

SALERNO BAY

10 CORPS (BRITISH)

VI CORPS (U.S.)

45 DIV (U.S.)
FLOATING RESERVE

3d DIV (U.S.)

36 DIV (U.S.)

56 DIV (BRITISH)

COMMANDOS (BRITISH)

RANGERS (U.S.)

SALERNO

VIETRI PASS

MAIORI

AMALFI

CASTELLAMMARE DI STABIA

SORRENTO

MONTECORVINO AIRPORT

BATTIPAGLIA

EBOLI

MONTECORVINO ROVELLA

ALTAVILLA

PERSANO

TOBACCO FACTORY

PAESTUM

AGROPOLI

OGLIASTRO

MT. SOPRANO

ROCCADASPIDE

PONTE SELE

assigned positions to cordon off the Anglo-American beach-head.

Streaming steadily toward the Salerno fighting, German grenadiers and black-uniformed panzer troops often broke out in song. The melodic strains of the *Wehrmacht* soldiers' favorite wartime ballad, "Lili Marlene," rang out from long columns of German infantrymen marching to battle, confident and eager. Echoing in their beings was the cry that came from *Feldmarschall* Kesselring urging the destruction of the Allied invaders: "Be ruthless! Annihilate them! Throw them into the sea!"

Ragged Italian civilians in a wide sweep of central Italy looked on in fear and dismay at the passing parade of the armed might of Nazi Germany. To the war weary and poverty-stricken natives the scene unfolding before their eyes vividly foretold the widespread death and destruction that was about to descend upon their once peaceful villages, green fields and majestic mountains.

As the German *Wehrmacht* was rapidly moving overland to Salerno, the sea lanes between Sicily and North Africa and the embattled beachhead were clogged with Allied ships of many shapes and sizes. All were loaded with troop reinforcements, supplies and the weapons of war. Early on D + 1 (September 10) the U.S. 45th Infantry Division, commanded by Major General Troy H. Middleton, came ashore over the American landing beaches.

That same morning, General Mark Clark, leader of Fifth Army, climbed down a rope ladder on the USS *Ancon* and into a tiny assault boat which took him to shore for the first time. Clark had been closely monitoring events on the beachhead since H-Hour, but there had been little he could do to influence developments ashore. In the early hours of an amphibious assault, a commanding general is impotent. He must rely on junior officers and noncoms to carry out a carefully conceived plan.

Clark was walking along the sandy beaches with his long strides when he heard the insistent barking of a dog. Looking around, much to his surprise, he discovered the source of the canine uproar—Mike, the general's German police dog. Clark thought his pet was back in North Africa.

Named Mike although a female, the animal had been given to General Clark by a sergeant several months previously in Oujda, North Africa, then headquarters of Fifth Army. Since that time the German dog had been the general's constant companion.

There were strict regulations against taking dogs on navy ships, so the Fifth Army commander, on leaving Algiers several days before the assault on Salerno, had bid goodbye to his pet. But, unknown to General Clark, Sergeant Chaney, Clark's orderly, had put a tag on Mike's collar and turned her over to some soldiers before they went aboard ship.

The tag, cleverly inscribed by the wily Sergeant Chaney to be subtly intimidating in tone, read: "This is General Mark Clark's dog. She is going to Salerno."

As no rational officer in Fifth Army had any desire to assume the responsibility of ejecting the commanding general's pet from the vessel, Mike made it to the embattled Salerno beachhead on D-Day. There, with shot and shell all around, she had the time of her life, leaping up and down on the beach and dashing hither and fro.

Pleased as Clark was to see Mike, he also realized that her hyperactivity had become something of a distracting influence to those involved in beachhead functions. So with a gentle pat on her head, the commanding general ordered that, in effect, she be restricted to quarters until further notice. Mike was promptly tied up.

By the conclusion of the next day, the eleventh, the Allied hold in the Salerno area was 11 miles at its deepest point and stretched in a huge semicircle from Agropoli on the south to Amalfi on the north with a circumference of 44 miles. Allied reinforcements continued to pour ashore and by now Clark had more than 140,000 troops in the beachhead. *Operation Avalanche* was off to a good start but the Allied high command braced for the inevitable blow—a coordinated, hard-hitting German counterattack to throw the invaders back into the sea once sufficient *Wehrmacht* forces had been gathered.

The massive enemy assault would not be long in arriving.

By midnight of September 11—D + 2—General von Vietinghoff had ringed the Gulf of Salerno with five and a half
divisions to confront the equivalent of four Anglo-American
divisions. The Germans were winning the Great Buildup
Race.

Earlier that day, unaware that the Germans had been able
to concentrate such a powerful force around the beachhead
in such a short period of time, a confident Mark Clark prepared to leave the *Ancon* for the shore. As he started to climb
down the rope ladder, the USS *Savannah* passed within 200
yards of his headquarters ship. Clark paused to watch the
cruiser and moments later he and others over a wide expanse
of the Gulf of Salerno heard an eerie screeching noise. Allied
sailors and army men alike on ships anchored offshore knew
instinctively the source of the sound—the approach of a new
type of German bomb.

Clark scanned the sky for *Luftwaffe* planes. He saw none.
The radio-controlled German bomb had been released from
high-flying enemy aircraft several miles away. Those on the
Allied vessels had received their introduction to these frightening new enemy bombs the previous day when several ships
were struck, a few plunging to the bottom of the Tyrrhenian
Sea.

The screeching sound grew louder. Clark and the others
on the *Ancon* sensed that the glide-bomb was heading directly
for the command ship, easily identifiable to the *Luftwaffe* due
to its forest of antennae. The noise of the approaching missile
became ear-splitting and moments later it crashed into the
nearby *Savannah*, just forward of her bridge. The bomb
plunged through the cruiser's deck and exploded below. An
orange flame erupted high into the clear blue sky and the
Savannah shook from bow to stern. Several hundred American navy men were killed or wounded.

The *Luftwaffe*, which apparently had not been reading Allied communiques telling of Anglo-American superiority over
the Salerno beachhead, had been heavily pounding Allied
ships offshore. In the first three days of the invasion, the
Luftwaffe, taking off from nearby bases in central Italy, flew
more than 500 sorties against shipping in the Gulf of Salerno,

using both conventional bombs and Adolph Hitler's frightening new "secret weapon"—the remote-controlled glide
bomb.

Launched at distances of nearly three and one-half miles
from a target, these electronically directed explosive devices
traveled 650 miles per hour and could not be seen by the
human eye. The psychological impact upon Allied military
men on vessels in the gulf was devastating. The physical dam-
age was extensive. Several Allied warships had been sent to
the bottom without personnel aboard realizing they had been
under attack from the air.

While the battle of Salerno beachhead was building into a
massive showdown, British General Bernard Montgomery was
inching methodically northward in the toe and heel of Italy.
His Eighth Army had landed unopposed in the toe of Italy
on September 3, and Montgomery had been issuing daily
communiques reporting his troops in "hot pursuit of the retreating Germans." Several days after Montgomery had
landed, German forces before him had broken off contact and
were withdrawing northward.

If Montgomery was in "hot pursuit," the Anglo-American
high command was unaware of the fact. General Harold Alexander, the British commander of Fifteenth Army group and
Montgomery's boss, had become increasingly disturbed over
Eighth Army's lack of progress. On September 10 Alexander
fired off a radiogram to Montgomery urging him to advance
more rapidly. The communication received no reply.

General Alexander, on September 12, dispatched his Chief
of Staff, Major General A. A. Richardson, to Eighth Army
headquarters to explain the increasing high level concern and
the urgent need for Montgomery to hurry northward. Richardson received no satisfaction.

"The Jerries have blown many bridges in the mountain
passes which have to be repaired before I can push on,"
Montgomery told the Fifteenth Army Group Chief of Staff.

Early on the morning of the twelfth at the embattled Salerno beachhead, General von Vietinghoff was ready to strike
back. His steel noose around the thin slice of Italian real

estate held by the Allies was strengthened by more than 600 tanks and hundreds of artillery pieces and mobile guns.

As dawn broke over the Apennines that day, German assault troops were read an exhortation from the Tenth Army commander, Von Vietinghoff, to "drive the enemy into the sea." Less than an hour later, Von Vietinghoff's infantry and panzers struck the Allied beachhead a furious blow. As planned, the *Wehrmacht* assault hit at the weakest point in the Anglo-American perimeter—a five-mile gap between the U.S. VI Corps and the British X Corps, which was patrolled only by a small armored unit.

It was Von Vietinghoff's intention to split the Fifth Army, drive to the shoreline, then destroy the predominantly British force on the north and the American formation on the south, one at a time.

Within an hour of the German jumpoff, troops and tanks began pouring through the five-mile gap. Von Vietinghoff hoped to reach the Tyrrhenian Sea by nightfall.

That same morning, unaware that Tenth Army had launched a major coordinated counterattack against his strung-out forces, Fifth Army commander Mark Clark, buoyant and confident, established his headquarters ashore. He was glad to be on dry land where he could more effectively direct the battle. Within a few days, Clark felt he would be able to launch a major thrust northward out of the bridgehead and drive toward the invasion's initial major objective—Naples.

Clark's staff had selected a large castle-like structure for his headquarters on shore, its location providing ready access to the road network on the beachhead. But the commanding general was not pleased. "It sticks out like a sore thumb," Clark stated. He moved into his personal trailer secluded in a brush-filled wood near the beach.

At his command-post early that morning, General Clark had been advised by his staff that the Germans had launched a number of local counterattacks around the 44-mile perimeter of the bridgehead, but they were thought to be efforts to keep the advancing invaders off balance.

Still confident that the Salerno operation was proceeding

as planned, Clark climbed into a jeep beside a driver and set out on a tour of the beachhead. He promptly discovered a new enemy—dust. Clouds of swirling, choking dust, churned up by crashing shells and heavy vehicular traffic on narrow unpaved roads behind Allied lines, hung over the landscape like a pall. Clothes and bodies were covered with dust. It seeped through outer garmets and saturated under clothing. Clark and the others ate dust and breathed dust.

All day the Fifth Army leader drove and walked through the choking fog. In desperation, the gasping Mark Clark tied a handkerchief over his nose and mouth. It did little to keep out the annoying dust. Aware that he may have looked slightly ridiculous in his improvised face mask, Clark mused to his driver: "I guess some of our fellows think I'm a bank bandit!"

As General Clark continued his tour of the front, his early morning optimism began to fade. In its place emerged a mood of concern. At each sector the word was the same: The Germans are attacking with great ferocity and firepower. A military fact of life became evident: These were no longer local probing attacks designed to slow down the onward rush of the Anglo-Americans. Rather it was now painfully evident that the *Wehrmacht*, in less than three days' time, had concentrated a massive force and launched a major counterattack along the entire perimeter.

Savage fighting continued all day on the bridgehead, and by sundown German troops and panzers, which had poured through the five-mile gap between British and American forces, were only six miles from the water. Von Vietinghoff had failed to reach his goal for that day—smashing through to the shoreline. But he was elated. His troops had torn open a large hole in the center of the Allied line and were in position and had the momentum to continue the onslaught in the morning. Then, he was confident, the German forces would push on to the sea, splitting the Anglo-Americans in two.

Although darkness halted the spirited German advance temporarily, Von Vietinghoff would allow no respite for the staggering Allied troops. Massed virtually hub to hub on three sides of the beachhead, *Wehrmacht* artillery pounded the front lines and rear areas through the night.

Earlier that evening of D + 3, as a rosy Mediterranean sun began its daily journey behind the western horizon, a beleaguered Mark Clark was striding along the sandy beaches. The gentle waves of the Tyrrhenian Sea lapped softly at his heels. A short distance away enemy shells crashed to earth, the violence of their explosions seeming to rock the shoreline where the army commander was walking. A worried Mark Clark, at the end of the third day of an operation he had entered with high hopes, was confronted with a military reality: His Fifth Army was in danger of being driven into the sea.

Dirty, tired and deeply concerned, Mark Clark's mind was awhirl. As he trudged through the sand he sorted out the options available to him to prevent another Dunkirk for Allied forces. An unthinkable eventuality. Yet Clark had to think of it. On his narrow but strong shoulders rested the ultimate responsibility for the destiny of Fifth Army.

The young American general had slept only a few hours in four days and nights of constant activity and decision-making. His body was weary and his mind tormented. His spirit was pierced by thoughts of the young American and British soldiers, many seeing armed violence for the first time, who were being cut to pieces by the veteran, numerically superior German *Wehrmacht*.

All that afternoon at his trailer command post Clark had been beset by continuing reports of Allied setbacks. A green battalion of the U.S. 36th Infantry Division had been driven out of Altavilla, a small town high on a hill overlooking the American sector of the beachhead, and suffered heavy losses. At Battipaglia, a key communications center in the British sector, Tommies, after a savage fight, were forced to abandon the battered old town.

General Richard McCreery, commander of the British X Corps, telephoned to tell Clark that men of his 56th Division were near exhaustion after many hours of constant fighting. McCreery asked for reinforcements. Clark's answer was brief: "There are no reinforcements."

Minutes after McCreery signed off, Clark received an urgent call from General Ernest "Mike" Dawley, commander of the U.S. VI Corps, who said tersely: "The Germans have broken through my center in great numbers."

"What are you going to do about it?" Clark replied, erasing any trace of undue concern from his voice.

"There's little I can do. I have no reserves. They're all in the line."

"Well, do what you can. I have no reserves, either."

Now, striding along the sandy beaches, General Clark saw the tons of supplies stacked in neat rows for hundreds of yards along the shoreline. These provisions were to support Fifth Army in its impending drive northward to capture the prized port of Naples. The German *Wehrmacht*, which was holding the aces in this deadly game of battlefield poker, had dramatically altered these Allied plans.

Clark's main concern at the moment was to arrive at a decision on what to do with these vast piles of critical supplies. The looming disaster at Salerno would be of even greater magnitude if this huge amount of stores was to fall into the hands of the Germans.

His thoughts harkened back many years to his West Point days. He recalled the stern admonitions of his instructors if a student one day in the future should be confronted with a situation which required abandonment of a battlefield: "Never, under any circumstances, allow your supplies and equipment to fall into the hands of the enemy!"

West Point instructors, Clark knew, would have flunked a cadet if he had theoretically failed to destroy these tons of supplies to keep them out of the hands of the Germans.

But Salerno beachhead on September 12, 1943, was no "paper" exercise. No instructor at West Point or the Army War College could have foreseen a situation such as Clark now faced on the Italian mainland. He realized that any order calling for preparations to destroy Allied supplies would plummet the morale of his fighting men, even create irreversible panic.

"Never, under any circumstances, allow your supplies to

fall into the hands of the enemy!'' The haunting warning of yesteryear echoed repeatedly through Clark's being.

Suddenly, the Fifth Army commander barked to an aide: ''To hell with the damned theory! I'm not going to issue any such orders!''

He paced on for a few yards and again spun around to the officer at his side. ''The only way the Germans are going to get us off this beach is if they push us, step by step, into the sea!'' he rasped defiantly. Pausing briefly, he added, ''And I don't intend to let that happen!''

Brave words. Inspirational words. Defiant words. But in themselves they did little to alter the impending Allied debacle on Salerno beachhead. More troops. More firepower. That was what was needed, Clark knew.

With a mantle of darkness beginning to enfold the battle-field, a spiritually rejuvenated Mark Clark returned to his headquarters in the brush. He was approached by a member of his staff.

''General,'' the grim-faced officer stated, ''I've got some bad news.''

Clark winced. ''Just what I need,'' he replied resignedly. ''What is it?''

''You know that new air strip our engineers scraped out north of Paestum yesterday?'' the aide continued. ''Well, two British Spitfires came in for a landing and our own antiair-craft gunners shot them both down.''

Now, seated in his blacked-out trailer with the sound of gunfire a short distance toward the front serving as a back-drop, the Fifth Army commander began to implement the options available to him which he had mulled over in his lonely walk along the beach. With him were Major General Alfred M. Gruenther, his Chief of Staff, and several other top aides.

Gruenther, at 44, was one of the U.S. Army's youngest major generals. He was noted for an incisive mind and an incredible power of recall.

Aware that a commander must formulate contingency plans for any battlefield eventuality, General Clark faced up to a cogent reality: Fifth Army might be driven from the Salerno beachhead. Consequently, he contacted U.S. Vice Admiral H. Kent Hewitt, commander of the naval task force at Salerno, and requested that he prepare two emergency plans immediately.

One plan would withdraw the British X Corps and land it again on the U.S. VI Corps beaches. The other would take VI Corps back over its beaches and disembark it in the British sector. If such a dire operation were necessary, it would be one fraught with peril. Disengaging troops from in front of the enemy and conducting a "landing in reverse" would be a most difficult procedure. At his headquarters on the USS *Biscayne*, Admiral Hewitt and his staff began work on the contingency plans.

Hewitt ordered unloading operations to halt in the VI Corps area, and placed ships and landing craft on a half-hour alert for movement out to sea beyond the range of enemy shore artillery. While this procedure was in progress and until General Clark actually ordered an evacuation, Hewitt's warships continued to pound enemy troops and facilities.

Clark next began to muster all the firepower that was readily available to help repel the continuation of the massive *Wehrmacht* onslaught the next morning. He received assurances from General Eisenhower, the Supreme Commander, in Algiers that "every plane that can fly" in the Northwest African Air Force would pound the enemy around the shrinking Salerno perimeter. Admiral Hewitt told Clark that his warships would bombard attacking Germans with "every gun that can fire."

This massive destructive power would be a big boost. But would it be enough to stem the rolling German tide heading relentlessly for the beaches?

What was direly needed was more Allied troops on the bridgehead to offset to a degree the *Wehrmacht* numerical superiority. General Eisenhower ordered elements of the U.S. 34th Infantry Division moved by LSTs from North Africa to the beachhead. General Alexander, commander of Fifteenth Army Group, directed the U.S. 3rd Infantry Division in Sicily to head for the shrinking bridgehead. In North Africa, the U.S. 1st Armored Division was alerted to move to Salerno.

These substantial reinforcements would be of immense value to General Clark—once they arrived. The logistical fact of life was that it would be anywhere from several days to two weeks before these formations reached the beachhead and were able to go into action. The crisis at Salerno demanded immediate action.

"Get Bill Yarborough in here," General Clark directed an aide. Within minutes Lieutenant Colonel William P. Yarborough, the 31-year-old airborne advisor to the Fifth Army commander, reported to the general.

Son of a retired army colonel, Yarborough had been one of the young pioneers of the infant United States Army airborne service when it was timidly launched with a test platoon in mid-1940 following startling successes by German *fallschirmjaeger* (paratroopers) and glider forces in Belgium, Holland and Norway as Adolph Hitler was overrunning much of Europe.

Yarborough had planned the airborne phase of *Operation Torch*, the Allied invasion of North Africa in November 1942, in which the independent 509th Parachute Infantry Battalion flew 1,600 miles from England to seize the key LaSenia and Tafaraoui airports south of Oran in front of seaborne landings. Yarborough went along on that mission, the first combat jump by any American airborne unit.

Several days later Yarborough jumped with elements of the 509th Parachute Infantry at Youks les Bains airfield in North Africa to take control of that facility, and in July 1943 he bailed out over Sicily as a battalion commander in the 504th Parachute Infantry Regiment of the 82nd Airborne Division.

Yarborough left the 82nd Airborne after the 38-day campaign in Sicily and became General Mark Clark's advisor for the crucial assault against Adolph Hitler's continental Europe.

Now, just before midnight of D + 3 at embattled Salerno beachhead, the Fifth Army commander was seeking expert opinion on the most rapid and effective means for employing his "ace in the hole"—the elite 82nd Airborne Division and its attached 509th Parachute Infantry Battalion.

"Bill, as you know we're in a lot of trouble here," Clark said to Lieutenant Colonel Yarborough. "The Germans have rushed in reinforcements much faster than anyone had anticipated. I want to bring Matt Ridgway's men in as soon as possible. What do you propose?"

Yarborough set out a precise course of action. He proposed that the two parachute regiments of the 82nd Airborne be dropped behind Allied lines on the beachhead for "numerical and psychological reinforcement" of the hard-pressed Anglo-American ground forces. "There's not sufficient airlift to bring in both regiments at the same time, so they would have to be dropped in two operations," he observed.

He also stressed that the mass jumps would have to be at night due to the *Luftwaffe* strength over the bridgehead. Lumbering, unarmed C-47s, filled with paratroopers, would provide juicy daytime targets for swift German fighter planes based at airfields in central Italy.

Colonel Yarborough recommended that the third major component of the 82nd Airborne Division, the 325th Glider Infantry Regiment, be brought to Salerno by sea. "A glider strip near Paestum is to be ready by tomorrow night," he pointed out. "But it may or may not be completed by then."

Another factor involved with glider reinforcement was one that concerned Yarborough: Could sufficient gliders be assembled rapidly in Sicily to fly in the 325th Regiment? "I doubt it," he concluded.

Moving over to a large wall map of the beachhead region, Colonel Yarborough pointed to a town 20 miles north of Salerno and stated, "As you know, general, there is the *real* German bottleneck in reinforcing and supplying their main forces around Salerno. We've got to stick a cork in that bottleneck."

Clark was well aware of the town—sleepy, unpretentious Avellino. The general and his airborne advisor had discussed the traffic center numerous times during the past three days.

Yarborough reviewed the reasons for his next recommendation: Dropping a battalion of paratroopers on Avellino, deep behind German lines. All road and rail traffic from Rome and northwest Italy had to pass through Avellino to reach enemy lines at Salerno. *Wehrmacht* forces could not be reinforced or supplied through the two mountain passes on the rugged Sorrento Peninsula at the extreme north of the Allied enclave at Salerno. Commandos and American Rangers, hard-pressed and under heavy attack, were blocking these two key defiles.

Alternative roads east of Avellino were circuitous, steep and traveling was slow and uncertain on them. Should the *Wehrmacht* be forced to use these inferior roads to supply and reinforce its Salerno positions, the task would prove ponderous, difficult and sluggish.

Yarborough, the veteran of three combat jumps, knew that dropping a battalion 20 miles behind German lines would be a perilous mission. He knew there were heavy enemy troop and armored concentrations in that region. "I'm certain our paratroopers can do the job without undue losses," the advisor stressed. "I have the utmost confidence in these men."

Yarborough's briefing concluded, there were several moments of silence as General Clark mulled over his advisor's recommendations. "Thanks, Bill," the weary Fifth Army commander said. "I'll think about it and make up my mind in the morning what I want to do."

Having achieved all that he could for the present to prepare for the resumption of the German onslaught on the morrow, Clark, fully clothed, crawled onto a cot to steal a few hours of sleep. Yet his tormented mind refused to permit him a brief respite.

High overhead in the star-spangled sky could be heard the distinctive throb of *Luftwaffe* bombers. Minutes later heavy explosions rocked the shoreline. Off in the distance was the incessant rumble of German artillery shells crashing into frontline positions. Much nearer was the loud roar of American gunners firing large-caliber projectiles into *Wehrmacht* troop concentrations and facilities.

With this gloomy backdrop of violence dinning his ears, a bone-tired Mark Clark was beset by one overriding thought: As serious as the situation was for Fifth Army, it would be even worse on the morrow.

As 140,000 Anglo-American fighting men clung by their fingernails to the Italian beachhead that night, a newscaster in London took to BBC with the latest communique from Allied Force Headquarters in Algiers:

The heaviest fighting of the Italian campaign is now going on at Salerno, but the Fifth Army is advancing steadily.

Far removed from the violence at Salerno that night, a worried General Dwight Eisenhower was holding a press conference at his headquarters in North Africa. The clock was approaching midnight. Reporters crowded the conference room, seeking clarification of repeated whispered rumors that General Mark Clark had one foot in the sea at Salerno.

Eisenhower, trim in his neatly pressed uniform with the four silver stars on his shoulders, avoided specifics and instead briefed the newsmen on reasons for the Salerno invasion:

"We're playing in the big leagues now. You can't hit a home run by bunting. You have to step up there and take your cut at the ball. The time has come to discontinue nibbling at islands, and hit the Germans where it hurts the most. I don't believe in fighting battles to chase someone out of some place. Our object is to trap and smash them."

In the dark vineyards, olive groves and deep defiles around the Allied bridgehead at Salerno, German grenadiers and panzers, spirited and self-confident, were massing to launch dawn attacks which *Wehrmacht* commanders were convinced would drive to the beaches.

5

An Allied
Disaster Looms

GENERAL DER PANZER Truppen Heinrich von Vietinghoff, the energetic commander of the German Tenth Army who had first attracted Adolph Hitler's attention for his successes as a corps commander on the Russian front, was up shortly after dawn at his headquarters in the Apennine village of Sant Angelo di Lombardi. He was in fine fettle. This well could be the day of decision at Salerno—September 13.

Von Vietinghoff no longer was satisfied with merely driving the Americans and British into the Tyrrhenian Sea. He was determined to prevent their escape, to inflict upon the Allies a massive disaster which would result in *herrenvolk* in the Fatherland forgetting the *Wehrmacht* debacle at Stalingrad the previous winter.

Over Salerno, eager young pilots of *Luftflotte 2* (Second Air Force) also had the scent of victory in their nostrils. Throughout the night heavy bombers and fighter-bombers had attacked the mass of vessels anchored offshore. Among the ships were the brightly lighted *Newfoundland*, *Leinster* and

Somersetshire, all hospital vessels with huge red crosses on them, crosses large enough to be seen miles away.

Inside the holds in the shades of a gray dawn, terrified wounded soldiers and medical personnel heard the roar of enemy airplanes diving toward the brilliantly illuminated hospital ships. Several German bombs barely missed the *Leinster* and *Somersetshire*, damaging the vessels slightly. One attacking *Luftwaffe* fighter-bomber pilot was more accurate than his comrades—his bomb exploded directly in the center of the *Newfoundland*, killing and wounding scores of soldiers and medical personnel.

Within minutes the *Newfoundland* was burning fiercely from bow to stern.

That morning a broadcaster over Radio Berlin, barely able to restrain the jubilation in his voice, told the Third Reich:

> The enemy is steadily falling back at Salerno. In some cases the Anglo-Americans are fleeing in panic. But they have no place to go. Another Allied Dunkirk is in the making!

At Fifth Army headquarters in the woods near the shoreline of the Gulf of Salerno, General Mark Clark was hard at work shortly after daybreak. Almost without exception, field reports arriving overnight from his hard-pressed army were gloomy in content. Alone in the trailer which served as his office, Clark was deep in thoughtful meditation. He pondered over the monumental ramifications should the Allies lose their first foothold on continental Europe and Fifth Army was destroyed in the process.

On a personal basis, the 47-year-old Clark was aware that a debacle for his command at Salerno would mean the end of a highly promising military career. A general who planned and then led the force in an invasion which ended in only a few days with the destruction of his army would be returned to the United States in disgrace—forever marked in history as a total failure in his first major battle command.

Painful as this looming eventuality might be for Mark Clark, professional soldier, it was the least of his concerns as he sat alone in his office that morning. A disaster on the Italian bridgehead in the Allies' initial confrontation on continental Europe with the military might of the Third Reich would result in a tremendous hue and cry back home, both among deeply worried citizens and in the hallowed halls of Congress.

It would be conceivable that not only would Clark have his neck figuratively lopped off, but the Allied Supreme Commander, General Eisenhower, might soon follow the Fifth Army commander to the public guillotine. Eisenhower would be a likely candidate for the American public's shrill demand for a Salerno scapegoat. It was Eisenhower who had approved the "disastrous" military venture onto the Italian mainland.

An Anglo-American debacle at Salerno, Clark knew, would inflict severe despair and a frightening drop in morale in the Allied world, not only among civilian populations but with fighting men as well. Maybe, the free world would conjecture, Adolph Hitler was right: Nazi Germany and its *Wehrmacht* were indeed invincible.

On the other side of the coin, a mammoth German victory at Salerno would result in a tremendous boost to morale in the German *Wehrmacht* and among the war-weary *herrenvolk*. *"Deutschland uber Alles!"* ("Germany over all!") would ring out again with renewed vigor across the length and breadth of the Third Reich as tens of thousands of British and American soldiers on Salerno beachhead marched into prisoners of war cages, while thousands of their comrades were lowered into the ground.

All of these monumental consequences sifted through Mark Clark's mind early that morning of the thirteenth—D + 4. He and his men had been on fireswept Salerno beachhead for 100 hours. Yet, to the commanding general, as well as his hard-pressed soldiers, it seemed more like a lifetime.

With attacking German formations only a short distance to his front, General Clark sent for a stenographer and began dictating an urgent letter to General Matt Ridgway, leader of the 82nd Airborne Division and its attached 509th Parachute Infantry Battalion, which was bivouacked around scattered airfields in Sicily. These airborne formations were Clark's only reserve, yet they were more than 300 miles from the embattled Italian bridgehead.

"The fighting at Salerno has taken a turn for the worse," Clark began, "and the situation is touch and go. I realize the time normally needed to prepare for a drop, but this is an exception. I want you to make a drop within our lines on the beachhead, and I want you to make it tonight. *This is a must!*"

Clark explained that one parachute regimental combat team was to drop behind friendly lines onto the beachhead that night and the second regiment was to jump the following night, September 14, on the same DZ (drop zone).

The Fifth Army commander also requested that at least a battalion of paratroopers be dropped on Avellino, 20 miles behind enemy lines, to plug the German traffic bottleneck through which reinforcements and supplies were flowing to the bridgehead.

Enclosed with Clark's letter would be a document drawn up by Lieutenant Colonel Yarborough, which contained a map designating the drop zone in the American sector of the beachhead and outlining operational procedures for receiving the parachuting regiments on the DZ that and the next night.

Although 82nd Airborne Division pathfinder platoons, equipped with Krypton lamps, radar devices and radios, would help guide the C-47s loaded with paratroopers into the DZ, Colonel Yarborough injected a new technique for maximizing the ability of carrier pilots to locate the drop zone south of the Sele River, near Paestum.

Troops already on the ground at Salerno were at work placing Jerry cans, cut in half and filled with gasoline-soaked sand, in the shape of a huge T, with each "arm" a half-mile in length. These improvised containers would be lighted when the first C-47s were heard approaching the beachhead. After the transport planes had delivered their paratroopers and turned toward their bases in Sicily, the burning cans of gasoline-soaked sand would be extinguished.

Completing his urgent letter, General Clark turned to Colonel Yarborough and his Chief of Staff, General Al Gruenther, and remarked, "I added a few other details to be sure Ridgway will understand why I am asking the impossible of him and his men, that they make a drop only a few hours after receiving this letter."

Clark then said to Gruenther, "Al, send someone out to locate a fighter pilot to deliver this message."

U.S. Army Air Corps planes had landed periodically that day on the hastily scraped-out strip just north of Paestum, and it was there that General Gruenther's emissary collared a pilot to deliver the message to Sicily. He was Captain Jacob R. Hamilton, who was on a tactical reconnaissance flight when he touched down on the Paestum air strip, not knowing that he would be entrusted with carrying one of the most crucial communications of the war—a message which could determine the fate of 140,000 American and British fighting men.

Captain Hamilton was quickly bundled into a jeep and rushed to Mark Clark's trailer. Hamilton would, in effect, become the Paul Revere of the Twentieth Century. Ushered into the army commander's presence, Hamilton was rapidly briefed on the situation.

Handing the large envelope containing the crucial letter, map and instructions to the awed pilot, Clark stated, "I want you to leave immediately for Licata, Sicily. This is a matter of the highest priority. You are to deliver this envelope personally to General Ridgway—personally to General Ridgway and to no one else. No one else. Do you fully understand these instructions?"

"Yes, sir," Captain Hamilton responded crisply, taking the envelope from Clark. He saluted, turned on his heel and bolted out of the trailer. Jeeping to the air strip at Paestum, Hamilton heard enemy shells crashing a short distance away. The explosions punctuated the dire urgency of his mission.

Arriving at the air strip, Hamilton leaped into his P-38 fighter plane, which had been warmed up and awaiting his arrival. With General Clark's vital message on his lap, Hamilton sped down the dirt runway and lifted off. He banked the twin-bodied craft and set a course for Licata, some 300 miles distant.

As Captain Hamilton in his P-38 raced for Sicily, the Fifth

Army commander, in between issuing orders and dispatching a flood of messages, heard a newscast over BBC in London:

> The Fifth Army remains under constant attack at Salerno and the situation there is touch and go. Meanwhile General Bernard Montgomery and his British Eighth Army are dashing up the Italian boot in an effort to reach the hard-pressed troops at Salerno.

General Clark and his aides were furious. The implication in the British newscast was clear: Clark was about to be thrown into the Tyrrhenian Sea and Montgomery was "dashing" to his rescue.

Montgomery, who had landed unopposed in the toe of Italy 10 days previously, had been making snail-like progress northward, even though the two enemy divisions before him had broken off contact and were withdrawing northward. Eighth Army was still 100 miles south of the bitterly-contested bridgehead.

Mark Clark's indignation over the BBC newscast was hardly relieved when he received a personal message from General Montgomery later that day, which read: "Hold on. We will soon be joining hands."

Clark responded with a pointed: "I still have yet to feel the warmness of your grasp."

Meanwhile, on that morning of the thirteenth, British military government officers were desperately endeavoring to get the town of Salnero functioning once again. Fifth Army was still bringing supplies and equipment in over the open beaches, and the harbor facilities at the town were desperately needed—and soon.

British officers recruited 28 extremely frightened and hungry Salerno men to go about the considerable task of clearing rubble and debris from the streets. But *Wehrmacht* artillery, relentlessly pounding the town and its harbor, soon gave the 28 laborers cause for reassessment of the situation. By noon all had deserted, returning neither for food nor wages.

German commanders, knowing that the harbor at Salerno was vital to the invading Allies, trained their big guns on the

dock facilities which were soon a shambles. Just after noon
that day, with the enemy bombardment at its height, the Salerno harbor was closed down—indefinitely.

At 12:15 P.M. that day, Von Vietinghoff struck. Preceded
by a massive artillery barrage, elements of the 29th Panzer
Grenadier and 16th Panzer Divisions, paced by swarms of
tanks churning up huge clouds of dust, moved out of Battipaglia, Eboli and Altavilla and crashed into the lightly-held
gap between British and American forces in the center of the
beachhead line.

The attackers soon overran American and British front
lines, killing or capturing hundreds and sending demoralized
remnants reeling back toward the beaches. Elsewhere, all
around the shrinking Allied perimeter on the beachhead, veteran *Wehrmacht* units, sensing a major Anglo-American disaster was in the making, assaulted the hard-pressed and
outnumbered defenders.

The Allied situation had gone from one of deep concern
to one of desperation. At this point, early in the afternoon,
General Clark threw every available man into the defense—
cooks, mechanics, drivers and clerks suddenly found themselves in the forefront of the action. They were fighting as
infantrymen to ward off the furious charges of the enemy,
who by now were flushed with the heady scent of victory.

On area roads to the rear, American officers were stopping
every vehicle that came along. Despite protests from some
that they were on important tasks, the occupants were handed
guns and told, "Go across that field and start fighting."

Walking wounded and those who had been sick were
rousted out of aide stations, given weapons, and ordered to
head for the front. General Clark, who moved from unit to
unit in an effort to rally his forces, noticed a key hill that was
not manned.

"Who's supposed to be defending that hill?" Clark rasped
out to a battalion commander.

"No one, sir," the harassed officer replied. "I don't have
anyone left to send up there. All my men are already fighting."

Clark promptly issued orders for the regimental band to be rushed to the crucial elevation and to "hold at all costs."

"What's the name of the hill?" Clark inquired.

"It hasn't got any name, sir," a begrimed young officer replied.

"Well, now it has," Clark responded, aware that GI musicians were taking up positions there. "It will be called 'Piccolo Peak.' "

Two hours after the Germans struck the massive blow along much of the Allied front, *General der Panzer Truppen* Traugott Herr, commander of LXXVI Korps, whose troops had plunged into the yawning gap in the center of the Allied line, was on the telephone to his superior, General von Vietinghoff, at Tenth Army. Herr's assessment of the battle situation was a glowing one. He told Von Vietinghoff that his troops had nearly broken through in the center and that the Americans and British were reeling back in confusion. Herr predicted his assault forces would reach the beaches in a few hours.

Over on the Allied side of the flaming battle lines, Fifth Army commander Mark Clark, had he been able to listen in on the telephone conversation between the two *Wehrmacht* generals, would have agreed with Herr's assessment. Clark could have added that the Anglo-American picture was even more gloomy than the enemy general had interpreted it to be. Clark knew that every able-bodied Allied man had been committed—walking wounded, clerks, truck drivers, musicians, and other service troops had been handed guns and told to start fighting. The *Wehrmacht* had poured troops and panzers into the five-mile-wide gap in the center and there was little to stop the Germans' onward rush to split the Allied beachhead in two.

However, standing in the path of the enemy drive were two battalions of field artillery—unlikely candidates for halting an all-out German ground attack. By training these men were to support the infantry, but due to the exigencies of the battlefield, the American artillerymen found themselves without infantry to support and alone between assaulting panzers and grenadiers and the sea.

Both of these units belonged to the U.S. 45th Infantry Division. Lieutenant Colonel Hal L. Muldrow, Jr., commander of the 189th Field Artillery Battalion, and Lieutenant Colonel Russell D. Funk, leader of the 158th Field Artillery Battalion, aware that it was up to them and their cannoneers to slow down or halt the German thrust, promptly went into action.

With guns positioned on a gentle slope overlooking crossings over the Calore River, the two battalion commanders kept skeleton crews by the guns, sent the others down the slope with rifles, machine guns and a few bazookas. These gunners-turned-infantrymen receive simple orders: "Stop the bastards!"

When the German spearheads, as expected, appeared shortly to cross the river, men of the two artillery battalions opened up on the enemy with every available weapon. At one point the perspiring, dust-covered American gunners were firing eight rounds per minute per gun into the ranks of the oncoming Germans. Soon German bodies were piling up along the banks of the Calore River. Staggered by heavy losses from the relentless American artillery fire, the attacking Germans wavered and began to fall back. By sunset the enemy force was licking its wounds. At least for the present, the *Wehrmacht* smash to break through to the sea at this point had been thwarted.

Elsewhere along the hard-pressed American defensive line, German grenadiers and tanks had punctured a hole in infantry positions and were heading for the guns of the U.S. 132nd Field Artillery Battalion. With the enemy force charging in his direction, a battery commander telephoned the battalion commander, Lieutenant Colonel John N. Green, with an urgent question: "The Krauts are almost on top of me. What'll I do?"

"Put out local security," Colonel Green replied.

"I've done that," the captain nervously responded. "Then what?"

"Then fight the bastards with your rammer staffs!" the colonel roared.

Thus was born the artillery battalion's battlecry: "Rammers to the ramparts!"

A short distance away from where the three American artillery battalions had stopped the assaulting Germans from breaking through to the sea, an entire gun battery panicked and prepared to abandon their positions. Passing by was an American tank platoon heading hell-bent for the rear. Neither unit had orders to withdraw.

Hopping onto the retreating tanks, the artillerymen hung on as the tracked vehicles clanked down a narrow, dirt road toward the relative safety of the beaches. Towering plumes of dust trailed in the wake of the racing tanks. Approaching a small bridge, the fleeing tankers and their piggy-back riders spotted a lone figure in an American uniform standing in the center of the structure, one arm upraised in a signal for the tank platoon to halt.

Brigadier General Raymond McLain, assistant commander of the 45th Division, called out to a nervous young lieutenant in the leading tank, "Where do you think you're going and why?"

The armor officer replied that they had been "overrun" by the enemy and were heading for the rear.

"You are like hell!" McLain barked, still standing in the center of the bridge. "The fight's up that way, not back here. Now get the hell back up there!"

Jolted out of their near-hysteria by the stern words of General McLain, the tanks, with the artillerymen aboard, reversed course and headed back to the front. Less than an hour later the men in the fleeing column were again fighting Germans.

At his forward command post, close to the front lines, General Troy Middleton, commander of the 45th Infantry Division, was worried. A college educator whose professorial countenance and calm demeanor belied his fighting heart, he had heard rumors that the beachhead was to be evacuated. Unless these reports were squelched, Middleton knew, panic could spread like wildfire throughout the entire division.

General Middleton called in an aide and told him: "I want

food, ammunition and supplies put behind the division. We are here and we're going to stay here!''

Meanwhile that early afternoon of the thirteenth, with Allied panic and the specter of a monumental catastrophe starkly evident on Salerno beachhead, Captain Jacob Hamilton was winging through the clear blue heavens toward Licata, Sicily, with his crucial message from Fifth Army. The P-38 fighter plane dipped low over olive groves surrounding the Licata airfield, along Sicily's rugged southern coast, and glided in to a smooth three-point landing. Hamilton taxied to the vicinity of the main hanger, a structure battered by the heavy fighting two months previously.

Bringing the P-38 to a halt, the pilot cut off the motor, threw back the canopy and leaped to the ground. He cast a quick glance at his watch. It was 1:35 P.M.

Face and uniform covered with grime, Hamilton approached the first officer he spotted and asked for directions to General Matt Ridgway's headquarters. He was told that the commander of the 82nd Airborne Division had taken off from the same airfield a half-hour previously, bound for Termini, Sicily, on an inspection trip.

By happenstance, Colonel James Gavin, leader of the division's 505th Parachute Infantry Regiment, was at the airfield. Gavin approached the pilot-messenger and offered to accept General Clark's letter for Ridgway. The paratroop colonel assured Hamilton he would give Ridgway the letter as soon as the 82nd Airborne commander returned from his inspection trip.

The Air Corps pilot refused to give the letter to Gavin, explaining that General Clark had been most emphatic that the communication be given only to Ridgway.

Aware that the written message was of major importance, Colonel Gavin promptly contacted the division's Chief of Staff, Colonel Ralph Eaton, who radioed Ridgway in his airplane to return to Licata immediately. As the commanding general winged back to his base, Captain Hamilton, Colonel Gavin and other airborne officers impatiently awaited his arrival.

It was a tedious wait. Gavin had heard rumors, as had

other commanders in the 82nd Airborne, that "Mark Clark is having a little trouble over at Salerno." The parachute colonel was convinced that the ultra-secret message was a mission to aid Fifth Army. The long minutes ticked by at the dusty, battered airfield.

Even before General Ridgway returned, word of an "urgent job" spread through much of the 82nd Airborne Division, bivouacked in olive groves and on the dusty terrain around the Licata airfield. "Yeah, old Matt's been out looking for work—and he's found some," a crewcut young corporal mused to his tent mate.

Staff Sergeant Sam DeCrenzo, a draftsman in the 504th Parachute Infantry Regiment, only one hour before the rumor raced through the ranks that "something big is up," had written into his daily diary:

> Boring around here. Nothing going on. "Mental Case"
> _____is awaiting a civilian who will bring *freschi teschi* (fresh eggs). "Mental Case" never eats—but he loves eggs.

As a solemn-faced Matthew Ridgway briskly leaped down from the C-47 that had returned him to Licata, Captain Hamilton, the pilot-courier, approached him, saluted sharply and handed the envelope with the secret message to the airborne commander. Ridgway moved to one side, tore open the envelope, and read the contents of the letter from General Mark Clark. Ridgway looked at his officers and said simply, "Let's get going, boys. We've got a job to do. Mark Clark's in big trouble."

Colonel Gavin and most of those in the 82nd Airborne felt a tinge of excitement. Venturesome spirits by nature, most loved to fight.

In planning for the parachute drops into Sicily two months previously involving both regiments of the 82nd Airborne, seven weeks had been available for mounting the airborne operations. Now Matt Ridgway's men were being asked to plan and launch a mission of comparable size to the one in Sicily in only a few hours' time.

General Ridgway expected no protests. He received none. Almost to a man, the All Americans were proud of their cavalry-to-the-rescue mission.

"Old Mark Clark can rest easy," a husky, red-haired trooper called out to his comrades, not yet knowing the details of the mission. "The 82nd is on the way!"

Sergeant Sam DeCrenzo, who would drop with his 504th Regiment that same night, took time to scribble his thoughts in his diary: "Mission is on. Great to hear the news!"

In a stroke of good fortune, top officers of the Troop Carrier Command, who were posted at scattered airfields in Sicily, happened to be at Licata airfield that afternoon. This made rapid coordination possible. A quick decision was reached to use the same teams of paratroopers and C-47s which had been earmarked to make the drop along the Volturno River, 40 miles north of the beachhead at Salerno, a mission that had been recently cancelled.

After hurried consultation with his airborne commanders, General Ridgway wrote a reply to Mark Clark on the embattled Salerno bridgehead. He handed his letter to Captain Hamilton, the Air Corps pilot who had flown the urgent request to Sicily. Hamilton dashed to his waiting P-38 at the Licata airfield, revved the engine and sped down the runway, bound for Salerno. He glanced at his watch. It was 3:22 P.M.—less than two hours since his speedy fighter plane had touched down at Licata.

Winging his way back to Fifth Army headquarters on his third lengthy mission of the day, Captain Hamilton was struck with a worrisome thought: What if he were to be shot down at sea and the crucial letter he was carrying from General Ridgway would go to a watery grave with him?

Hamilton landed without incident on the makeshift strip north of Paestum and caught a ride in a jeep. While racing along a narrow dusty road, the Air Corps captain heard the roar of airplane motors. He glanced back over his shoulder to view an alarming sight: Four *Luftwaffe* fighter planes were bearing down on him at tree-top level with machine guns blazing.

Clutching the vital letter from General Ridgway in one

hand, Hamilton leaped out of the jeep and into a ditch, landing hard on one shoulder. He felt a sharp pain shoot through
the upper part of his body. A split-second later streams of
bullets from the German fighter planes were hissing past and
thudding into the ground all around his flattened body.

As the *Luftwaffe* tormentors raced out of view, Hamilton
got to his feet. He did not know at the time that his shoulder
had been dislocated. Reaching Mark Clark's trailer office
minutes later, the courier handed General Ridgway's reply to
the Fifth Army commander.

Clark tore open the envelope and his face glowed with
relief—and admiration. The first two words in the message
from the airborne general were: "Can do!"

Clark was proud of his old West Point classmate and close
lifelong friend, Matt Ridgway. "He's the kind of man you
can depend on," the Fifth Army leader told his aides. "And
his men are tops."

In his reply to General Clark, Ridgway expressed deep
concern over one factor: The ingredients were at hand for a
repeat of the Sicily jump by his 504th Parachute Infantry
Regiment on the night of D + 2 when 23 American C-47s
loaded with paratroopers were shot down by "friendly"
ground and sea antiaircraft weapons.

"Rigid control of antiaircraft fire is absolutely essential,"
Ridgway stressed.

The Fifth Army commander had no intention of taking
halfway measures to prevent another Sicilian airborne tragedy. He promptly conferred with Admiral Hewitt, commander of naval forces off Salerno, and General Dawley,
leader of VI Corps in whose sector 82nd paratroopers would
drop.

"At precisely twenty-one hundred (9 P.M.) tonight and
until further notice from me, personally, not a single antiaircraft gun on this beachhead or offshore is to fire for any reason," General Clark emphasized. "Barrage balloons will be
taken down at the same time."

As a secondary precaution, the Fifth Army commander
dispatched an officer to each antiaircraft-gun battery to make
certain these strict don't-shoot orders had been received and

understood. Clark told his emissaries to use the strongest terms possible in making known to battery commanders his instructions.

Back at Licata airfield in Sicily late that afternoon, airborne and troop carrier command officers were putting the final touches on plans for the urgent parachute mission. In only four hours since the Air Corps pilot, Captain Hamilton, had touched down at Licata in his P-38, paratroop and C-47 squadron commanders had been briefed on that night's mass drop at Salerno.

General Ridgway selected Colonel Reuben Tucker's 504th Parachute Infantry Regiment, less its 3rd Battalion which was going to Italy by sea, to jump that night. Other elements of Tucker's combat team would be the 376th Parachute Field Artillery Battalion and Company C, 307th Airborne Engineers Battalion. Tucker would have 1,300 paratroopers bailing out with him over the bridgehead.

Relatively short of stature but extremely long on heart, the 31-year-old Tucker was regarded in the army as a fierce combat leader. He was known to many friends as Tommy after the popular big-band conductor of the era, but most fellow officers called him Rube. Tucker had commanded the 504th Regiment since it was activated on May 1, 1942, at Fort Benning, Georgia.

At 6:15 P.M. Colonel Tucker's paratroopers had gathered around their C-47s and were hurriedly briefed by junior officers, who themselves had received sketchy outlines of the mission from company and battalion commanders. There was no time for lengthy presentations even if briefing officers had known more about the situation at Salerno.

A young lieutenant at Comiso airfield held a map against the fuselage of a C-47 and told his troopers:

"Men, here's the poop. Those goddamned Krauts are kicking the hell out of our guys over on Salerno. Mark Clark wants us to bail the straight-legs out. When the green light comes on, jump. When you hit the ground, be ready for anything. We're supposed to drop behind our lines—but no one knows what the situation is there. Any questions?"

Staff Sergeant Sam DeCrenzo pulled out his diary while waiting for the order to board his C-47, and wrote:

> Fifth Army is in precarious position. They need our troops. Briefing in fast time—two minutes. Dust all over field. Colonel Tucker dashing about.

The operational plan for the 504th Parachute Infantry drop that night called for Major Dan Danielson's 2nd Battalion, flown by the 313th Carrier Group, to take off from Trapani airfield, in western Sicily. The 1st Battalion, under Lieutenant Colonel Warren R. Williams, would liftoff from Comiso in C-47s of the 61st and 314th Carrier Groups. The flights would rendezvous over Cape Rasocolmo on the northeast tip of Sicily.

The air armada carrying the two battalions of paratroopers would fly successive doglegs to Cape Vaticano, Cape Fonifati and Cape Palinuro, then head northward up the western coast of the Italian boot. Agropoli, a town five miles south of the drop zone, would be the major checkpoint.

Colonel Rube Tucker and his regimental staff would ride in the lead C-47 of Lieutenant Colonel Williams' 1st Battalion flight.

At an airfield near Agrigento, near the coast of southern Sicily, Air Corps Lieutenant Colonel Joel L. Crouch, operations officer of the 52nd Troop Carrier Wing, climbed into the cockpit of a C-47. It was 8:40 P.M., less than seven and one-half hours since General Mark Clark's pilot-courier reached Licata with the urgent message for help.

Colonel Crouch had been a strong proponent of the newly developed pathfinder technique in which a small number of specifically trained paratroopers jumped on a drop zone 15 minutes in advance of the main body. Armed with electronic homing devices, the pathfinder's job was to guide succeeding C-47s to the designated DZ. Now Crouch was piloting the first aircraft to drop pathfinders in an American airborne operation.

Crouch taxied his C-47 onto the dark, dusty runway and was followed by two more C-47s with the remainder of the pathfinders. The three troop carriers sped down the strip and lifted into the air, bound for Salerno beachhead, 300 miles away. The three "crash" parachute missions to reinforce beseiged Fifth Army had been launched.

Fifteen minutes after Crouch and his pathfinders took off from Agrigento airfield, 36 C-47s with Major Dan Danielson's 2nd Battalion on board departed from Trapani, in western Sicily. In his lead aircraft, Danielson noted that his flight had taken off on time. "That's always a good omen for a parachute mission," the battalion commander reflected.

Meanwhile, another airborne force was aboard a little fleet of LCIs (landing craft-infantry) at a harbor in southern Sicily. The 325th Glider Infantry Regiment, under Colonel Harry L. Lewis, plus the 3rd Battalion of Colonel Reuben Tucker's 504th Parachute Infantry, were also bound for the Italian beachhead—the slow way. They would move by boat and land at a site on the beachhead yet to be determined.

Several correspondents attached to the 82nd Airborne Division, including Cy Korman of the *Chicago Tribune* and syndicated columnist Richard Tregaskis, had elected to go into the beachhead by ship. At about the time Major Danielson's paratroopers were flying off from Trapani airfield, Lieutenant William Graffis, a public relations officer with the Troop Carrier Command, came to the boat carrying the correspondents just before they sailed. His purpose was to give the reporters the latest radio news.

"It looks rough for our boys at Salerno," Graffis solemnly told the correspondents. "The BBC says the Krauts have thrown in more tanks. I sure hope you'll be able to land someplace when you get there."

"Gee, thanks a lot," Korman replied with a straight face. "Do you have any more cheerful news for us before we hoist anchor?"

At Comiso airfield, with liftoff for the 1st Battalion of Lieutenant Colonel Warren Williams fast approaching, Colonel Rube Tucker had worked himself into a near frenzy. The regimental commander, who would fly with the 1st Battalion, was particularly eager to get into action with his Five-O-Fours. He was still fuming inwardly over the fact that his fellow

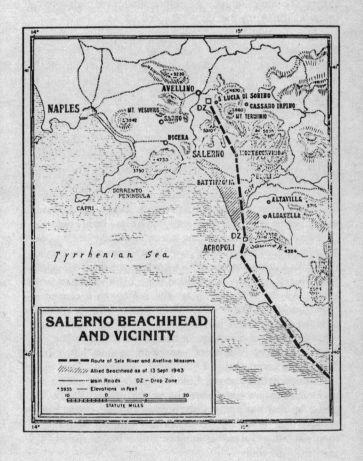

NAPLES

AVELLINO

S. LUCIA DI SORINO
CASSANO IRPINO
MT. TERMINIO

DZ

MT. VESUVIUS
SARNO

NOCERA

SALERNO

MONTECOSVINO

EBOLI

BATTIPAGLIA

SORRENTO
PENINSULA

CAPRI

ALTAVILLA
ALBANELLA

DZ
ACROPOLI

Tyrrhenian Sea

SALERNO BEACHHEAD
AND VICINITY

━ ━ ━ Route of Sele River and Avellino Missions

░░░░░ Allied Beachhead as of 13 Sept 1943

──── Main Roads   DZ — Drop Zone

*5935 ──── Elevations in Feet

10   0   10   20
STATUTE MILES

parachute colonel and friendly rival, "Slim Jim" Gavin, had been selected to spearhead the invasion of Sicily two months previously, while Tucker and his regiment, due to lack of airlift, had to remain behind for 48 hours.

As the Five-O-Fours were loading their C-47s at Comiso, Rube Tucker bolted from plane to plane in his jeep. As he reached each aircraft, Tucker halted his jeep, stood up, shook his fist vigorously and shouted: "Men, it's open season on the goddamned Krauts. Let's give the bastards hell!"

Now, at 9 P.M., with his flight of 51 C-47s loaded with paratroopers and ready to take off from Comiso to rendezvous with Major Danielson's armada flying from Trapani, Tucker heard someone running toward his C-47 and calling his name.

The regimental commander, anxious to get started, thrust his head out the door and growled, "Yeah, what is it?"

The Air Corps officer hurriedly explained that several of the C-47s were having engine trouble and the sky convoy would not be able to depart until repairs had been made.

Tucker was furious over the last-minute delay. He was beginning to think that, indeed, his 504th Regiment was jinxed. First it had to stay behind for 48 hours in the Sicily invasion, then when it had been committed there 23 of its planes were shot down by "friendly" fire, and now, with a chance to show the world what his Five-O-Fours could do on a battlefield, he was forced to sit idle on a dark Sicilian airfield while other elements of his regiment headed for battle.

The Gods of War were conspiring against him, Rube Tucker was convinced.

For nearly three hours, Colonel Tucker fumed and fussed as mechanics worked feverishly on the balking C-47s. He paced up and down the dusty airfield runway, much like a restless tiger in a cage. Troopers had climbed back out of their aircraft and were standing or sitting beside their C-47s in small gatherings.

Finally an Air Corps officer rushed up to Colonel Tucker and advised him that the repair work had been completed and the sky train could take off. Shouts of "Load 'em up!" rang out through the night and hundreds of troopers, burdened with heavy combat gear, waddled to their C-47s, pulled their way up the short ladders and into the doors of the aircraft.

A tremendous roar of motors raced across the bleak terrain as the C-47s headed for the runway and one by one lifted into the air. Destination: Salerno beachhead. It was midnight when the final plane carrying the 1st Battalion and Colonel Tucker's headquarters staff was airborne.

The Five-O-Fours, seated shoulder to shoulder in bucket seats in the 51 C-47s winging for the Italian bridgehead, rode mostly in silence. Banter and joking were left behind in the puptents of Sicily. Each man, in his own way, was solemnly steeling his spirit for the ordeal just ahead. "It's just a routine drop behind friendly lines," each assured himself. "But . . ."

British bombers were over Berlin that night of the thirteenth as a *Luftwaffe* aircraft with several passengers aboard was winging from Vienna to *Wolfsschanze* (Wolf's Lair), Adolph Hitler's military headquarters tucked away in dense woods behind the Russian front. One of those on the German aircraft was an obscure *Hauptsturmführer* (SS Captain) named Otto Skorzeny. Another was a short, balding, heavy set man who sat in silence, a tattered black overcoat draped around his body and a wide-brimmed hat pulled down over his eyes. His name was Benito Mussolini and until the previous July he had been in nearly absolute control of Italy's destiny for 22 years.

Only the day before, September 12, Captain Skorzeny, an engineer by profession in civilian life before the war, and a handful of *fallschirmjaeger* (paratroopers) had swooped down on a towering peak in the Apennines known as Gran Sasso, snatched the deposed dictator from under the noses of more than 200 Italian guards, and bundled the famous prisoner into a light *Storch* aircraft.

The hulking Skorzeny, six foot five and 240 pounds, wiggled his way into the little plane designed to carry two passengers and, along with Mussolini and a daring *Luftwaffe* pilot, *Hauptman* (Captain) Heinrich Gerlach, lifted off from a short, boulder-strewn plateau on Gran Sasso. On reaching the edge of the plateau, the *Storch* plunged downward into a yawning valley and Gerlach was able to right the aircraft just before it crashed. The pilot, flying at tree-top level, set a course for Rome.

In the Italian capital, Mussolini was transferred to a *Luftwaffe* JU-52 airplane and along with his liberator, Otto Skorzeny, flew to Vienna where the two men checked into the closely-guarded Imperial Hotel. Hardly had the exhausted Skorzeny reached his room than there was an urgent phone call for him. His boss, Heinrich Himmler, commander of the *Schutzstaffein* (SS), was on the line from Berlin to congratulate his subordinate. Skorzeny, Himmler knew, had been sent on the "impossible" mission to rescue Benito Mussolini by Adolph Hitler. The operation had been a spectacular success.

Now Himmler wanted in on the glory achieved by his obscure SS captain.

Minutes later the daring Skorzeny's heart skipped a beat. He was informed that the *Führer* himself was calling from *Wolfsschanze*. Barely able to control the deep emotion he felt, Hitler said, "I congratulate you. You have fulfilled a mission that will go down in history. The eyes of the entire world are upon you. You have given me back my old friend, Benito Mussolini."

Pausing momentarily, the *Führer* added: "Skorzeny, I have awarded you the Knight's Cross and promoted you to *Sturmbannführer* (Major)."

At *Wolfsschanze* on September 13 Mussolini, once robust and bombastic, was ushered into the presence of his close friend and political partner, Adolph Hitler. The *Führer's* wide smile vanished. What he saw standing in front of him was not the confident strutting *Duce* he had known for years. This was a trembling, ashen-faced relic of a man—broken in body and spirit.

Adolph Hitler did not shock easily. He was shocked.

As Nazi Propaganda Minister Josef Goebbels proclaimed Otto Skorzeny's rescue of Benito Mussolini a "first-class moral victory," at his headquarters outside Rome as midnight of the thirteenth approached *Feldmarschall* Albert Kesselring was anticipating an impending triumph of a more tangible nature—the destruction of Fifth Army at Salerno.

Kesselring was talking on the telephone to his superior at the *Oberkommando der Wehrmacht, Feldmarschall* Wilhelm Keitel, in Berlin. Kesselring told Hitler's right-hand military confidant that it would be only a matter of hours until the Anglo-Americans on the bridgehead were driven into the Tyrrhenian Sea.

Inside General von Vietinghoff's Tenth Army headquarters in the Apennines, the scent of the forthcoming Allied kill was wafting through the nostrils of staff officers. A young *Wehrmacht* lieutenant picked up a pen and wrote in the Tenth Army war diary:

> A wonderful present for our beloved *Führer*. The battle for Salerno appears to be over.

6

Parachutes over
the Beachhead

LIEUTENANT COLONEL WILLIAM Yarborough, General Mark Clark's airborne advisor, was standing on the dark drop zone on Salerno beachhead. He peeked at his luminous watch. It was 11:55 P.M. At any minute the leading elements of Colonel Reuben Tucker's 504th Parachute Infantry Regiment were to arrive over the drop zone—if the operation was carried out as planned. A nervous Bill Yarborough knew that the "if" was a big one.

He was aware that in an airborne operation involving thousands of men and scores of aircraft things were far more likely to go wrong than they were to go right. The "crash" nature of the current mission, with its hasty planning and sketchy briefing, would be far more susceptible to this accepted military axiom than would an operation in which there had been adequate time to carefully prepare.

Many thoughts raced through Yarborough's head as his ears strained to pick up the sound of airplane engines from the south which would signal the approach of Colonel Reuben Tucker's paratroopers. Many of the C-47 pilots were inex-

perienced and might come under fire from Germans ringing
the beachhead. Would they drop their troopers over the sea
by mistake? The water was only a stone's throw from the DZ.
Would faulty reckoning result in dropping the Five-O-Fours
onto the German-held heights ringing the beachhead? Would
the *Luftwaffe* appear and shoot down the lumbering, low-
flying, unarmed C-47s?

Earlier that day General Clark had gone to great lengths
to assure there would be no repeat of the Sicily tragedy in
which 23 C-47s were shot down by "friendly" gunfire. And
since 9 P.M., three hours earlier, not an Allied antiaircraft
gun on shore or at sea had fired a round, as Clark had ordered. But Yarborough knew that if a lone rattled young Allied gunner would open up on Colonel Tucker's flight as it
passed over the beachhead, others, also tense and nervous,
might follow suit as men in the strain of combat were prone
to do.

All that day Colonel Yarborough had been busily involved
in supervising the placement of the Jerry cans filled with
gasoline-soaked sand so that at the proper time the containers
would ignite to form a huge flaming T. As Reuben Tucker's
C-47s were heard in the distance Yarborough would fire a
Very pistol, an instrument designed to shoot a brilliant green
flare high into the sky. This would be the signal for the soldier
standing by each Jerry can to light the gasoline-soaked sand.

The containers had been positioned on a drop zone 1,200
yards long and 800 yards wide. It was situated on flat land
north of Paestum. Four miles to the south of the DZ was the
front. Along the massive heights just inland German observers would have a choice view of the mass parachute drop as
it unfolded and be in position to bring down highly accurate
artillery fire on the DZ as the paratroopers landed and began
assembling. That alarming possibility had to be accepted—
the drop zone was the only site on the shrinking Allied
bridgehead suitable for a mass parachute landing.

Yarborough was convinced that everything possible had
been done to assure that the American paratroopers dropped
directly onto the DZ. Now all that he could do was to stand

in the center of the dark DZ and wait . . . and wait . . . and
wait some more.

About two hours earlier a curious phenomenon had suddenly blanketed the bloody Salerno beachhead. Allied antiaircraft gunners, in keeping with General Clark's stern order,
had refrained from firing at *Luftwaffe* bombers overhead.
Soon other guns, Allied and German, fell silent. Rifle and
machine-gun fire in the front lines dwindled and then halted
entirely.

Along the entire sweep of the Gulf of Salerno, from Agropoli on the south in a curving arc to Amalfi on the Sorrento
Peninsula, 35 miles away, an eerie hush fell over the landscape. There was not a sound to be heard on the war-torn
beachhead where 300,000 Allied and German soldiers were
locked in a death struggle. It was as though some huge supernatural force had magically intervened to bring a brief
respite to the tormented, weary and bleeding gladiators on
both sides.

"My God, what's happened?" Yarborough mused to a
young officer.

"Beats the hell out of me, colonel," was the reply.

Within the hour *Luftwaffe* planes were overhead and dropping flares which bathed much of the beachhead in brilliant
iridescence. German battle commanders apparently believed
that Allied antiaircraft guns having gone silent at 9 P.M. was
an indication that the Anglo-Americans were starting to evacuate the bridgehead. The *Luftwaffe* was rushed in to reconnoiter Allied activities. Not a single gun fired at the German
aircraft as they flew up and down the beachhead, bombing
and strafing, before heading back for their bases.

Almost an hour after the *Luftwaffe* had departed, the faint
hum of airplane motors was heard far to the south. The noise
became louder as the flight of C-47s approached the drop
zone. Lieutenant Colonel Yarborough felt a tingle of elation
sweep through his being. This had to be the approach of
Reuben Tucker's paratroopers.

Standing in the open door of the lead C-47 pathfinder was
Lieutenant William B. Jones, a young officer from New Jer-
sey in the intelligence section of Lieutenant Warren Williams'

1st Battalion. Standing behind Jones, hooked up and ready to jump, were Sergeant Milton V. "Fuzzy" Knight, Sergeant Regis J. Pahler and other pathfinder troopers.

Pahler would jump carrying the large homing beacon, an assignment he was handed because he was the biggest and strongest in the stick. The others in the C-47, in addition to the normal heavy burden of weapons and equipment, also held parts of electronic homing devices as they prepared to bail out.

At the controls of the lead pathfinder C-47 was Air Corps Lieutenant Colonel Joel Crouch. Behind him were the two other troop carriers with pathfinders aboard.

Favored by fair weather, light winds and a bright full moon, the three pathfinder C-47s flew to the drop zone with no difficulty. It had not been an easy task. Crouch and the two other pilots had to locate a relatively tiny dot of ground more than 300 miles from their takeoff point at Agrigento airfield in Sicily.

Just as Colonel Crouch turned in his seat to call out, "This should be the DZ," a green flare burst forth in the dark sky ahead. It had been fired by Lieutenant Colonel Bill Yarborough's Very pistol and was the signal for each soldier to ignite his Jerry can of gasoline-soaked sand. Moments later a huge flaming T exploded over the landscape.

With a cry of "Let's go!" Lieutenant Jones leaped from the door of Colonel Crouch's C-47, followed at split-second intervals by others in the stick. Troopers from the three pathfinder planes landed in routine fashion in the center of the DZ, and within three minutes had set up their electronic homing devices. The burning T was extinguished.

Although the pathfinder teams had been organized only a week earlier at Agrigento, most of the men had had previous training in the new airborne technique. So skilled were these pathfinders at their crucial job that they were capable of assembling and operating the equipment while blindfolded.

Minutes later the sound of more approaching C-47s was heard. A green flare shot into the air and the half-mile-long T burst into flame. Crouched in the door of the lead aircraft, Major Dan Danielson was peering intently downward. When he saw the burning T he bailed out of the yawning door followed by the 16 men in his stick. Tumbling out of other C-47s were the remainder of Danielson's 2nd Battalion. In moments the sky was dotted with scores of swaying white parachutes, floating majestically to earth directly in the center of the drop zone. It had been a tight landing pattern, textbook perfect.

After depositing their loads of paratroopers over the Salerno DZ, pilots of the 35 C-47s which had carried Major Danielson's battalion banked sharply toward the sea and climbed rapidly to 6,000 feet. The airmen wanted to get well above nervous Allied gunners on vessels down below. Flying by way of Cape Palinuro, exotic Stromboli and Cape Milazzo all C-47s returned to Sicilian bases without a single casualty.

At 3:15 A.M., some six hours after having lifted off with their paratroopers for the flight to the Italian bridgehead, the Troop Carrier Command pilots were in bed. Exhausted as they were, physically and emotionally, the airmen slept fitfully. They had been too keyed-up and one factor loomed in their minds: They would have to repeat the same operation that night with Colonel James Gavin's regiment and the Germans might be ready and waiting for the C-47 convoy this time.

As the hours ticked by on the DZ along the Gulf of Salerno, Lieutenant Colonel Bill Yarborough was beset with mixed emotions. He was elated that Major Danielson's battalion had landed directly on the drop zone and had assembled without incident. But what had happened to Lieutenant Colonel Williams' 1st Battalion and Colonel Tucker's headquarters group, both of which should have reached the beachhead at about the same time as did Danielson's battalion?

Major Danielson could shed no light on the absence of Tucker's flight, which was to have taken off from Comiso airfield and rendezvoused with Danielson's air convoy over northeast Sicily. When Tucker's C-47s did not appear at the rendezvous point, Danielson's 2nd battalion continued on to the beachhead.

As strict radio silence was in effect so as not to alert the enemy that an airborne mission to reinforce the bridgehead was in progress, Colonel Yarborough had no way of knowing that Colonel Tucker and Lieutenant Colonel Williams and their troopers had been delayed on takeoff for three hours while defective C-47 engines were repaired.

Continuing his lonely vigil on the drop zone and straining incessantly to hear the sound of C-47 motors in the south, Yarborough hoped for the best and braced for the worst. Reuben Tucker's flight should have reached the DZ long before.

As the Fifth Army airborne advisor waited, a curious thought puzzled him: With German observers and troops on the massive heights overlooking the drop zone, which provided front-row seats for the parachute-and-flaming-T extravaganza, why had not the *Wehrmacht* poured devastating artillery fire onto the DZ? A heavy concentration of shells conceivably could have seriously disrupted the parachute mission.

While these worries and thoughts flowed through Colonel Yarborough's mind, Reuben Tucker and Lieutenant Colonel Warren Williams' 1st Battalion were in C-47s burrowing through the starry Mediterranean night—three hours late but now on their way to battle. Tucker was in the lead plane and still figuratively pacing about like a caged tiger. Actually, like all troopers, Rube Tucker was in his bucket seat, loaded with heavy combat gear and wedged into place by the shoulders of the man to either side of him.

Colonel Tucker, happy to be on his way to Salerno, had his share of concerns. His C-47 flight from Comiso was strung out for miles instead of winging to the beachhead in a neat pattern of Vs as called for in the operational plan. Due to the balky engines in several aircraft, the C-47s had taken off from Comiso individually, in pairs and tiny groups and immediately set a course for Salerno without waiting to rendezvous with the remainder of the troop carrier planes. Tucker wondered if all of his paratrooper-laden C-47s would reach the bridgehead.

Long after Colonel Tucker's flight was to have reached the bridgehead, Colonel Yarborough, on the DZ, picked up the soft hum of airplane motors to the south. This had to be Rube Tucker's flight of 51 C-47s, Yarborough was convinced. As the roar of engines grew louder, Yarborough fired a green flare into the air and moments later the huge T leaped into flame.

There were six C-47s in the first group to reach the beachhead, and in seconds the sky was filled with nearly 100 blossoming white parachutes. Colonel Tucker was among the first to reach the ground. He landed heavily, but leaped to his feet, spilled the air from his chute, and rapidly rolled the silk into a ball. Shucking his chute harness, Rube Tucker glared around fiercely to appraise the situation. He was ready to fight; all he needed was to be shown in which direction were the Germans.

Colonel Yarborough's instructions had been to promptly locate the commander of the 504th Parachute Infantry Regiment, Rube Tucker, and escort him to VI Corps headquarters for orders. Despite the darkness and the customary confusion of a nighttime mass parachute drop, Yarborough located Tucker in a short period of time.

"Glad to see you made it okay, Rube," Yarborough said as the two parachute leaders shook hands.

"So am I," replied the barrel-chested, deep voiced Tucker. "I was beginning to think I wasn't going to get here."

Tucker quickly inquired: "Where the hell are the goddamned Krauts?"

Despite the drama surrounding the meeting between Colonel Tucker and Lieutenant Colonel Yarborough on the dark beachhead drop zone, the episode was strained. A coolness between the two paratroop officers had existed since the tragic shoot-down by "friendly" antiaircraft guns of 23 C-47s carrying members of Yarborough's battalion on the night of D + 2 in the invasion of Sicily two months previously. Yarborough was serving under Colonel Tucker at that time.

After the Sicily action, Yarborough made no secret of his views that the disaster had resulted from bad planning. Tucker, looking ahead to months of heavy combat, did not participate in his battalion commander's vocal protestations, and a short time later a critical Yarborough was reassigned from the 504th Parachute Infantry Regiment to Fifth Army headquarters. There he became airborne advisor to Mark Clark.

Yarborough's separation from the 82nd Airborne Division came as no surprise to the principals involved or to paratroop officers who were aware of the nature of the problem. His departure was not impeded by the fact that General Matt Ridgway, the division commander, did not approve of Yarborough's vocal complaints as to the true cause of the decimation of his battalion by ''friendly'' gunfire over Sicily—poor planning.

Meanwhile, for nearly an hour, the sky over the drop zone was periodically dotted with billowing parachutes as C-47s, alone and in tiny knots, reached the beachhead. These were the remaining troop carriers in Colonel Tucker's flight.

One of those floating to earth as Colonel Tucker and Lieutenant Yarborough were conferring on the DZ was Lieutenant Colonel Warren Williams, commander of the 1st Battalion. As his parachute popped open on leaping from his C-47, Williams' reserve chute on his chest struck him a heavy blow across the mouth, dazing him and knocking several teeth loose.

Looking downward, Williams saw that he was heading toward a rocky portion of terrain, and he tugged strenuously on his parachute risers to avoid what would be a jolting landing on boulders. His efforts were in vain. He crashed heavily onto the inhospitable surface.

Dragging himself to his feet and shucking his parachute, Williams began to assemble his battalion. Most members had landed on or adjacent to the DZ. But on counting noses the battalion commander discovered that eight planeloads of Company B men—some 120 troopers—were missing. Williams was distressed by the unexplained absence of the Company B parachutists. He feared they may have bailed out over the nearby sea and drowned or landed in heavy German troop concentrations hemming in the beachhead, in which case their chances for survival would be minimal.

Waiting for orders to move out, Williams spotted a shadowy figure walking toward him. When the man reached the battalion commander, Williams immediately recognized his features despite the darkness. Lieutenant Colonel Charles J. Denholm, a West Point classmate and longtime friend of Williams and now on the staff of General Mike Dawley's VI Corps, warmly shook hands with the paratroop leader.

"Damn, are we glad to see you fellows!" Denholm observed enthusiastically. "The situation around here is tense as hell."

"Where're the Krauts?" Williams wanted to know.

Denholm pointed to the hulking elevations silhouetted against the sky in the foreground. "See those hills over there?" Denholm asked. "Well, if it was daylight the Krauts up there could see you and I standing here talking."

Colonel Reuben Tucker, the pugnacious commander of the 504th Parachute Infantry Regiment, had been dashing about the drop zone like a demon possessed. He was anxious to learn if all or most of his troopers had landed and to get into action. Tucker was elated—the parachute drop had been successful. A force of nearly 1,300 paratroopers had been deposited on the Italian bridgehead by 85 C-47s of the 52nd Troop Carrier Wing in less than 15 hours since receiving the Fifth Army commander's urgent plea for immediate reinforcement.

Only one trooper had been seriously injured in the jump. Not a single C-47 had been lost. Tucker held out hope that the missing 120 parachutists of Colonel Williams' battalion would turn up later on the beachhead. There was the possibility, he knew, that the aircraft carrying the absent men could have developed engine trouble and returned to base with the paratroopers aboard.

Within one hour after the last Five-O-Four had touched down, both parachute battalions assembled and headed for a nearby column of trucks. With Colonel Tucker and Lieutenant Colonel Yarborough in a jeep at the head of the convoy, the troopers were driven to the headquarters of VI Corps. At 4 A.M. on September 14 Tucker reported to General Mike Dawley that his two battalions and headquarters group were present and ready for action.

Dawley told Colonel Tucker that he was attaching the parachute regiment to General Fred Walker's 36th Infantry

Division, the Texas National Guard outfit. During the previous afternoon, powerful German attacks had broken the center of the Allied line and threatened to drive to the sea. General Mark Clark had stripped his southern sector to strengthen his center, where the breakthrough to the shoreline appeared imminent. It was to this denuded southern front, defended only by a handful of infantrymen of the 45th Division and a few beach engineers, that the parachute battalions were rushed.

Tucker's airborne men took up positions southwest of Albanella, a little town perched on the heights overlooking a wide sweep of the American bridgehead. Only the previous afternoon, elements of the 36th Division had been driven out of Albanella. Locating the assigned sector in the inky darkness, without the benefit of prior reconnaissance and in a fluid battle situation, proved a difficult task for the paratroopers.

Moving along a narrow secondary road at the head of his battalion, Lieutenant Colonel Warren Williams detected shadowy figures and vehicles to his front, coming along the road toward his marching men. Williams alerted his column for imminent action, but at the final moment determined that approaching silhouetted forms were stragglers from the 36th Division heading for the rear. They were remnants of a battalion that had taken a bloody beating the previous afternoon at Altavilla and on nearby heights.

Williams halted a jeep carrying only the driver. The man was sullen and had the ashen-faced, haunted look of one who has had a narrow brush with death.

"How about turning around and taking me on up ahead so that I can reconnoiter the ground to position my battalion when they get there?" Colonel Williams asked.

"Hell, no, I'm not about to go back up there," the corporal driver responded. "I'm heading for the beach. You can have this goddamned jeep if you want it as far as I'm concerned."

"All right, I'll take it," Williams replied. The corporal of the Texas division climbed out of the jeep and soon disappeared into the darkness toward the rear. The parachute

officer got into the vehicle with an aide and drove off in the
darkness toward the German lines. He breathed a sigh of
relief on reaching the designated positions for his battalion
without encountering enemy troops or panzers.

Williams' 1st Battalion and Major Dan Danielson's 2nd
Battalion, which had also moved into position near Albanella
without difficulty, spent the remainder of predawn darkness
digging in and strengthening their lines. Shortly after the gray
of dusk dissolved into the light of day, a lookout in Colonel
Williams' battalion called out, "There's a column of men
approaching us from the rear. Can't make out who in the hell
they are."

The paratroopers had been warned before moving out from
VI Corps headquarters a few hours before that the situation
around Albanella was "highly fluid." The passing stragglers
from the 36th Division told the troopers that there were
"Krauts crawling all over the place." So troopers in the vicinity of the lookout cautiously prepared for the approach of
the unidentified column from the rear.

Minutes later weapons were lowered and apprehension
vanished. These were the 120 men of Company B reported
"missing" when Colonel Williams counted noses on the drop
zone several hours before.

"What in the hell happened to you?" Williams inquired
of a young Lieutenant when the column filed into battalion
positions. "We thought you might have plunged into the
drink."

"Well, sir, we were coming along in good shape until our
eight planes got near what the fly boys thought was the DZ,"
the lieutenant responded. "They spotted a few lights down
on the ground, gave us the green light and out we went. We
came down in a neat pattern about 10 miles southeast of here
and out of the beachhead perimeter. There were no Krauts
around so we oriented ourselves and began marching toward
the DZ."

As a rosy Mediterranean sun peeked timidly over the Apennines that morning of the fourteenth, a curious phenomenon swept through the ranks of embattled American and
British troops on the fireswept bridgehead. Word that Amer-

ican paratroopers had leaped onto the battlefield during the
night electrified the hard-pressed fighting men. In some infantry companies, dwindled to skeleton-size through five days
and nights of almost constant struggle with a skilled and aggressive enemy, some haggard soldiers stood in their foxholes
and cheered the news.

The exhilaration sweeping through Allied ranks that morning was not limited to front-line soldiers facing a resumption
of the heavy German blows that had struck them repeatedly.
Mark Clark, the Fifth Army commander, who had snatched
a few hours of fitful sleep, at dawn was approached by an
excited staff officer. "Matt Ridgway's boys jumped during the
night," the aide exulted. "They're already in the line!"

Clark beamed. "I knew Matt's parachute boys wouldn't
let us down," he exclaimed.

The arrival of 1,300 tough, experienced paratroopers, like
a bolt from the dark nighttime sky, infected all ranks on the
beachhead with a new buoyancy, a new sense of purpose, a
new confidence. The spiraling boost to Allied morale was
incredibly disproportionate to the relatively small number of
paratroopers involved.

In those early hours of daylight, while American and British fighting men were imbued with a new will to resist, on
the other side of the front the German Tenth Army commander, Heinrich von Vietinghoff, was intent on keeping the
pressure on reeling Allied forces. He was convinced that his
assault troops would break through to the sea at some point
if the *Wehrmacht* continued to attack with vigor and elan.

Shortly after dawn, Von Vietinghoff telephoned his two
corps commanders, General Traugott Herr and General Her-
mann Balck. He gave identical orders to each: They should
hit the Anglo-Americans with all their resources and break
through to the Tyrrhenian.

At 8 o'clock that morning, the Germans struck again. Preceded by a massive artillery bombardment, *Wehrmacht* infantry and panzers poured out of their positions in an all-out
effort to destroy Fifth Army. The Germans hit the British 46th
Division in the Vietra area at the far north of the bridgehead
and in front of Salerno City. Combat weary and depleted in

strength, the 46th Division fought back tenaciously. The assaulting Germans then shifted the weight of their drive and smashed into the British 56th Division near the key communications center of Battipaglia. Only the day before General McCreery, commander of the British X Corps, had reported that the 56th Division was exhausted and reinforcements were crucial. But the Tommies hung on—by their fingernails.

Just south of the British sector, *Wehrmacht* infantry and panzers moved out of the morning mist and assaulted the lines of the hard-pressed U.S. 36th and 45th Infantry Divisions. German grenadiers, supported by the flat-trajectory fire of tanks, charged American positions and were cut down. Other waves of grenadiers followed to the muzzles of rifles and machine-guns manned by dogfaces of the two U.S. divisions. Soon German bodies were piled in grotesque masses in front of American positions.

Allied fighter-bombers swept in over the beaches and strafed and bombed the attacking German forces. American and British heavy and medium bombers ranged the sky to the rear of *Wehrmacht* lines and pounded enemy installations, communications centers and command posts.

Offshore, British warships moved in close to fire huge 15-inch rifles at the attacking Germans until the barrels were white-hot. So intensive was the naval gunfire that German commanders were unable to maneuver reinforcing units to the front lines.

On the flatlands along the sea, in mountain passes and on the heights looking down on the Allied beachhead, the thunderous Anglo-American air and sea bombardment took a heavy toll among German forces. Bloody and mutilated German corpses saturated the landscape, and twisted and burning enemy panzers, sending plumes of black, acrid smoke soaring into the sky, dotted the landscape.

Despite the enormous Allied curtain of fire, German grenadiers, passing over the bodies of previous assault waves, pressed forward. The battle cry remained: "Throw them into the sea!"

The death struggle for Salerno beachhead had erupted anew.

Earlier that morning, spirits buoyed by the arrival of Colonel Reuben Tucker's tough and resourceful paratroopers during the night, Mark Clark hauled his lanky frame into a mud-splattered jeep with the three stars of his rank prominently displayed in front. His mission: Rally the troops.

Much like generals of the previous century who galloped on horseback up and down their lines of wavering troops and exhorted them to hold firm, Clark drove along the roads and byways behind his hard-pressed fighting men. He was deeply worried that a potentially fatal malady had infected his troops—"Dunkirk-phobia."

With Sergeant Holden at the wheel and Captain Warren Thrasher, his aide, in the back seat of the jeep, Clark sped from one hot spot to another. Everywhere it was the same: Officers and men dispirited, near exhaustion, recipients of a severe drubbing at the hands of the *Wehrmacht.*

The Fifth Army commander talked to small groups of solemn fighting men wherever he found them. "Our situation is improving, reinforcements are arriving, our Air Corps is pounding the enemy," he told his troops. "This is where we quit giving ground."

After delivering his exhortation to a group of his soldiers, Clark and his aides would leap back into the jeep and race to another threatened sector. Always the general's theme was the same: Fifth Army would retreat no farther.

"There mustn't be any doubt in your minds," Clark declared in a confident tone time and again. "This is it. We don't give another inch. Don't yield a damned thing. We're here to stay!"

Despite his morning-long efforts to rally and inspire the exhausted and demoralized men in his command, alarming signs continued to point toward imminent panic erupting among the Anglo-American invaders-turned-defenders. Clark's jeep passed a line of American trucks racing from the front back to the rear. The general was startled to see that the men in them were wearing gas masks.

Clark promptly halted the convoy. "What's going on here with all these gas masks being worn?" he asked in a stern tone.

"Gas!" the frightened driver replied, pointing back toward the front. The man answered without taking off his mask. He was nearly petrified with fear.

"Where's the gas?" Clark demanded. "Who said so?"

"Somewhere up front," the man replied, still wearing his mask. "I don't know who said it. There's just gas and everyone's putting on masks."

An exasperated Mark Clark allowed himself the luxury of a few curse words. "There isn't any damned gas," he exploded. "Now take off those damned masks and get on with your business."

Still fearful, the soldier slowly removed his gas mask. Others in the convoy followed suit.

Climbing back into his jeep, Clark said to Captain Thrasher, "That's what happens in a tight battlefield situation when men are on edge. It probably started when someone spotted some heavy clouds of dust."

He added resignedly: "If I hadn't put a stop to that, in two hours every man in Fifth Army would be wearing his gas mask, and the panic would be on."

Returning to his headquarters near Pontecagnano in mid-afternoon after a tour of the front, General McCreery, commander of the British X Corps on the north sector, was startled to find the facility in a state of disarray and near panic. Soldiers were dashing about and packing equipment and belongings into trucks.

McCreery was furious. "What the bloody hell is going on here?" he demanded of his chief of staff.

"Headquarters is now virtually in the front line and we're in danger of being overrun at any minute," the aide replied.

"Stop this damned packing at once," the aggressive McCreery exploded. "Put out some men for security. We're staying here."

At about the time McCreery was putting a damper on the near-panic in his headquarters. *Feldmarschall* Albert Kesselring—"Smiling Al" to the Allies—was indeed grinning broadly at the *Wehrmacht's* Mediterranean headquarters at

Lt. Gen. Mark W. Clark,
Fifth Army commander

Lt. Col. William P. Yarborough
conceived parachute missions.

View looking east shows area on lower half of photo onto which two regiments of the 82nd Airborne Division dropped on successive nights. Right rear is Monte Soprano where Col. James Gavin and an aide made a recon out in front of American lines. Old Roman watch tower is at lower right.

Italian armistice principals. From left: British Brigadier Kenneth Strong, *Generale di Brigata* Giuseppe Castellano (Italian emissary), U.S. Major General Walter B. Smith, and Castellano's interpreter.

Lt. Gen. Mark W. Clark, Fifth Army commander, with his Salerno airborne advisor, Lt. Col. William P. Yarborough, in back.

Col. James M. Gavin
(Picture taken after promotion)

Headquarters Company, 505th Parachute Infantry Regiment, entering Naples, the primary objective of Operation Avalanche.

Ruins of old Greek temples outside Paestum on Salerno beachhead. Germans occupied high ground to rear.

Lt. Charles C.W. Howland (left) led raiding force in capture of Ventotene Island. Later killed in Battle of the Bulge. Capt. Archie Birkner (right) was captured near Avellino.

Ready for the Avellino jump. Edward Pawloski (left) and Carl Dunphy.

Lt. Charles H. McKinney receives Silver Star from Lt. Gen. Mark W. Clark for Avellino mission.

James B. Ray (left) and
Samuel Callahan

In Sirico marketplace are Signora
Margherita Ciccone, daughter Anna and a
child relative.

Elements of the U.S. 3rd Infantry Division advancing through Avellino after Fifth Army broke out of the beachhead. Down this road the Germans were pouring troops and supplies to Salerno, 20 miles to the south.

Frascati, near Rome. He had just read an urgent message from Tenth Army:

> Troops and some tanks of the LXXVI Korps report breaking through to the beach in the American sector.

The field report was accurate. A small German force had reached the shoreline. A burned-out panzer, struck by Allied artillery fire, sat in mute testimony to that fact.

While Salerno beachhead was engulfed in flame that afternoon, at advanced Allied headquarters at Carthage, several hundred miles across the blue Mediterranean in North Africa, the Supreme Commander sat tensely at his desk. A furrowed brow creased the forehead of the self-styled Kansas farm boy, General Dwight Eisenhower. He was worried—highly worried.

Only minutes before a staff officer had handed Eisenhower a message from General Clark on shell-swept Salerno beachhead. The message had become garbled in transmission and conveyed the impression that the youthful Clark, in his first battle assignment, had panicked and was preparing to evacuate the beachhead—if such were possible under the relentless pressure of massed German artillery, attacking infantry and the *Luftwaffe*.

More than 3,000 miles to the west, Eisenhower's boss, General George Marshall, the Army Chief of Staff, was slipping on his eyeglasses to peruse a top-secret message from the Supreme Commander in North Africa. In terse yet revealing terms, the message stated:

> We are very much in the touch-and-go stage of the Salerno operation. We have been unable to advance and the enemy is conducting a major attack . . . I am using everything bigger than a rowboat (to get reinforcements) to the beachhead.

Earlier in the day a little fleet of LCIs had sailed out of a harbor in southern Sicily and for hours had been inching along at low speed through the gentle blue swells of the Mediter-

ranean Sea. On board were two elements of the 82nd Airborne Division: The 325th Glider Infantry Regiment and the
3rd Battalion of Colonel Rube Tucker's 504th Parachute
Infantry.

The flotilla presumably was on its way to Salerno bridgehead—but no one on board knew for sure, including the senior officer, Colonel Harry Lewis, commander of the glider
unit. After the craft had been at sea for many hours, the airborne men spotted a land mass to their starboard, and the
LCIs headed into what was thought to be a harbor on the
Italian mainland in control of the Allies. Soon the identity of
the harbor became known to the airborne men—Palermo. The
flotilla, after hours at sea, was not yet away from Sicily.

Colonel Lewis went ashore for orders. He returned in
about an hour, expressionless and silent as to the future course
of the little convoy. "All I can say," Lewis finally stated,
"is that we are proceeding to Italy and will land sometime
tomorrow."

"How do you know there'll be anywhere to land?" an
inquisitive war correspondent inquired.

Lewis turned around without a word and went below deck.

In the meantime, back on the beachhead, it was not long
after Colonel Reuben Tucker's 1st and 2nd Battalions dug into
a defensive position southwest of Albanella that the *Wehrmacht* announced dramatically it was aware of the presence
of the paratroopers in that locale—artillery shells began
screaming into the line of 504th foxholes. But, to the surprise
of the parachutists, the Germans did not attack their position
with infantry.

Earlier that day, after inspecting his positions, Lieutenant
Colonel Warren Williams, the commander of the 1st Battalion, was suffering increasing pain from the teeth that had
been knocked loose when his chute popped open in the jump
several hours before. He approached Captain Charles Pack,
his battalion surgeon.

"Say, Doc," Williams began. "I got some of my teeth
knocked loose in the jump and they're giving me fits. No big
deal, but is there anything you can do for me?"

"Oh, they'll probably tighten up in a few days," Captain

Pack replied. "Come on back to the station when you get a chance and I'll write you up for a Purple Heart."

"You must be kidding," Williams replied. "What would I tell an amputee when he asks me how I got my Purple Heart?"

That afternoon of the fourteenth, while powerful German forces were making an all-out effort to break through to the sea, men of the 509th Parachute Infantry Battalion were idling in their bivouac area near Licata, Sicily. Officers and men were spoiling for action. Elements of the 509th Battalion had previously made three combat jumps in North African fighting and had been engaged in bitter action as straight infantry. But since that time—more than five months—the rugged paratroopers of the battalion had been involved in tedious, boring training.

"For Chrissake," a Five-O-Niner exploded one day, "now we're training to learn how to train!"

The battle-tested men of the 509th Parachute Infantry Battalion had been fuming for 24 hours. Most of their ire was directed at General Matthew Ridgway, commander of the 82nd Airborne Division to which the battalion was attached. On learning the previous afternoon that Colonel Rube Tucker's regiment would jump that night behind friendly lines on the Salerno bridgehead with only two of his three battalions, the 509th veterans thought that their unit would be taken along as the third battalion in the regiment.

Colonel Tucker's other battalion, the 3rd, had previously been sent off with the 325th Glider Regiment to go to the beachhead by sea. As a result, Tucker's regiment was "short" a battalion for the Salerno jump.

Most troopers in the attached 509th Battalion considered Colonel Tucker's failure to take the experienced outfit along that night to be a slur on their fighting abilities. What the parachutists of the 509th, in their puptents and quonset huts scattered in olive groves around Licata airfield, could not be told was that the veteran unit had been selected for an even more crucial mission than reinforcing the Italian bridgehead.

It was just past 3 P.M. that day, September 14, when a message was received at the CP of the 509th Parachute Infantry. Lieutenant Colonel Doyle R. Yardley, the battalion commander who had been a school teacher in civilian life in Texas, hurriedly read the communication. It stated that in precisely one hour General Ridgway would arrive at the 509th command post. All staff and line officers were to be present.

"Wonder what we've done to rate a personal visit from old Ridgway, himself?" a 509th officer in the CP mused to no one in particular.

"Maybe he wants to find out if we've been getting enough booze and broads," replied another with a straight face.

Lieutenant Colonel Yardley immediately ordered his adjutant, Lieutenant Laverne P. Wess, to have the designated officers clean up, shave and report to the battalion command post within a half-hour. At the appointed time, all officers were present to await the arrival of the 82nd Airborne's commanding general.

Knowing that General Ridgway was a stickler on the personal grooming of troops under his command, Yardley was irate when Lieutenant Jack Pogue, the battalion communications officer, turned up badly in need of a shave. Ridgway would interpret Pogue's slovenly appearance as lack of discipline in the 509th Parachute Infantry, Yardley was convinced.

Pogue, who had received a battlefield commission in North Africa, explained to the battalion commander that he had been up all night repairing radios.

"You might have been up all night," Yardley barked. "But it sure as hell wasn't to repair radios."

Yardley turned to his adjutant, Lieutenant Wess, and snapped, "Take Pogue off jump status for a month."

As the 509th officers settled down to await the arrival of General Ridgway, Yardley began to count noses. Among those present were the battalion executive officer, Major William Dudley; the battalion adjutant, Lieutenant Wess; the communications officer, Lieutenant Pogue, and company commanders Captain Erven E. Boettner, Captain Casper E. "Pappy" Curtis, Captain Ralph H. Whitmore, Jr., Captain Archie Birkner and Captain Edmund J. Tomasik. All had previously seen combat.

All the officers knew that Ridgway was extremely punctual and invariably arrived on visits to his command precisely to the minute. Noting that the commanding general would not appear for another 22 and one-half minutes officers bided their time with conjecture as to the purpose of Ridgway's visit. The consensus was that the general would reveal that the battalion was to make a reinforcing jump behind Allied lines on the Salerno bridgehead.

Much to the astonishment of the awaiting officers, a dusty staff car ground to a halt in front of the battalion CP and out hopped General Ridgway—several minutes ahead of schedule. "Mark Clark's in even bigger trouble than we've been hearing," a Five-O-Niner whispered to a comrade.

Ridgway strode into the command post amid calls of "Ten-shut!" and the rustling of chairs as the officers jumped to their feet. His face was a portrait of solemnity as he shook hands hurriedly with Colonel Yardley and gave an "At ease." Those acquainted with Ridgway's command habits noted another indication of an extreme urgency at hand. At such meetings Ridgway customarily shook hands with each officer present. Now he immediately began speaking.

"Gentlemen, Fifth Army's in serious trouble over at Salerno," the general observed. "They need our help—and they need it now. Colonel Tucker's two battalions jumped behind our lines on the beachhead last night and are at the front fighting Germans. Colonel Gavin's regiment will jump tonight on the same DZ. If we can't give Mark Clark more help he may lose the beachhead.

"You and your men will jump tonight well behind German lines, at a town called Avellino. It is 20 miles north of Salerno. Your mission will be to seize or occupy, prior to daylight, a crucial three-point crossroads just south of Avellino and deny its use to the enemy. Most German reinforcements and supplies to the beachhead are being brought in through Avellino."

The airborne general said that the 509th Battalion was to hold the crossroads until Fifth Army pushed ahead to link up with the paratroopers. If Fifth Army did not reach the parachutists after three to five days the men were to break up into pairs or small groups and infiltrate back to Allied lines on the beachhead.

As Ridgway continued with his briefing dark thoughts raced through the minds of the veteran parachute officers. If Fifth Army was hanging on by its fingernails, how could it suddenly drive forward against a tenacious foe and link up with the paratroopers in three to five days? If the hard-pressed Fifth Army did manage to link up with the 509th Battalion at Avellino, how long would it take? Days? Weeks? Months?

The experienced Five-O-Niners knew that any parachute force far behind enemy lines would have to carry all their weapons, supplies, ammunition and equipment with them when they jumped, and that there would be no method for resupply except through uncertain air drops. While the enemy could bring to bear the full force of his combat arms to root out and destroy the invaders from the sky, the lightly-armed paratroopers would have no tanks, artillery or antitank weapons (except for the ineffective 2.36-inch bazookas).

General Ridgway was keenly aware of these circumstances, yet he had great faith in the courage and resourcefulness of the veterans of the 509th Parachute Infantry Battalion. He also knew that the situation at Salerno was desperate. It called for desperate countermeasures.

"I cannot stress too much the crucial significance of your mission," Ridgway told the assembled and grim-faced parachute officers. "This Avellino jump is much more than just another important combat jump. There are tremendous stakes involved. The life of Fifth Army at Salerno may well depend upon how you do your job,"

He continued: "This is going to be an especially dangerous mission, but I know I can count on you. You'll get plenty of trouble from the Germans. But it is absolutely essential that you and your men do everything within your power to disrupt enemy reinforcements and supplies pouring through Avellino to the beachhead. Fifth Army's fate is in your hands. Good luck and Godspeed!"

There were more shouts of "Ten-shut!" and the officers leaped to their feet. Ridgway shook hands with each officer. When he arrived in front of Lieutenant Pogue he glanced at the communications officer's heavy facial stubble but said nothing.

Hardly had Ridgway's staff car sped away in a cloud of dust than Lieutenant Colonel Yardley and his staff plunged into the tedious task of drawing up plans for the jump at Avellino. With takeoff only a few hours away, Yardley and his officers were worried over the total lack of intelligence as to German troop dispositions in the Avellino region. Intelligence officers of the 82nd Airborne could say only that "there are thought to be several Kraut units stationed around and in Avellino."

In addition to lack of information on German troop dispositions, the 509th staff began uncovering other difficulties. Surrounding the little town of Avellino were towering mountains, most of which were 4,000 feet or higher. This would require C-47s to stay above 4,000 feet before lowering altitude for the bail out. Even then, the Five-O-Niners would jump from heights of 2,000 to 3,000 feet. This height in itself would almost assure a wide dispersal of the parachutists, even if they were to jump directly over the drop zone.

By contrast, Colonel Rube Tucker's two battalions of the 504th Regiment bailed out over the Salerno beachhead from 600 to 800 feet, resulting in tight patterns in the landings.

At Avellino, there would be tricky air currents to be encountered, as in most mountainous regions. If a stick of paratroopers bailing out from 3,000 feet were caught in these powerful, swirling mountain air currents, their billowing chutes might be carried for miles.

Those hurriedly making sketchy plans for the 509th drop at Avellino were also deeply concerned as to the ability of Troop Carrier Command to locate the DZ. Most members of the battalion were participants in the combat jump which spearheaded the invasion of North Africa 10 months previously. The 509th flew 1,600 miles from England to make the drop ahead of seaborne forces. Plagued by inexperienced pilots, inadequate navigational instruments, turbulent weather, darkness and assorted unforeseen factors, the C-47s had become widely dispersed. Planeloads of paratroopers, flying alone and in pairs or tiny groups, made landfall over North

Africa along a stretch of several hundred miles. Three plane-loads had landed in Spanish Morocco—the wrong country.

Only two months before, in the Allied invasion of Sicily, heavy gales, inexperienced pilots and navigators and inadequate navigational equipment resulted in Colonel James Gavin's spearheading regimental combat team to be scattered over a 60-mile swath of southeast Sicily.

As a result of these two previous experiences, 509th confidence in Troop Carrier Command's ability to locate a tiny drop zone at night in the mountains of central Italy was minimal—even indiscernible.

A flight route for the Avellino mission was selected by Troop Carrier Command at Licata which would minimize the possibility of C-47s being shot down by "friendly" fire from the beachhead and Allied ships offshore. The route also would avoid heavy German antiaircraft batteries known to be in the Salerno City region.

The C-47 pilots carrying the 509th Parachute Infantry to Avellino would follow the identical route up the western coast of Italy that was traveled by Colonel Tucker's parachute regiment the previous night. Only instead of veering out to sea after the beachhead was reached as the C-47s of Tucker's flight did, the Avellino sky convoy was to continue northward to Montecorvino and on through mountain valleys to the crossroads DZ south of Avellino.

Despite its numerous advantages, this route would add to the burdens of pilots trying to locate the drop zone. The route was improvised too late to obtain complete photographic coverage around Avellino, so the first time C-47 pilots would have a chance to view the terrain would be when they were flying over it in the darkness.

Once the flight carrying the 509th flew northward from the beachhead the route to the DZ would be devoid of easily identifiable checkpoints. Without the coastal highway and the towns along the shoreline which would help guide the flight to the bridgehead, pilots would soon find that one mountain valley and peak looked almost identical to another mountain valley and peak.

As the frantic minutes ticked by late that afternoon and

time approached for lifting off for the Italian crossroads near
the hamlet of Santa Lucia di Sorino, a staff officer hurried up
to Lieutenant Colonel Yardley, the battalion commander. He
told him that the 51st Carrier Wing had decided that instead
of dropping the paratroopers at 2,000 to 3,000 feet, the jump
would have to be made at 4,000 feet. The Air Corps had
become increasingly concerned about its C-47s crashing into
the lofty mountains around Avellino.

Minutes later the same paratroop officers approached
Yardley and told him that the Troop Carrier Command had
also decided that no downward recognition lights were to be
used on the C-47s. Air planners were concerned that *Luftwaffe* night interceptors might be active north of Salerno and
would have a "Turkey shoot" with the slow-moving, bulky,
unarmed troop carrier planes.

Hasty planning concluded, Colonel Yardley assembled his
battalion and climbed onto the hood of a jeep to address the
troopers. This would be his first combat mission as battalion
commander, having been promoted to that post from executive officer earlier in the year.

As the troopers listened intently, Yardley briefed them on
what few details were known. "Men, we're going to drop
around a little Eytie town called Avellino in a few hours. The
place is alive with Krauts, although we have no specific info
on their dispositions. The Germans are rushing reinforcements and supplies to the beachhead. You might have to start
fighting the bastards the moment you hit the ground—or on
the way down."

Seeking to relax his eager but anxious fighting men, Colonel Yardley concluded his short talk with an offhand effort
at humor: "One final thing, men. For Chrissake when we're
up there at Avellino tonight don't get shot in the ass!"

Within a few hours, this parting admonition would have
an especially ironic significance to Colonel Yardley.

7
"If We Don't Come Back . . ."

IN OLIVE GROVES around Licata there was a beehive of activity. Members of the 509th Parachute Infantry Battalion, combat veterans and a few green replacements who had yet to hear a shot fired in anger, were making personal preparations for the jump that night near Avellino.

Solomon Weber the battalion communications sergeant from New York City, checked his Tommy gun to make certain that it was clean, oiled and in perfect working condition. He might have to fire it on landing—or on the way to earth. Then he examined the weapon again. And a third time.

Lieutenant Ernest R. "Bud" Siegel, also of New York, whose perpetual smile belied his fighting tenacity on the battlefield, was concerned that new parachutes had not as yet been issued for the jump. So were all Five-O-Niners. For many weeks, the troopers had literally been living with their old chutes. During the recent campaign in Sicily, the 509th Battalion had been alerted for one mission after another, but each was cancelled as ground forces overran the drop zones.

In order to jump in Sicily on brief notice, the Five-O-

Niners had retained individual chutes and had been using them to sit on, as pillows and as miniature eating tables. The troopers of the battalion had been carrying the same parachutes for so long that one man, in getting ready for the mass jump that night, called out with a straight face to his comrades: "Say, where in the hell did all these silkworms crawling out of my chute come from? Do you guys have them in yours, too?"

No one laughed.

Lieutenant Segal asked his company commander, "Where do we get our new chutes for the jump tonight? These old ones are probably full of holes."

Came the response: "We don't. We jump with what we've got."

Lieutenant Jack Pogue, whom Colonel Yardley had ordered taken off jump status because of his beard stubble at the meeting with General Ridgeway two hours previously, was getting ready to go on the mission—even though officially he had been grounded. Glancing around to see that no one was watching, Pogue, a Texan who had studied history in college, slipped a half-pint of Four Roses whiskey into a pocket.

Several weeks before, an old friend from Fort Benning jump school had arrived in North Africa with the 82nd Airborne Division. Sergeant Tommy Gore smuggled the half-pint of Four Roses overseas with him, and on arrival had given it to Old Pal Pogue. The gift in the Mediterranean region was a more valuable commodity than a bushel of diamonds.

Pogue guarded the whiskey diligently. He could not bring himself to drink it, but rather would wait for a significant occasion. Pogue knew that if his comrades discovered he had a half-pint of whiskey in his possession the Four Roses would vanish much like the early-morning dew. Twice, in order to protect his valuable commodity, Pogue buried the bottle and its contents in the desert.

Now, the battalion communications officer concluded, was an appropriate occasion to consume the Four Roses with his comrades—when they landed on Adolph Hitler's continental

Europe. "As soon as we touch down, I'll drink it with my buddies," Pogue vowed to himself.

Nearby, Captain Carlos C. "Doc" Alden, battalion surgeon, was diligently checking the Tommy gun and two pistols he would carry when he bailed out of his C-47 in a few hours. He knew, as did all troopers, that when he landed on the dark Italian mainland his weapons might be his only friends.

Doc Alden—he was called Doc by generals and privates alike—was not the stereotyped combat surgeon. He went into combat fully armed. The Geneva Convention, which laid down rules for killing and mutilating in a civilized manner, forbade medics to carry weapons. But in North Africa, where he made two combat jumps and was wounded, Alden had seen his unarmed medics shot down by the enemy on occasion. He concluded that the German enemy respected the provisions of the Geneva Convention only when such served a purpose.

From that point on, Alden went into battle with a Tommy gun or Garand rifle, a .45-caliber Colt pistol on his hip, a .38-caliber pistol in a shoulder holster, a nasty-looking trench knife in a boot, another knife for emergencies hidden in his clothing, and one large pocket was crammed with hand grenades and the other pocket with bandages and splints.

Captain Alden's 31 medics also were armed during combat, except for two troopers whose religious beliefs precluded their carrying weapons. None wore red cross armbands or the large red crosses painted on helmets, as Geneva Convention provisions dictated. "Aiming points for enemy riflemen," Doc Alden called the crosses.

Due to its relatively small size and its role of being a bastard outfit (that is, not being a part of a division), the 509th Parachute Infantry Battalion was an extremely close-knit fighting machine. Its members were fiercely proud, keenly loyal to each other and to the battalion, and intensely determined not to conduct themselves on the battlefield in a manner which would bring disfavor upon themselves in the eyes of their comrades.

Paratroopers of the battalion sprang from a wide spectrum of American society. There were the wealthy and the destitute and those in between. There were law enforcement officers and ex-convicts. White collar and blue collar workers. School teachers and grave diggers. Regardless of their background as civilians, in the 509th Parachute Infantry Battalion all men were "equal" and were judged solely on how they performed on the battlefield. All were volunteers for hazardous duty and had one common denominator: Each was a tough, resourceful fighter.

As the afternoon dissolved into evening, Troop Carrier Command headquarters in the old schoolhouse near Licata received a message from embattled Fifth Army on the Salerno beachhead:

> Situation remains critical, Parachute missions tonight on beachhead and at Avellino most urgent.

Elsewhere in southern Sicily, at Castelvetrano, Colonel James Gavin was immersed in a whirlwind of last-minute activities just before he and his 2,100 men of the 505th Parachute Regimental Combat Team took off for Salerno. A flurry of orders had to be rushed out, arms, equipment and ammunition had to be assembled, and detailed coordination with Troop Carrier Command had to be implemented.

Like his men, Colonel Gavin was apprehensive about that night's drop behind Allied lines on the bridgehead. The specter of the 23 C-47s shot down over the beachhead at Sicily by "friendly" fire was too fresh in his mind. Could this recent tragedy repeat itself in the confusion on mainland Italy?

Still, Gavin was too engrossed in the myriad of preparation details to dwell unduly on his personal safety or that of his troopers. He had a job to do.

Gavin—called "Slim Jim" by his men—had enlisted in the army as a private at age 17 and received a commission at West Point, graduating in 1929. He was not flamboyant and bombastic like the other 82nd Airborne parachute colonel, Reuben Tucker, but was a highly inspirational leader and held in great affection by his troopers, who regarded their commander as "one of us."

The night's mission to Salerno beachhead would follow

the same flight route as did Colonel Tucker's regiment the
night before. Gavin's sky convoy would be much larger than
the one that carried Tucker's men into battle. One hundred
and thirty-one C-47s would be required to fly Gavin's 505th
Parachute Infantry Regiment and Company B of the 307th
Parachute Engineers to the Salerno DZ.

Plans called for Gavin and his men to bail out over the
beachhead at midnight, the same time Doyle Yardley's 509th
Parachute Infantry Battalion was to jump at Avellino.

As the light of a beautiful Mediterranean day began to fade
into twilight and then into darkness, at scattered airfields in
southern Sicily, Colonel Gavin and his men were grim but
ready for whatever Dame Fate had in store for them.

At one encampment, Sergeant Buffalo Boy Canoe, a full-
blooded Oglala Sioux Indian, who had gained wide recognition in the 82nd Airborne for his fierce fighting in Sicily,
was energetically honing his trench-knife to razor-blade
sharpness.

"You've been sharpening that goddamned pig-sticker so
long, Buffalo Boy, that you could split a hair in two with it,"
injected a nearby comrade.

"It'll make my job easier," the 20-year-old Indian warrior
replied, not looking up from his honing. "I got two Kraut
scalps in Sicily and I'm going to get a couple more before
the night is over."

Sergeant Otis L. Sampson, a mortarman, was cramming
his pockets with grenades. "Aren't those a little heavy for
you, Pop?" a comrade needled. "You're getting a little old
for all this."

Sergeant Sampson, who it was said could drop a
.60-millimeter mortar shell into a cup of coffee at 500 yards,
merely grinned. He was the oldest man in the company—all
of 32.

Private Edward J. Bisso, Jr., just turned 20, was exchanging pre-battle confidences with his close friend, Private Rocco
Rubino. Talking in hushed tones, the grim-faced Bisso exclaimed, "We're going to get the hell shot out of us tonight
flying over the beachhead. We were lucky in the Sicily
mission. But tonight we're not going to make it."

There was no hysteria in the voice, no display of excessive fear. Only a calm and candid reaction of how the young paratrooper felt about his chances in that night's mission to Salerno.

At Agrigento airfield along the rugged coast of southern Sicily darkness had draped the landscape as Lieutenant Colonel Joel Crouch, operations officer of the 52nd Troop Carrier Wing, slipped into the pilot's seat of his C-47. As in the jump by Colonel Tucker's regiment the night before, Crouch would fly the lead plane in a flight of three C-47s, which would drop pathfinders from the 505th Parachute Infantry Regiment onto the DZ at Salerno.

Colonel Crouch and the two other pilots of the pathfinder aircraft revved their motors and, trailing thick clouds of dust, sped down the runway and lifted off. It was 9:47 P.M. The second paratroop reinforcing mission to bring relief to Mark Clark's embattled Fifth Army had been launched.

It was a beautiful autumn night. The moon was round, smiling and brilliant. The flight of three C-47s burrowed on into the Mediterranean sky without incident and some two hours later they were approaching the beachhead at Salerno. Once again, a green Very-pistol flare shot into the dark sky to the front, followed by a huge T leaping into flame. Lieutenant Colonel Bill Yarborough, the Fifth Army commander's airborne advisor, and his men were again on the job, unseen in the darkness far below.

As the three pathfinder C-47s zoomed in over the DZ, the moonlit sky was dotted with white billowing parachutes as the troopers, swaying gently, descended to earth. All landed directly on target. It was 11:38 P.M. Only three minutes after reaching ground, pathfinders had assembled and were operating radar and radio homing devices and Krypton lights to guide in the main body of Colonel Gavin's regiment to a point where the huge blazing T could be clearly seen by the C-47 pilots.

Meanwhile, unforeseen delays were plaguing the takeoff of Colonel Gavin's first formation of 54 aircraft which would carry Gavin and his staff, Colonel Edward "Cannonball" Krause's 3rd Battalion, and the attached parachute engineers company. Planes and pilots were from the 313th and the 314th Carrier Groups.

Scheduled to liftoff precisely 15 minutes after Colonel Crouch's pathfinder planes headed for Salerno, tire blowouts, engine trouble and some confusion as the result of the necessarily hasty planning all contributed to delaying the departure of the initial formation of the 505th Parachute Infantry.

Finally, one hour behind schedule, Gavin's C-47s began rolling down the runways at Castelvetrano and Borizzo and headed for battle. Knowing that the parachutists were to land near the ancient Roman town of Paestum, one man called out as his C-47 lifted into the air, "We're jumping near Paestum and that's exactly what we're going to do to the goddamned Krauts—paste 'em!"

Shortly after the first formation to liftoff rendezvoused and set a course for the beachhead, Colonel Gavin said to Captain Alfred W. Ireland, his personnel officer seated in the adjoining bucket seat, "I'm going to have a look around."

In his burdensome combat gear, the angular colonel struggled to his feet and waddled to the open door. It was a beautiful Mediterranean night. Calm and peaceful. A round iridescent moon, hanging aloof high in the heavens, smiled down mockingly at Colonel Gavin. Well it could—Mr. Moon was wisely far removed from the madness of man on the bloody battlefield he watched over at Salerno.

Shortly after the dark northeast tip of triangular-shaped, mountainous Sicily passed under the wing of his C-47 and the craft headed out over water, Colonel Gavin was encouraged to view the shadowy silhouettes of massive heights to his front—mainland Italy. That was good news. The flight appeared to be on course. Knifing across the Italian shoreline, shimmering in the moonlight far below, the flight veered sharply to the left and set a course northward, up the western coast of the peninsula, directly to the DZ near Paestum.

The Five-O-Fives, seated shoulder to shoulder in bucket seats on each side of the C-47s, were weighted down with the heavy gear. Some men would jump with 100 pounds of weapons and equipment. They were burdened with personal weapons, ammunition, rations, gas masks, musette bags, first-aid kits, maps, binoculars, steel helmets, heavy jump boots and other paraphernalia of war.

Distributed among the troopers to carry to earth were bazookas and rockets, radios, steel cases with machine-gun ammo, mortar components and shells, and land mines.

The men rode along in silence. Tension was thick inside the dimly-lit cabins. This was to be a routine jump behind friendly lines—that's what the briefing officers declared—but the experienced paratroopers knew there was no such thing as a "routine" combat flight into a hotly-contested battle zone. Too many things could go wrong, of that they were certain.

A few troopers dozed—or pretended to dozed. Tiny orange gleams speckled the dark cabins where men nervously took drags on cigarettes before grinding out the light with their heels. Here and there a trooper vomited from the stress, splashing his inner contents over the floor or into his steel helmet. Foreheads and palms perspired. Stomachs churned and knotted. On occasion a parachutist's lips moved ever so slightly in a rhythmic cadence. Prayers. Perhaps his final prayers.

Ears were cocked and strained for the sound of *Luftwaffe* motors above the roar of the C-47 engines and the rushing of angry Mediterranean air through the open doors. German fighter pilots could leisurely pick and choose which of the lumbering C-47s, filled with paratroopers, they would shoot down first. Few parachutists, if any, would have time to bail out if a bulky C-47 were shot down in flames.

If *Wehrmacht* gunners around the beachhead did not shoot them down, there was the possibility of a repeat of the Sicily tragedy where 23 C-47s were sent plunging to earth or into the sea by "friendly" antiaircraft fire. Ever present in a paratrooper's mind was the frightening specter of parachutes that failed to open. "Streamers," the men called them.

Winging toward Salerno, minds flashed back to the young corporal at Fort Bragg who plunged, screaming, to his death when his parachute failed to open. No one ever learned why. The trooper landed with a sickening thud. As comrades touched down safely all around, they glimpsed the blond-haired youth's body—lying in a bloody heap, twisted and broken, much like a rag doll. None ever forgot the ghastly sight.

Parachuting into combat, a paratrooper could shatter a leg, and endure endless agony with bloody bone slivers protruding through the flesh. He could land heavily on his back or his head, breaking his spinal column and leaving him paralyzed and helpless. The possibilities for personal disaster on a combat jump were countless.

As Colonel Gavin's formation of 54 C-47s flew on toward Salerno, the flight had difficulty remaining together, and soon the armada became widely dispersed. Undaunted, the pilots pressed on in pairs and tiny groups.

Meanwhile, delays continued to hamper delivery of the 505th Parachute Infantry to the bridgehead. The second flight of 38 C-47s, with Lieutenant Colonel Mark J. Alexander's 2nd Battalion aboard, was over an hour late before lifting off at 11:20 P.M. Gavin's final formation, 36 aircraft carrying the 1st Battalion, lifted off from Comiso airfield at 1:00 A.M., three hours behind schedule. Aircraft of the 313th and 316th Carrier Groups had been tardy in arriving at Comiso from other fields to pick up the 1st Battalion.

Colonel Gavin's regimental combat team was strung out for more than 300 miles. AS the final flight carrying his 1st Battalion lifted off from Comiso at 1 o'clock in the morning of the fifteenth, Gavin's C-47 was nearing the bridgehead. The parachute colonel braced himself in the door against the onrushing blasts of air. The ominous red light flashed on—four minutes to go. Gavin peered intently into the darkness to glimpse the big flaming T on the drop zone. He could see nothing but the rocky landscape bathed in the light of the moon. Where was the T? Was this to be a repetition of the Sicily jump by the 505th Regiment two months before when Colonel Gavin was deposited 25 miles from the DZ?

Gavin's lumbering C-47 droned onward. He continued to stare into the darkness for the T. Suddenly the red light in the cabin cut off to be replaced by the green light—Go!

In seconds Colonel Gavin surveyed terrain features. He had but an instant to make a decision: Jump or not to jump. The landscape looked precisely like that of the drop zone in a photograph he had studied diligently back in Sicily only hours before. There was the long strip of white sand along the shoreline, the flat patch of ground on which the jump would be made, the mouth of a river emptying into the sea only a short distance ahead. All the geographic features matched up perfectly. But where was the flaming T? Had the Germans overrun the drop zone?

Gavin could conjecture no longer. "Let's go!" he shouted from his crouched position, and out the door he went. His stick bailed out rapidly, each trooper literally on the neck of the man in front of him as they plunged through the yawning door. Nearby troopers were tumbling out of the other C-47s and floating earthward.

Colonel Gavin felt the customary sharp blow across the back of his shoulders as his parachute popped open and felt the hurricane wind slapping him in the face. Instinctively he glanced upward. There he saw the world's most beautiful sight—a white, billowing parachute.

Moments later Gavin crashed into the ground. He and the other troopers, now landing all around him, had leaped out at 700 feet. The colonel cast a hurried glance at his watch and saw that it was 1:10 A.M.

Bailing out of the same plane as the regimental commander was Sergeant Buffalo Boy Canoe, the young trooper who had been so energetically honing his trench knife a few hours before to "get a couple of Kraut scalps before the night is over." A split second after his parachute popped open, the Oglala Sioux Indian felt a deep surge of concern flow through his being. He had reached up to touch the eagle feather he had placed in his hair before the jump—and the feather was missing.

Sioux Indians regarded an eagle feather as a sacred and powerful "medicine" to protect its wearer, a religious symbol. Now he feared the shock of his parachute opening had caused the feather to dislodge. Sergeant Canoe, frantically feeling about his head for the feather, breathed a sigh of relief. The eagle adornment had indeed been jarred loose, but was not lost. It had become lodged under his helmet. A split second later, Canoe struck the ground with a heavy impact.

Standing in the center of the drop zone and peering upward at the majestic sight of scores of white parachutes floating to earth in the moonlight, Lieutenant Colonel Yarborough, the Fifth Army airborne advisor, was puzzled once more: Why had not the Germans, with observers on the surrounding heights, brought heavy artillery fire down on the drop zone as the parachutists landed?

More immediately, Yarborough was concerned with promptly locating the commander of the 505th Parachute Infantry Regiment, Colonel Gavin, from among the hundreds of troopers landing on the mile-long drop zone. Yarborough's instructions were to escort Gavin at once to Fifth Army headquarters to receive orders. It might be a difficult task, locating Gavin promptly, as he could have landed anywhere on or near the DZ.

Yarborough knew that the only way he could quickly locate Colonel Gavin in the customary confusion of a night mass drop was to ask each paratrooper if he had seen the regimental commander. A parachutist had landed almost at the side of Yarborough and as the tall, shadowy figure was rolling up his chute the Fifth Army airborne advisor approached him for information as to Gavin's whereabouts. As the trooper turned around, Yarborough was astonished. By the light of the moon's bright rays he recognized the man as Colonel Gavin, himself.

Almost an hour after the 505th commander's flight had dropped its cargo of paratroopers on the DZ, the sound of C-47s approaching from the south was heard once more. These planes were carrying Lieutenant Colonel Mark Alexander's 2nd Battalion. Again the flaming T burst forth. Colonel Alexander, in the lead plane, bailed out and floated earthward. Just before Alexander hit the ground, his chute pitched violently and he struck with tremendous impact on his back.

Alexander was stunned by the heavy force of the blow. Through a bleary eyesight he saw that he had landed almost upon one of the burning containers of gasoline soaked sand. He was also aware that a figure was standing over him. The colonel focused his eyes to make out the form of a large soldier, a toothy grin spreading across his black face.

For an instant Alexander thought he was having hallucinations from the heavy blow he had received on landing. He knew that there were no black troopers in his battalion. Then he realized that the soldier belonged to a quartermaster company on the beachhead and had probably been one of those whose job it had been to ignite the flaming T on spotting LIeutenant Colonel Yarborough's green flare.

It was nearly two hours more before the final flight carrying the 1st Battalion reached the bridgehead. Within 45 minutes from the time the last of the Five-O-Fives touched down, the paratroopers were loaded into a truck convoy and headed for an assembly area. Colonel Gavin, accompanied by Lieutenant Colonel Yarborough, drove by jeep to Fifth Army headquarters, a complex of tents and Mark Clark's trailer. An exhausted army commander was snatching a few hours of sleep, but his Chief of Staff, General Alfred Gruenther, was awakened.

"General Clark wants you to take over the southern sector of the beachhead perimeter," Gruenther explained to Gavin. Pointing to a map, Gruenther continued: "You will tie in with Tucker's 504th near Albanella and your line will extend to the sea near Agropoli."

Minutes later Colonel Gavin was back at his regiment's assembly area. By dawn a combat team of Five-O-Fives was in action.

The two parachute missions to reinforce Fifth Army had been incredible achievements in planning, logistics and execution by both the 82nd Airborne Division and the 52nd Trooper Carrier Wing. In 24 hours, 3,400 superb fighting men had been airlifted from bases more than 300 miles away in Sicily, dropped on the beachhead directly on the DZ, and were at the front spoiling for a fight. This had been attained with only a few hours' advance notice.

Much like the little Dutch boy in folklore, Matt Ridgway's resourceful paratroopers had plugged the badly leaking Allied dike at bloody Salerno.

The innovative burning T on the drop zone had not been

learned from a military textbook. Rather it was an invention born of necessity. Two regiments had been dropped in neat patterns and not a single paratrooper or C-47 had been lost.

A Troop Carrier Command pilot returning to Sicily from the beachhead enthused to his comrades, "I first spotted that god-damned burning T when we were 17 miles from the drop zone!"

Meanwhile, as "Slim Jim" Gavin's parachutists were being dropped on the bridgehead, the 509th Parachute Infantry Battalion was winging its way toward the once inconspicuous mountain town of Avellino. This would be the third—and most perilous—parachute mission to relieve the pressure on embattled Fifth Army.

Earlier that afternoon, as dusk was descending on Sicily, members of the 509th Parachute Infantry Battalion boarded C-47s at Licata for the short flight to Comiso airfield, from where they would lift off in a few hours for their appointment with destiny at Avellino. Soon night had pulled its cloak over the island. Troopers, their gear on the ground beside them or stashed under the spreading wings of the C-47s, gathered about their aircraft in little knots, waiting for the word to move out.

There was no outward display of panic or undue concern. They had volunteered for hazardous duty when they joined the paratroopers. This was hazardous duty. The normal idle banter was at a minimum. Even women were not being discussed. What conversation there was took place in subdued tones. These fighting men had a job to do—and they intended to do it. Many felt they would not return.

Captain Carlos Alden, the battalion surgeon, was outwardly calm. Pulling out a small diary, Alden sat on his helmet under a C-47 wing and by the light of a tiny flashlight scribbled an entry for September 14:

> If we don't come back, there are thousands to take our place and win this war. I hope I make it. But more important, I hope I can do my duty as an American man.

Suddenly the ominous silence blanketing dark Comiso airfield was shattered. A lone C-47 motor sent a roar echoing across the bleak landscape, and the pilot of the aircraft sped down the dusty runway and lifted off. It was 9:20 P.M. On board were two officers, Lieutenant Fred Perry and Lieutenant Henry F. Rouse, and nine troopers. They were members of the pathfinder detachment.

The C-47 headed northeast to the Italian mainland, then turned northward to follow the identical route of Colonel Reuben Tucker's 504th Parachute Infantry the previous night Instead of dropping the pathfinders on the bridgehead, the C-47 would continue north to the Avellino DZ.

Approaching he Salerno beachhead, one man on the C-47 called out. "Look at those yellow flashed down below!" The others craned necks to glance out the window. The yellow flashes were German antiaircraft batteries on the ground—and the lone C-47 pathfinder was the target.

Shells exploded outside the lumbering C-47, causing it to heave and lurch. There were sounds like a handful of rocks being tossed against the wall—shrapnel spraying the aircraft's fuselage. Inside the men were tense. And silent. They wished it were time to jump. Even bailing out into the dark unknown was preferable to sitting helplessly in a slow-moving airplane while enemy guns blasted away at it.

Presently the red light flashed on near the door. It would be four minutes until the DZ was reached. Lieutenant Perry, as jump-master, took his place in the yawning door and scanned the moon-bathed landscape. He was alarmed: One valley and field looked much like another valley and field. There were no significant landmarks. How could the pilot possibly locate the DZ in this faceless terrain?

Perry did not have long to dwell on his immediate concerns. A crossroads loomed up below, the green light switched on near the door, and with a cry of "Let's go!" the pathfinder commander bailed out. Lieutenant Rouse and the other nine troopers followed Perry out the door at split-second intervals and in less than eight seconds all 11 members of the detachment were floating earthward. As the men hit the ground and hauled in their chutes, several checked the time the first members of the 509th Parachute Infantry Battalion had set foot on Adolph Hitler's continental Europe. It was 11:30 P.M.

Hurriedly reconnoitering the drop zone, Lieutenants Perry and Rouse discovered a significant factor: They had been dropped on the wrong crossroads, this one a mile south of the designated DZ at the three-point road junction near the village of Santa Lucia di Sorino. A short consultation was held. It was concluded that there would not be time to march the mile to the correct drop zone, as the first aircraft carrying the main body of Five-O-Nines would arrive in less than 15 minutes. The jump would have to be made at the wrong crossroads and after landing the battalion could assemble and march the one mile to the designated DZ.

Perry, Rouse and the other pathfinders knew there was not a minute to lose and feverishly began setting up their equipment. In one respect, Dame Fortune had smiled broadly on the little group: Their homing devices, though dropped separately from the C-47, had landed in plain sight almost directly among the parachuting pathfinders. Precious minutes would not be squandered in searching for the equipment. Within five minutes, homing devices were in operation.

The pathfinders' equipment to guide in C-47s carrying the main body of the 509th Battalion consisted of a radio transmitter and two Aldis lamps. Only much later would the pathfinder team learn that the equipment had been virtually useless. The towering mountains deflected electronic signals aimed at the approaching C-47s and the narrow beam of the Aldis was nearly impossible to pick up unless a pilot were precisely on course.

Back at Comiso airfield, the pathfinder C-47 had barely lifted off when shouts rang out across the bleak terrain: "Okay, load 'em up! We're shoving off!" Burdened with heavy combat gear, the Five-O-Niners, grim-faced and silent, filed into their aircraft. It was 9:35 P.M. when the lead airplane, carrying the battalion commander and his headquarters detachment, lifted off, followed at close intervals by the other 38 C-47s.

Blacked-out Messina at the northeast tip of Sicily passed beneath the wings of the 39 troops carriers. The troopers rode in silence. They recalled what one of their own, an Old Army sergeant, had joked that afternoon when informed of the crash mission 20 miles behind enemy lines: "They're throwing the Krauts a bone. The 509th is going to be a nice, juicy, 600-man bone to take Fritz's mind off our boys on the beachhead."

Here and there a grim face cast an eerie glow, lighted by the fire on a cigarette, before slipping again into darkness moments later. A sergeant traced semaphoric-like patterns with his hands as he checked his harness straps and gear—then checked them again. A young crew-cut corporal quietly chanted a few words from the old training school song which nightly had echoed across the bars around Fort Bragg, North Carolina: "Gory, Gory what a helluva way to die . . ." before falling into silence under the icy glares of comrades. The song's title: "Blood on the Risers."

On occasion, in the confines of the C-47s, subdued mirthless laughter, shaky and contrived, would break out among a few men. Moments later that, too, was gone. Now there was only the relentless pounding of the motors, an occasional lurch of the metal bucket seats as men weighted down with gear shifted positions, and the rush of air through the yawing door. Always the rushing air.

Through the small windows the troopers could occasionally spot the vague silhouettes of other C-47s in the cloudless Mediterranean sky. There was an indefinable assurance in knowing that others were moving through the night also.

It was not just the haunting specter of what awaited each man on the ground when he bailed out into the unknown a short time ahead. That thought, in itself, was bad enough. It was partly that but it was mostly the traumatic experience of soon having to face up to the ordeal of leaping through the yawning door at the rear of the airplane. It was not a normal human function to jump out of a high-flying aircraft.

The Five-O-Niners heading toward their unknown destiny thought of the two comrades climbing sullenly into a truck on the sun-baked field near Kairouan, a few months before. Both were old hands at the jumping business, but now they were on their way to a replacement pool—beaten by The Door.

They never knew when they would have to jump. It gnawed on their nerves—relentlessly. That made each time going out The Door more nerve-racking than the last time.

The tense paratroopers in their C-47s recalled the teen-ager, back in sun-baked Oujda, walking bootless off the parade ground. He had been stripped of his prized jumpboots. Tears of anguish and humiliation streamed down his cheeks. The youth had jumped many times. Suddenly he could no longer go out The Door.

These were bad thoughts, but there were others more frightening. Unthinkable thoughts. Yet they thought them.

There were the piercing screams of two paratroopers just over from the States in a practice jump in Tunisia. They had landed on cactus trees which grew profusely in the desert and were skewered by giant needles two to three feet long. Impaled and unable to move, their screams and anguishing wails echoed across the bleak landscape as comrades were unable to remove the men from the cactus tree. They died in agony and were buried with the needles still in their bodies.

These fighting men on their way to bailing out near Avellino remembered the trooper in the practice jump at Mason Caree who was slammed into a stone wall by turbulent winds. His head split open, he died instantly. And there was the parachutist at Oujda, lying in the desert in agony with the fireball sun blasting him in the face. His back was broken.

Those were only practice jumps. Now the Five-O-Niners would soon leap from an airplane in the darkness from levels four to five times as high as most mass parachute drops, onto jagged, mountainous terrain laced with deep ravines, 20 miles or more behind enemy lines, into a region known to be infested by the Germans, with 100 pounds of battle gear strapped to their bodies. It would take God's benevolent help to get a trooper to the ground, out of his parachute harness and ready to fight.

8
Dropping onto a
Hornets' Nest

COMPLETE BLACKOUT WAS in effect as the sky train of C-47s carrying the 509th Parachute Infantry Battalion on its mission deep behind enemy lines at Salerno burrowed through the Mediterranean night. Flying northeast across Sicily and then north up the western coast of Italy, the aerial armada held its formation for the first 45 minutes. Then one C-47 drifted away from the main body, followed shortly by another aircraft slipping off. Two more planes broke away.

Now the pilots started climbing drastically to reach 5,000 to 6,000 feet in order to avoid crashing into the towering, ominous mountains around the drop zone. At this point any semblance of flight formation discipline evaporated like a wisp of smoke into the night. The once tidy pattern of C-47s proceeded to the drop zone individually and in tiny groups.

On his bucket seat next to Lieutenant John R. Martin, a platoon leader, a trooper was cursing the heavy burden of equipment and weapons with which he was jumping into battle. Locked shoulder to shoulder with the men on each side, the angry trooper began wiggling about in an effort to loosen his bulky life preserver and gas mask. He tossed the items contemptuously to the floor of the dark cabin.

As though on cue, there was a sudden flurry of activity in that C-47 as others followed suit. Soon the aisle was awash with discarded life preservers and gas masks. Elsewhere in the scattered C-47s, other troopers also were pitching these two items of equipment.

"If the bastards gas me, they'll just have to gas me!" a parachutist summed up the sentiment of all.

The moment of decision for the 641 paratroopers winging toward a rendezvous with the unknown was drawing closer. The Salerno beachhead, over which the C-47s would fly, was looming just ahead. Strained attempts at nonchalance in the aircraft now disappeared as loud cracks outside were followed by a severe rocking of the troop-laden C-47s—exploding antiaircraft shells. Down below and unseen in the darkness *Wehrmacht* gunners were furiously firing at the scattered transport planes. The flaming beachhead had been reached.

Most of the men, foreheads damp with perspiration, awkwardly turned their heads to peer out the windows behind them. On the pitch-black ground they could see the winking yellow bursts—ack-ack guns firing at them. The C-47s pressed onward.

In the headquarters plane carrying Colonel Yardley's staff Captain Carlos "Doc" Alden, the battalion surgeon, glanced out a window to look for other C-47s. Although the moon was out in all its brilliance, Alden could not spot a single transport plane. All he saw were the little lavender lights on the wing tip of his own aircraft.

Sergeant Gordon Hahn, one of Alden's medics, felt a nudge from the man along side who held out a package of Camels. Hahn took a cigarette. It required two matches to get the smoke flaming.

Knowing they were only minutes away from bailing out, an especially heavy pall fell over the paratroopers winging into battle. In most planes there was only the sound of the powerful airplane engines and the roar of wind rushing through the open door. In one C-47, a trooper, summoning his voice from a remote area deep inside, shouted: "Is everybody happy?" It was the traditional tongue-in-cheek morale booster among American fighting men in tight situations. Came back a full-throated chorus from the other 15 parachutists: "HELL, YES!"

In Lieutenant John Martin's plane the bright red panel light near the yawning door flashed on explosively in the darkness. Its haunting glare sent chills racing up the spines of the paratroopers. Four minutes to go before bailout.

A call "stand up and hook up!" rang through the cabin. It took an effort to stand. The troopers felt huge and bloated with their burdensome combat gear as they staggered into position, one behind the other, and snapped static lines onto the anchor cable that ran the length of the dimly-lit cabin. Now the waiting stress returned—harder, more nerve-racking than ever. The lurching of the plane seemed more pronounced. Hearts beat faster—and skipped beats. It would be only seconds now.

The thing to remember, all knew, was to get out that door fast, right on the neck of the man ahead. A one-second delay would mean a huge gap on the ground from the nearest comrade. This could prove fatal—to the trooper and to the mission. Fast . . . fast . . . fast. Out the door fast!

Lieutenant Martin glanced out the window. What he saw alarmed him. Off in the distance he spotted volcanic Mount Vesuvius, where the fabled ruins of Pompeii cuddled serenely at the foot of the towering elevation. Something had gone wrong, Martin knew. Vesuvius was nearly 30 miles west of the drop zone near Avellino.

Suddenly the green light—Go!—flashed on and troopers began leaping into the eerie, dark unknown. Clearing the C-47, Martin saw the enormous rectangle of black sky and felt the angry hurricane blasts ripping at his body. Moments later there was the white flash of exultation—his parachute had popped open. Martin knew he had a long way to drop as the transport planes had been flying high to avoid the mountains. Even if he wanted to, there could be no turning back. Whatever lay below him in the ominous blackness, the die had been cast.

Swinging beneath his canopy, the young lieutenant felt a surge of relief to view the dim outlines of other white parachutes floating to earth around him. Not many, but a few. Come what may, John Martin would not land alone.

Seconds later the black sky suddenly burst into flaming iridescence. Steams of angry white tracers laced the sky around Martin and the other troopers as they traveled earthward under their billowing white canopies. Bullets hissed past the helpless Martin and ripped through his parachute. He glanced around to see his comrades dangling in air were also being raked by machine-gun bullets fired from the ground. There was no question about it: Martin and his comrades were dropping onto a lethal hornets' nest.

Moments later the lieutenant could detect great masses of black foliage rushing up toward him, and then he crashed into the ground—hard. The heavy impact was jarring and sent shock waves of pain rushing through his legs. He tumbled over and lay on his back on the rugged terrain for a few seconds, staring upward at the fascinating yet frightening sight of his comrades floating to earth with white tracers stabbing long fingers into the sky all around them.

Martin rejected a sudden impulse to run his hands over his jump suit, to satisfy an inner urge to determine if all his parts were intact. Other than the customary shock of any parachute landing, the lieutenant knew he was all right physically. Although Germans were quite obviously in force all around him, he felt a twinge of relief to know that the worst part was over—he was on the ground.

Moments later, Martin was reminded that the war wouldn't wait, nor was his part in it over. He heard the rustle of movement in the darkness. Rapidly and quietly shucking his parachute, the lieutenant whipped out his nasty looking trench knife from his boot and waited tensely in a crouched position. All around him he could hear the rattle of small arms fire echoing down the valleys as descending paratroopers, on touching down, began engaging German troops. Neither Martin nor the other parachutists had any way of knowing that they had leaped onto the bivouac area of a panzer division headquarters.

The rustling sound Martin had detected moved closer. Seconds later the lieutenant spotted the silhouette of a helmet-clad soldier stealthily slipping past. Not knowing if the figure was German or American, Martin began silently tip-toeing after the shadowy apparition. As he stalked the unknown man, trench knife at the ready in the event the soldier were an enemy, Martin noticed with suspicion that the man he was surreptitiously pursuing would halt and resume walking on occasion, often crouching down for long seconds.

After Lieutenant Martin had stalked his quarry across the forbidding landscape for 15 minutes, the unknown shadowy figure paused atop a little knoll and the bright moonlight's beam flooded his face. He was wearing an American jump suit and helmet. And Martin recognized his face. It was Sergeant Lloyd Bjelland of the battalion's demolitions platoon, know affectionately to the troopers as "Mother BJ."

Lieutenant Martin called out the night's password— "California"—in a stage whisper, and a startled Bjelland answered with "Grapefruit," the countersign.

Martin walked up to the sergeant. "Mother BJ, what in the hell do you think you've been doing, halting and crouching and all that?" the relieved officer inquired of the veteran Bjelland.

"Hell, I'm stalking some guy going along up there in front of me," was the reply. "I can't tell if he's a Kraut or one of our guys."

Martin and Bjelland promptly moved out together, quietly stalking this unidentified soldier together. After nearly 10 minutes of a cat-and-mouse game over rugged Italian terrain, Martin and Bjelland caught sight of the man's facial features. He was a member of Bjelland's demolitions platoon who was, himself, in the process of silently moving through the countryside on the trail of yet another unidentified shadowy figure.

The three troopers hurriedly took stock of their situation and tried to orient themselves. By the muted glow of a tiny flashlight the men studied a large-scale map that had been issued the previous afternoon to various squads and officers involved in the mission. They were unable to pin-point their location.

Looking for the railroad which ran through Avellino, Lieutenant Martin, Sergeant Bjelland and the other trooper set off in the direction they concluded would take them there. Walking along in the darkness over the inhospitable terrain they heard a cacophony of small arms fire off to their right, perhaps a mile away. There were the familiar rapid bursts of German Schmeissers which sounded like bed sheets being ripped in two, followed by the slower-tempoed bark of American Tommy guns or Browning automatic rifles.

The knowledge that other paratroopers were in the region and dueling with enemy patrols spurred Martin, Bjelland and the other man to an even more brisk marching pace; they wanted to hook up with a larger force of comrades and join in raising havoc among *Wehrmacht* contingents and facilities.

Picking their way along in the darkness over the rock-strewn landscape with Lieutenant Martin leading the way, the three troopers skirted a hill when a shadowy figure suddenly leaped out from behind a huge boulder and stuck the muzzle of a pistol into the startled Martin's ear.

The lieutenant froze in place. Simultaneously with thrusting the pistol barrel at Martin's head, the shadowy figure called out, "California!" Martin, fleetingly fearful that his precarious predicament would render him incapable of speaking, blurted out "Grapefruit!" It was the American password and countersign for the night.

The pistol was lowered. Martin turned and recognized the figure as Ralph H. Whitmore, Jr., Martin's company commander. Huddled in the nearby shadows, weapons trained at Martin, Bjelland and the other trooper, were two men with Whitmore. Now the fighting force had doubled—to six members.

Elsewhere, Private Otto D. Weer, a 19-year-old bazooka man, landed alone. As with many others comrades that night, he fleetingly conjectured if he was in the right country. He saw neither American nor German. Silence prevailed in the area.

Weer began roaming the countryside and within an hour had hooked up with three other Five-O-Niners. They were from other companies and he knew none of them. Together the four troopers began marching along a narrow road in what they thought was the direction of the DZ south of Avellino. Rounding a bend in the road where it sloped gently downhill, the four Americans, by the rays of the moon, spotted 50 or 60 German soldiers moving up the road directly toward them. Two armored cars were inching along in support of the marching column.

Weer and his three comrades hurriedly scrambled behind bushes to either side of the road. The heavily armed *Wehrmacht* force soon reached the point where the four American paratroopers had secluded themselves. Weer could feel his heart thumping furiously and feared its pounding would be heard by the Germans whom he could almost reach out and touch.

Suddenly strident shouts in German rang out from the head of the column and the force halted precisely where Weer and his comrades had taken refuge. It was almost as if the Germans knew the troopers were there. More loud shouts were heard. The enemy force promptly fanned out to either side of the road and systematically began probing bushes with vigorous swipes of razor-sharp bayonets.

Two Germans reached Weer's bush and were about to plunge their bayonets into it when the parachutist did all that could be done—he stepped out and surrendered. Minutes later Weer's three comrades were collared.

In the meantime, miles away, Sergeant Robert Akers had bailed out of his C-47 at 2,500 feet, after the aircraft had been rocked repeatedly by German antiaircraft shells. Floating earthward, he had a curious fleeting thought: The white German tracers crisscrossing the sky all around him resulted in a brightness that would have allowed him to read a newspaper on his way to earth.

Akers and his stick, like many others that night, were dropping into a lethal hornets' nest.

Expecting a hand-to-hand fight for survival as soon as he touched down, Akers pulled out his trench knife and clutched it tightly in his fist. He knew there might not be time to assemble his Tommy gun or even reach for his .45 Colt in his hip holster. He was glad that he had taken a few minutes earlier in the afternoon to hone the weapon to razor sharpness. If he were going to die, Akers was determined to take as many Germans as possible with him on the business end of his trench knife.

Moments later Sergeant Akers crashed into the ground. He felt a sharp pain jab him in the head. Vegetation stubble had struck him in the left eye, which caused tears to flow profusely from both eyes. He got to his feet, cut the harness holding him to his parachute, hurriedly assembled his Tommy gun and stood crouched in the darkness ready for any eventuality.

At a time full vision was crucial, Sergeant Akers' eyes were flooded with copious tears. He was virtually blind.

Nearby in the darkness, enemy machine guns were raking the terrain in search of American paratroopers. Akers could not see the gun flashes, but bullets whipping past him sent the mortar noncom flopping onto the ground. As he lay there for several minutes, his vision began to return. He could see that much of the intense German automatic weapons fire was concentrated on a large bundle nearby which had been dropped separately. The large bundle, its colored parachute starkly visible in the brilliant moonlight, held a vitally needed mortar and shells as well as rations. It was a juicy target for German machine gunners who knew the concealed American invaders would try to recover it.

Sergeant Akers waited for nearly a half-hour to try to recover his mortar and shells from the equipment bundle, lying tantalizingly in front of him some 30 yards away. Yet each time he got to his haunches to dash to the bundle, the German machine gunners opened fire. Knowing that daylight was approaching, Akers decided he would have to abandon the mortar bundle and set out in search of comrades. He would gain nothing trying to fight a one-man war. The sergeant stole off silently into the night.

A short time later he located his company commander, Captain Casper E. "Pappy" Curtis. Soon Curtis had rounded up 16 troopers and another officer, making 18 in the combat party. The little band of parachutists located railroad tracks and began walking along them, a trek and direction that, hopefully, would take them to Avellino, the key German traffic center through which enemy reinforcements bound for the embattled Salerno beachhead had to pass.

After marching for nearly an hour, Captain Curtis and the

others could see ahead the shadowy outlines of a good-size town. Having had no significant landmarks with which to orient themselves, Curtis and his troopers did not know where they were. Approaching the dark town, the parachutists, with weapons at the ready, began moving down the main street in single file. It was an eerie sensation. House shutters were all tightly closed. There was a hushed quietude hovering over the old buildings. A black cat, its back arched in fear of the unknown invaders, scampered across the cobbled street and disappeared.

Captain Curtis and his men moved watchfully and stealthily along. Where are we? each wondered. Are we walking into a trap? each silently conjectured. Reaching a street intersection, deserted and forlorn in appearance, the moon's bright beams flashed onto a crudely painted sign along the front of a rickety building—Avellino!

The parachutists, tense and ready for anything, pressed onward. Soon they arrived at a large, shadow-filled square, like other parts of town deserted. Halfway across the square, Captain Curtis halted his men. A dim light, barely discernible from the outside, could be seen inside a store. Outside the building was parked a vehicle immediately identifiable to the veteran combat men—a German weapons carrier.

As the troopers took cover in the shadows, one man was sent forward to investigate. He reported back to Curtis minutes later, and whispered, "There're five or six Krauts inside the store, looting. The weapons carrier is loaded with radios, china, and other goods. They'll probably be coming out soon with some more stuff."

As the scout had predicted, the unknowing German looters did emerge minutes later, and were greeted by angry bursts of American Tommy gun and rifle fire. The startled Germans, arms loaded with valuable goods, tried to fire back, but it was over in seconds. The bodies of five *Wehrmacht* soldiers lay sprawled in the square—dead.

The small arms fire alerted the enemy garrison to the presence in town of an American force, and within minutes Captain Curtis, Sergeant Akers and the other troopers heard a frightening sound echoing through the night just to their front—the roar of enemy tank motors and other vehicles, no doubt loaded with *Wehrmacht* grenadiers, grinding to the scene of the sudden outburst of shooting.

"Okay, men," Captain Curtis hurriedly told his troopers. "We can't fight tanks with rifles and fists. Let's break up into small groups, get the hell out of town, and raise hell with the Krauts in any way we can."

Sergeant Akers promptly told five men to follow him, and George Watson, Willie Beal, Wilfred Dugan, Roy Carr and a trooper from another company stole out of the dark city and into the hills nearby. As the last parachutist cleared the main square of Avellino, German tanks clanked into the clearing, just missing their quarry. It had been a close call for the lightly-armed little band of paratroopers. As they scooted out of town and disappeared into the night, Sergeant Akers and his men could hear the strident shouts of German officers behind them, directing enemy soldiers in a house-to-house search for American parachutists.

Meanwhile, some 30 miles to the west of the drop zone just south of Avellino, Corporal Adolph Fuessel was floating to earth under his billowing parachute. Known as "Tex" to his comrades, Fuessel was a machine gunner and a member of the original 509th Parachute Infantry Battalion. This was his third combat jump.

Fuessel was worried for a cogent reason over and above the fact that he was being shot at by German gunners on the ground. Off to his left he could see Mount Vesuvius erupting and even could hear its roar. Despite the sketchy briefing back in Sicily, Fuessel knew that Vesuvius was near Naples, not Avellino.

The machine-gun corporal and his stick had bailed out over a ridge nearly 1,500 feet high, and to the descending Fuessel the moonlit side of the ridge looked like water. A frightening thought flashed through his mind: During the invasion of Sicily two months previously, some paratroopers had been dropped over the Mediterranean Sea and drowned when unable to extricate themselves from their parachute harnesses. Was he about to end his war by drowning, his body, perhaps, never to be recovered?

Fuessel started furiously tugging on his parachute risers to guide himself to the dark side of the ridge. He was successful in his effort, but landed on one side of the towering, jagged elevation and his stick came down on the other side. Fuessel shucked his parachute and gazed around. He had come down on terraced terrain planted with grapes growing on arbors.

Knowing he had to find his comrades who had bailed out with him, he scrambled his way to the top of the ridge, six or seven terraces up. Fuessel descended the far side of the ridge—the one he thought was water—and wandered around for two hours. He finally located one trooper, his ammunition carrier.

As the blackness of night began to dissolve into the gray of another Mediterranean autumn day, Corporal Fuessel and his fellow trooper came upon two Italian boys, both appearing to be about 18 years of age. The two native boys appeared terrified and to be hurrying away from something. Fuessel and his companion stopped the pair, but in a few minutes let them continue on their way. The troopers had no way of knowing that they would be repaid in a dramatic manner—by treachery.

Earlier that night a C-47 carrying 18 members of a 509th bazooka team flew down a valley that the pilot thought would lead to Avellino and the DZ. Crouched in the open door was Staff Sergeant William W. Sullivan, who was jumpmaster for the drop. Sullivan's status as jumpmaster was a unique one. It had been standard procedure in the parachute service for an officer to be jumpmaster on a combat drop. Only the day before the officer who was to serve as jumpmaster of Sullivan's C-47 was badly injured when an Italian grenade he was practicing with prematurely exploded. The noncom replaced him.

In Sullivan's plane, the red light was on. It would be only seconds now until the bailout. He sensed the throttling of the engines, the lifting of the tail. The plane was slowing. Sullivan tensed to leap. Then . . . suddenly the engines revved, speed increased, tail dropped. No green light. It was much like a foot race, a brutally nerve-wrenching foot race. Ready . . . set . . . but no go.

Sergeant Sullivan turned to face the crew chief who had worked his way back from the cockpit. ''The pilot didn't like what he saw down there,'' the airman explained in a shout above the roar of engines and rushing wind. ''He's going to take another pass at locating the DZ.''

Paratrooper Sullivan felt an inner admiration for this conscientious Air Corps pilot. Sullivan knew that the safest course for the airman's personal well being would have been to flash the green light, dump his stick of parachutists, and high-tail it for his home base.

Now the pilot pulled out from the several C-47s he was with and banked to the left over a darkened town—Avellino. None aboard was aware at the time of the town's identity. Retracing his course the pilot sped toward the rear to make another pass at locating the DZ south of Avellino. Standing in the door, Sergeant Sullivan viewed a unique sight. His plane was going in the opposite direction from other C-47s carrying his comrades. ''Something like two trains passing in the night,'' Sullivan mused to himself.

The parachute sergeant's C-47 was flying at the same level as the oncoming aircraft. Plane after plane drifted past. Men were spilling out of the doors and dropping into space, white chutes above them blossoming against the dark background of the mountains and illuminated by the beaming moon hanging high in the heavens.

Presently the men on Sullivan's plane felt the craft banking sharply and the pilot began another run for the drop zone. Minutes later the green light flashed on and with a shout of ''Let's go!'' Sergeant Sullivan plunged into space. His parachute popped open and showered him with a cloud of African insects and dust. As with other members of the 509th battalion, Sullivan for months had been using his parachute pack as a pillow in the deserts of North Africa and Sicily, knowing that new parachutes would be issued for any impending combat jump. But the ''crash'' nature of the current mission did not permit time to bring in new chutes; the troopers jumped with what they had.

Sullivan had a soft landing in a grape vineyard. All around him he could hear rifle and Schmeisser automatic weapons

fire. He was startled to hear echoing across the valley to his
front the sound of church bells furiously tolling. Obviously,
he surmised, the enemy had established an anti-paratrooper
warning system through the ringing of church bells throughout the region.

In a short period of time Sullivan rounded up three other
troopers and a bundle of bazookas that had been dropped
separately. Loaded down with bazookas and rockets, the three
Americans started marching down a valley which they believed would take them to Avellino, from which direction they
could hear the ominous sounds of an intense firefight in progress.

Meanwhile, Private Edward W. Pawloski, a 21-year-old
member of battalion headquarters company, was floating to
earth—directly on top of enemy-held Avellino. He could hear
the loud pealing of church bells from somewhere within the
maze of dark buildings just below. Knowing it might be su-
icidal to land directly in the heart of the town, Pawloski
tugged furiously on his risers and managed to sideslip to just
north of the town. He landed in a heap in a small garden
patch.

Pawloski listened and watched intently. He was alone. No
enemy. No comrades. Making no effort to conceal his parachute, Pawloski headed for a nearby woods, and there located
Private J.J. O'Brien, a member of a battalion rifle company.
Discussing their situation, Pawloski and O'Brien, concluded
that they had landed among enemy occupied positions and
that the wisest course was to remain in the forest until daybreak. At that time, they decided, they would attempt to locate other troopers and make for the DZ, nearly four miles
away.

At the time Pawloski was nearly dropping into the heart
of German-held Avellino, a C-47 with Lieutenant Lloyd G.
Wilson, a platoon leader, standing in the door was flying up
a deep gorge with bleak, craggy mountains on both sides.
The aircraft had been under heavy ground fire as it passed
over the Salerno beachhead minutes before, but shells were
no longer rocking the C-47 and its paratrooper cargo. In the

bright moonlight Wilson could see the road network, the crazily-shaped fields, the terraces on the mountain slopes and the deep, jagged ravines which laced the countryside.

Up ahead, Wilson was convinced, was the drop zone. He had seen an aerial photograph of the DZ that afternoon and the terrain features matched precisely. Although the pilot had not flashed on the red warning light, Wilson gave the order to "stand up and hook up" and returned to the door. The red light came on and the lieutenant crouched to jump, but the green light never glowed. The plane and two companion C-47s were over the DZ but Wilson could not give the order to jump on his own because the plane had not slowed down to allow the troopers to bail out.

Wilson looked on helplessly as the DZ slipped beneath the C-47. He unhooked his static line, rushed to the cockpit.

"Goddamn it," Wilson exploded, "you've overflown the DZ! You're going to have to circle for a second crack at it."

The pilot checked the time and replied, "We've still got a couple of minutes to fly until we reach the DZ."

There was no time to argue. Wilson rushed back and hooked up his static line just in time to see the green light explode. The lieutenant leaped through the door followed closely by other troopers in the stick. Seconds later the moonlit sky was dotted with 48 parachutes as men in the other two C-47s in the little flight bailed out on command of the pilot in Wilson's plane.

Floating earthward, Wilson intently peered at the landscape trying desperately to orient himself. He had seen a photo that afternoon of the DZ, but now nothing on the terrain looked familiar. Soon the ground was rushing up to meet him and Wilson saw that he and others were going to crash onto the steep slope of a craggy mountain saturated with sharp-pointed tree trunks poking ominously into the sky. This slope apparently had been heavily bombed at one time, and the trees had been shorn of their branches. Seconds later Wilson hit the ground with great impact, narrowly missing being impaled on a lance-like tree trunk.

Shucking his chute, the lieutenant quickly located Staff Sergeant George Fontanesi, his rifle platoon-sergeant, and together they rounded up other troopers on the crater-dotted mountain.

Crawling under a poncho and by the light of a tiny flashlight, Lieutenant Wilson and Sergeant Fontanesi scanned a map of the Avellino region but could not orient themselves. They were convinced they had landed outside of the locale covered by the map, Utilizing navigational aids learned in army classrooms, the pair concluded that they were some 10 miles east of the drop zone.

Several of Wilson's men had received crippling injuries in the drop onto the jagged, crater-covered terrain and would have to be left behind on the mountainside. A medic was designated to stay with the incapacitated men. A few parachutists, including one who had plunged into a deep, dark ravine and was located only when his shouts for help were heard, insisted that they could navigate and wanted to go with the able-bodied troopers to fight.

Farther down the mountain slope Wilson and his men could hear the ominous rumble of heavy traffic moving along a road—German convoys on the way to the Salerno beachhead. From their vantage point, the paratroopers could detect the tiny cat's-eye slits in the enemy vehicle headlights.

Lieutenant Wilson took his platoon sergeant, Fontanesi, to one side. "We're in a hell of a fix, George," he said. "We're 36 miles behind German lines, we've got only a handful of men, and there's only three or four hours of darkness for us to march to the DZ and hook up with the rest of the battalion."

Wilson knew that there was no time to lose if the bank of parachutists was going to reach the drop zone under the protective blanket of night. There was a long way to go over uncertain terrain, and the enemy, quite obviously, was around the region in sizable numbers.

The lieutenant told his men that "my intuition tells me that the road at the base of the slope the Krauts are using will lead us to Avellino." He collected his able-bodied troopers, bid goodbye to the injured men and medic left to await the arrival of Fifth Army, and began picking his way down the craggy mountainside. Behind him were Sergeant Fontanesi,

George Gately, William Herb, James Ray, Samuel Callahan and six other troopers.

Reaching the road at the base of the slope, the troopers stealthily edged into a clump of trees which gave them a closeup of the passing German traffic. Along with trucks filled with enemy infantrymen, there were numerous staff cars, motorcycles and mobile guns. Most were heading toward Avellino and eventually the beachhead.

It was a tempting target for an ambush. But there were only 12 paratroopers and a firefight in the darkness would detain the little group indefinitely. Their principal duty was to join the battalion on the drop zone 10 miles to the west.

Wilson and Fontanesi decided to head for Avellino cross-country on a course parallel to the heavily-traveled road. They would soon learn of the folly of that decision. The country-side was cut to pieces by deep gorges with perpendicular walls and interlaced with thickets that even squirrels found difficult to penetrate.

The moon had disappeared and the night was inky black. The troopers stumbled, fell, picked themselves up, fell again. Curses rang out and thuds were heard where the marching men plunged into ravines or fell heavily into thickets. The pace was snail-like, but the parachutists pushed onward.

Crossing a level field, a trooper stumbled into what seemed to be a small shelter tent, lost his balance and fell heavily onto two sleeping forms inside. The suddenly awakened and angry figures began cursing. *"Schweinehund!"* (son of a bitch!), one shouted at the unknown bumbling intruder who had not only knocked over his tent but had clumsily flopped onto him as he slept. There was a squirming tangle of bodies in the darkness as the American sought to disengage himself from the forms under the canvas.

Nearby other paratroopers stumbled into pitched puptents and crashed down onto sleeping occupants. Soon a chorus of curses—German curses—filled the air. The Americans had wandered into a bivouac of a *Wehrmacht* unit, one probably on its way to the front at Salerno. The large field was dotted with camouflaged shelter tents.

Soon dim figures scurried about and shouts rang out as

the enemy troops, abruptly awakened, tried to locate the source of the uproar in their midst. Masked by darkness and the confusion, the paratroopers hastily withdrew. Early fears that the Germans would quickly send a force after the American intruders vanished as the minutes ticked by. The troopers concluded that the enemy in the bivouac had mistaken the clumsy interlopers for some of the thousands of Italian civilians wandering aimlessly about the countryside seeking safety from bombs being rained down on the villages and towns.

It had been a close call for Lieutenant Wilson and his men. And the episode dramatized the sheer folly of marching cross-country in the darkness over such treacherous terrain. If the tiny group was to join the battalion on the drop zone before dawn, bold risks would have to be taken. The troopers would march toward Avellino on the same hard-surfaced road being used extensively by the *Wehrmacht*.

Forming into two columns, one to each side of the road, the men moved out in rapid-time cadence. Daybreak was approaching; there was much ground to be covered. When an enemy vehicle was heard, the troopers scrambled into roadside ditches until it had passed. Lieutenant Wilson had told his men, "If we come to anyone on foot, or a group marching, just keep right on walking as though we belong here. It's so damned dark they'll think we're Krauts." He added: "At least I hope they will."

A short time later the paratroopers approached a tiny, blacked-out village. Detouring around the cluster of houses would have squandered much time. With weapons at the ready, as the village might have been occupied by German troops, Wilson and his men stealthily reached the first houses. Immediately the Americans were pounced on by a sea of humanity—excited Italian civilians who had heard the roar of airplane motors and seen white parachutes floating to earth.

The villagers were wildly ecstatic over the sudden arrival of American soldiers who had, literally, dropped in on them unannounced. The Italians clapped, cheered, shouted, *"Viva Americano"* and thrust wine and food on the men with the baggy pants and the ankle-length jumpboots.

"For Chrissake," a trooper called to a comrade, "if the

Krauts didn't know we were around before, with all this racket they sure as hell will now."

Lieutenant Wilson turned to Sergeant Fontanesi, who spoke fluent Italian. He was born in northern Italy but had been an American since boyhood. Wilson said, "George, see if you can find out from these people where in the hell we are."

Fontanesi held an animated conversation with one of the villagers as Wilson stood to one side looking on. "What's he saying?" the lieutenant asked Fontanesi anxiously.

"He says we're about eight kilometers from Avellino," the platoon sergeant replied. "And here's some good news. He says the joint's jumping with Krauts all the way there."

The Italian civilian erupted once more in a torrent of words, and pointed excitedly up the road in the direction the troopers were marching. "What's he talking about now?" Lieutenant Wilson asked of his interpreter.

"He says a German infantry company had marched through the village on its way to Avellino and that it was only a few hundred yards in front of us," Fontanesi replied.

"Good God!" Wilson exclaimed. "I wonder how long we've been marching through the dark right on the tail of that Kraut infantry company?"

Despite the presence a short distance ahead of the enemy grenadier formation, Wilson waved his men onward and soon the shadowy outline of the village and the tumult within it disappeared into the darkness. Wilson, Fontanesi and the other troopers were beset with one nagging concern: If the German infantry company up ahead halted for a brief rest, the little band of Americans would stumble onto them without warning in the darkness.

As the troopers walked briskly through the night, they became aware that the black Mediterranean sky was beginning to dissolve into irregular patterns of light. Dawn was nearly at hand. Just as the sun peeked over the towering Apennines, Lieutenant Wilson took out his map and made an encouraging discovery: He and his men were right on the objective—the drop zone south of Avellino. But where was the rest of the 641-man battalion? There was not an American to be seen.

Wilson's early elation on reaching the DZ turned to intense alarm. He and his men were alone on the objective and in desperate straits. With daylight present and Germans all around, the little knot of paratroopers edged into a dry stream bed with weeds almost shoulder high to await developments.

The exhausted Americans tried to sleep. But sleep would not come. There was almost an incessant sound of enemy activity reaching their ears—the grinding of tank treads and the rumble of trucks on a nearby road, an occasional shout from a German officer or noncom directing his men in their search for American invaders from the sky. Each trooper nestled in the high weeds had to remain perfectly still as the tedious hours ticked by. The danger of discovery was always present.

At four o'clock in the afternoon the Americans, huddled motionless and silently for many hours, heard nearby voices. Peeking carefully out of their weed cover the troopers discovered the source of the sounds—two elderly Italian women were picking greens in the dry stream bed and moving directly toward the band of parachutists.

The native women, deeply involved in conversation as they methodically went about their work, reached the point where Lieutenant Wilson was crouched in the tall weeds. He could have reached out and touched them. Suddenly the two women spotted Wilson, instinctively threw hands to their mouths in surprise and fear, choked and gasped. The officer pointed to the American flag sewn onto the shoulder of his jump jacket sleeve and whispered, *"Americano! Americano!"*

Wide-eyed and ashen-faced over the sudden appearance in the weeds of a helmeted soldier in an unfamiliar uniform, the women remained motionless and stared at Wilson. They cast quick, furtive glances and saw the helmets of other strange figures crouching in the shoulder-high weeds.

Abruptly, one of the elderly women turned on her heel and ran up the bank toward a nearby road which the Germans had been patrolling. In her fright she was screaming at the top of her lungs. The other woman, unsure of a course of action, followed her friend.

Knowing the Germans would rush the dry stream bed, the troopers, one by one, infiltrated into a thicket some 50 yards away which overlooked the spot they had just suddenly departed. Watching intently, the Americans saw a large detachment of Germans, probably in company strength, approach the dry stream bed in a long skirmish line. When 40 yards from the recent paratrooper place of refuge, the enemy soldiers unleashed powerful burst of Schmeisser automatic weapons fire into the stream bed.

Under cover of the fusillade of small arms fire, a crew armed with a flame thrower edged close to the bank and sent long streams of fire hurtling into the tall weeds. A whistle blown by a German officer echoed over the bleak landscape and the grenadiers charged the spot the paratroopers had abandoned only a half-hour previously. There, instead of finding dead, wounded or cowering American paratroopers, the *Wehrmacht* soldiers looked down on weeds burned to a crisp by blasts from a flame thrower's torrid breath.

Night was rapidly approaching and under its protective mantle the troopers edged their way out of the thicket and instinctively headed up the mountain for a more secure place of refuge. They located a shallow cave, partly hidden by vegetation. Exhausted, the 12 troopers climbed inside and in minutes all were asleep. As they dozed off, the roar of many guns in the valley firing at high-flying Allied bombers penetrated their beings.

Elsewhere, Lieutenant Dan A. DeLeo, a platoon leader in a rifle company, and his stick dropped almost directly onto the bustling headquarters of a German panzer division. Alerted by the roar of C-47 motors, enemy machine gunners around the facility began raking DeLeo and other descending paratroopers almost from the moment the Americans had leaped into space.

Two of Deleo's men landed with their chutes caught on tall trees just inside the large walled enclosure that was the water-pumping station for Naples but now was serving as a panzer-division headquarters. As the two Americans dangled helplessly, panicky Germans riddled the pair with bursts from Schmeisser machine pistols,

Lieutenant DeLeo and a few of his men landed in a cluster and were raked by machine-gun fire from nearby woods as they sought to shuck their parachutes. Flopping to the ground, DeLeo and his comrades returned the fire, but within seconds four of the paratroopers were wounded.

Sergeant Fred Miller was struck by a fiendish dum-dum bullet which entered his buttocks and emerged from the top of his thigh. A gaping hole had been torn in his buttocks large enough for a fist to be inserted. The dum-dum bullet also had smashed his leg, and bloody slivers of bone were protruding through tortured flesh.

Dragging and half-carrying their wounded comrades while continuing to fire at the German machine gunners with rifles and Tommy guns, DeLeo and his handful of men withdrew from the fiery cauldron into which they had dropped. The parachutists reached the relative safety of nearby hills without enduring more casualties, but knew that enemy patrols would be searching for them soon.

As daylight broke over the Apennines, Lieutenant DeLeo had to make a crucial decision. With several wounded men on his hands he concluded his only course of action was to remain in the troopers' present place of refuge and venture out at night to create havoc in enemy ranks.

That night, DeLeo and a comrade were stalking silently through a wooded area when each suddenly froze in place. By the light of the moon, their alert and searching eyes had spotted a shadowy figure ahead. His coalbucket-shaped helmet told the Americans that this was a German sentry. He appeared to be alone and guarding a small bridge. The enemy soldier was casually leaning against a large tree and facing the opposite direction.

Pausing only briefly, DeLeo handed his rifle to his comrade. Motioning for the other trooper to remain in place, the lieutenant whipped out his trench knife and, clutching it tightly, began silently creeping up on the unwary sentry. When DeLeo was four yards from the German and ready to leap and plunge the sharp-pointed dagger into the enemy soldier's vitals, a nearby voice called out in German. Only then did DeLeo spot the shadowy silhouette of another man approaching the sentry.

His heart already pumping furiously, the young American felt a new tinge of apprehension. Having moved into position to lunge for the enemy sentry, DeLeo was in the open, bathed in moonlight. The blade of his trench knife glistened in the bright rays of the moon. He felt naked poised statue-like in a half-crouch, only a few feet from an armed German.

On hearing the voice calling out to him, close the enemy sentry turned halfway around and replied, *"Jawohl, Herr Hauptman."* (Yes, sir, captain.)

As a tense Dan DeLeo looked on, a German officer with glossy black knee-high boots and a peaked cap with a bill strode into view. The *Wehrmacht* officer had called to his sentry before reaching him unexpectedly. With American paratroopers marauding about the region, the newcomer was taking no chances that a panicky sentry would shoot first if startled and ask questions later.

In the new direction the guard had taken to face his approaching commander, the German was turned sideways to DeLeo, crouched motionless only 12 feet away. Fortunately for the American, shadows from overhead trees broke up the contours of the paratrooper's figure.

Not conversant in the German language but able to understand bits and pieces, the eavesdropping DeLeo concluded that the *Wehrmacht* captain had asked the sentry if there had been any indication of American paratroopers prowling about. The sentry replied, *"Nein!"* (No!)

In less than two minutes, a span of time that seemed hours to the exposed and vulnerable DeLeo, the sentry joined his commander and the two men walked off into the darkness.

As the lieutenant silently returned to his nearby waiting comrade, the anxious trooper inquired in a soft voice, "What happened?"

"Nothing," DeLeo replied dryly. "I had a front-row seat for a Kraut changing of the guard ceremony."

As a result of his forays around the countryside, Lieutenant DeLeo was able to orient his group's position by comparing landmarks to his map. He concluded that he and his stick had landed somewhere in the San Stefano del Sol Valley, southeast of Avellino.

Back at the base of DeLeo and his men on the side of a rugged, wooded mountain, the troopers became aware that a German motorcycle courier sped by on a dirt road at the foot of the elevation at nearly the same time each day. A reception was organized for the unsuspecting *Wehrmacht* messenger.

A telephone wire was tied to a tree on the far side and allowed to lay slack across the road. Troopers hid in shrubbery along the road with the loose wire in their hands. Minutes later they heard the puttering of a motorcycle engine around a bend in the road and the German courier, on time as usual, approached the ingenious trap that had been laid for him.

As the unwary enemy cyclist neared the wire lying over the road, the troopers pulled it taut. The wire caught the speeding German's body and jerked him off the two-wheeled vehicle, which rolled on down the road as though the rider were still aboard. As the *Wehrmacht* soldier lay dazed in the dust, DeLeo's men pounced on him with knives; a rifle shot would have alerted other Germans in the area.

The luckless enemy soldier's body was dragged deep into the woods where it would not be found by comrades who almost certainly would come looking for the mysteriously vanished courier. Should DeLeo and his troopers eventually be captured, the enemy would not look kindly on the Americans who had ambushed and buried the German courier.

9
A German Trap
Is Sprung

IN THE VICINITY south of Avellino in which Lieutenant Dan DeLeo and his stick had landed, Captain Carlos "Doc" Alden, the battalion surgeon, was floating to earth under a blossoming parachute. Alden was concerned. He could not detect another parachute. A thought flashed through his mind: "Good God, I'm making a one man assault on German-held Italy!"

As he came closer to the ground, Alden could make out the farmhouses, trees and roads in the area. Suddenly, looming up under him, was a sight that ran cold chills up his spine. Only some 100 feet below him was a well about five feet wide with a circular stone wall around its opening to keep unsuspecting individuals from falling in—and Alden was heading directly for it. Should he plunge into it, he would probably drown. Should one foot land on the stone wall and the other foot go into the well he would break his leg, or back, or be split open much like a chicken wishbone at a dinner party.

Captain Alden began tugging frantically on his front riser,

his back and side risers to alter the course of his fall. To no
avail. He plunged into the well, missing by a fraction striking
one foot on the guarding stone wall. At the last second, the
doctor's blossoming parachute caught on a large overhanging
tree and he was jerked to a halt after he had plunged into the
well water up to his waist. Burdened with his combat gear,
had Alden descended three more feet before his parachute
had caught in the tree, he would have drowned.

Taking stock of his predicament, the unruffled Alden listened for any sound that might indicate a German presence
outside the well. He heard nothing. Then mustering his
strength, he began pulling himself out of the well in hand
over hand fashion, using the parachute risers for that purpose.
Weighted down with wet combat gear, it was not an easy
task. But within a couple of minutes, Alden's exertion paid
off. He reached the top of the well and pulled himself out.
Once on solid ground, Alden shucked his parachute harness,
which had miraculously saved his life. He concluded that he
was alone. At least if there were no comrades around, there
were no enemy soldiers either.

About a mile from where Doc Alden was clawing his way
out of a well, Lieutenant Colonel Doyle Yardley, commander
of the 509th Parachute Infantry Battalion, walked up to a
shadowy figure in the center of a large field. It was Lieutenant
Fred Perry of the battalion's pathfinder platoon. Recognizing
Perry in the moonlight, Colonel Yardley was encouraged, as
he felt that most of his men had dropped on the DZ and would
be assembling soon. Told that Lieutenant Perry and his pathfinders were not on the designated drop zone but a mile south
of it, Yardley was hardly discouraged. "That's close enough,"
he mused.

With Perry was Lieutenant Laverne P. Wess, who had
bailed out of Yardley's plane and had landed on the improvised DZ. Wess was also encouraged that the Five-O-Niners
had landed in a neat pattern on the correct drop zone as
planned because on divesting himself of his parachute Wess
heard fierce firefights break out a short distance away. Paratroopers engaging the Germans, Wess thought.

Unknown to Colonel Yardley, his men had been scattered

from south of Avellino northward to Caserta, many miles away, and even at the moment he was anxiously looking for their arrival individual troopers, pairs and tiny bands prowled the moonlit, rugged terrain of central Italy, trying to gain their bearings and make their way to the crucial crossroads south of Avellino. Few of Yardley's men had any idea where they were.

Meanwhile, Captain "Doc" Alden was walking stealthily along a narrow dirt road, heading in what he believed to be the direction of the Avellino crossroads. Crickets were chirping merrily away. Tall trees swaying gently in the mild breeze gave off rustling sounds that increased Alden's vigilance. Suddenly, ahead in the shadows, Captain Alden spotted the outline of a man standing along side the road. Garand rifle at the ready, the surgeon moved closer and could detect the white shirt of a man—probably an Italian native.

Weapon still at the alert, Alden approached the man, greeted him with broken Italian and was startled to hear a reply in perfect English: "Hello, friend. Glad to see you."

The civilian knew Alden was an American as an American flag was sewn on the jacket shoulder of each paratrooper in the jump.

"Seen any Germans around here?" Alden inquired.

"Not close by," the native replied. "But I know where there are 250 German army trucks parked together, about two miles from here, toward Avellino."

Alden's excitement mounted. This was precisely the kind of target the parachute battalion was seeking. If 250 trucks could be destroyed at one fell swoop, the *Wehrmacht* would be deprived of a huge amount of rolling stock for carrying reinforcements and supplies to the embattled Salerno beachhead.

"A lot of my comrades are assembling around here," the surgeon told the man, who said his name was Roger. "When I reach them, will you take us to those German trucks?"

"I'll be glad to," Roger replied. "I can take you there without having to use the main road where we might run into Germans."

Alden and Roger, side by side, moved off into the night.

*Avellino drop zones
and actual landings*

Map by Steve Brodhage

In a half-hour the surgeon discovered the field where Colonel Yardley was apprehensively awaiting the arrival of his parachutists. The surgeon could see the shadowy outlines of a small number of paratroopers. Alden said to a trooper, "There're only 25 or 30 men here. Where're the rest of them, I wonder?"

"That's the only guys who landed around here, it looks like," was the response. "Colonel Yardley's out there in the center of them, and he's worried as hell. Said it looks like things have gone haywire."

Doc Alden went up to Colonel Yardley, the Texas school teacher who was on his first combat mission as battalion commander. "What're you planning on doing?" Alden asked.

"I'm going to wait here for a half-hour to see if any more troopers come in," Yardley replied. "Then we'll move out to the crossroads area south of Avellino and either occupy it or seize it from the Krauts."

Alden said nothing of what he was thinking. He knew seizing the crossroads was the mission of the battalion. But how could 25 or 30 lightly-armed paratroopers, a hodge-podge collection from several units, possibly capture a key junction the Germans could be counted on to tenaciously defend or seize back from the Americans?

"Colonel," Alden said, nodding his head toward the Italian man at his side. "This is Roger. I ran into him a short distance from here and he knows where the Krauts have 250 trucks parked. He's willing to lead us there without using the main road."

"Good!" responded Yardley. "We can go knock them out and move on to the crossroads from there. We'll wait and see if some more men come in."

It was time to march on the *Wehrmacht* truck park. Disappointment mixed with deep concern was etched into the battalion commander's face. Not a single additional trooper had appeared. Thirty-six hours previously General Mark Clark, commander of the hard-pressed Fifth Army on the beachhead, had requested that a regimental combat team be dropped on the key three-point crossroads south of Avellino. Now Colonel Yardley had 28 men to do the job.

"Okay, let's go," Yardley called out in a low voice. Turning to Roger, the Italian native, the Colonel spit out, "You sure as hell better know where you're taking us."

Nodding his head affirmatively, Roger moved out onto the narrow dirt road and walked off at a brisk pace, moving toward Avellino with the paratroopers in single file behind him.

After walking through the night for a mile and a half, Roger turned off the dirt road onto a narrow path. Yardley and Doc Alden, at the front of the column, thought it curious that Roger would veer off the dirt road where good time was being made to take a narrow, twisting path. But, the troopers mused to themselves, no doubt Roger was taking a short cut.

Continuing for about a half-mile, with the white-shirted Roger some 10 to 15 yards out in the lead, the column turned a curve in the path and troopers at the head of the column noticed with alarm that Roger had disappeared. Considering it prudent to ponder this latest development, Colonel Yardley halted the column.

A hurried discussion was held. Had Roger had second thoughts of the wisdom of guiding the paratroop force? Had he gone off in one direction and the troopers had kept moving without noticing the turnoff by the guide? Or had Roger been engaged in a deadly game—cold calculated treachery?

There was no time for conjecture. Yardley calculated the troopers were about a mile from where the 250 German trucks were parked. The colonel waved the column forward.

Suddenly the hushed stillness in the vicinity was shattered. From out in front, several machine guns and scores of rifles raked the Americans as they scrambled for cover in ditches and behind trees. Fascinating geometric patterns of white tracer bullets crisscrossed the sky over the prostrate forms of the American paratroopers who had walked blindly into a lethal ambush because they had trusted one man—Roger.

Flat on his face in a ditch, with bullets hissing just past his head and cutting off tree leaves which fluttered down over his prostrate form, Doc Alden made an instant vow to himself: "If I get out of this, I'll return some day and kill that son of a bitch Roger!"

Seconds later the vicinity was bathed in a brilliant iridescence. The German force had fired flares into the air, the better to pick off the trapped American parachutists. Peeking toward the front, as machine guns continued to fire into the column, troopers saw a new and frightening development: The shadowy silhouettes of several German tanks.

Sharp cracks echoed across the bleak landscape as high-velocity .88-millimeter guns mounted on the enemy tanks began firing pointblank into the huddled little cluster of Americans. Paratroopers who had not been hit were firing back at their tormentors as the angry sounds of the fierce firefight sped through surrounding valleys and up mountain sides.

Cries of "Medic! Medic!" rose above the din of battle as German bullets and shells found their marks. Now enemy flak-wagons, vehicles mounted with multiple, large-caliber machine guns, raked the trapped American parachutists. Each trooper knew he would have to crawl away from this holocaust or not a man would survive against the overpowering German force. As if on cue, the Americans began to crawl and creep out of the direct line of lethal fire.

Staff Sergeant Leon Maenhout, while firing toward the enemy positions even as he was crawling away, glanced to one side and saw a comrade, bathed in the light of German flares, blasting away at the Germans with a pistol in each hand. The trooper was in a low crouch, and Maenhout noted that he was wearing a distinctive headgear—a bright red beret. The sergeant knew instantaneously who the man firing two guns was—Captain Carlos Alden, the battalion's surgeon.

One American who remained behind was the battalion commander, Colonel Yardley. In the initial burst of firing when the troopers walked into the ambush, a German shell had exploded near Yardley and a jagged white-hot fragment had torn a large, raw chunk of flesh from his lower buttocks. In excruciating pain but alive, the battalion commander was taken prisoner when the German force moved forward to mop up the remainder of the little band of Americans.

It was Yardley who, less than 12 hours before back at Licata airfield in Sicily, had joked to his assembled troopers,

"Now men, when we get to Avellino tonight, don't get shot in the ass!"

Lieutenant Jack Pogue, the battalion communications chief, who had been officially "grounded" by Colonel Yardley the previous afternoon for not shaving for the arrival of General Matt Ridgway, was one of those caught in the German ambush. After firing at the enemy until his ammunition ran low and it became obvious the troopers would have to abandon their position, Pogue arduously crawled and creeped away. He reached an adjacent cornfield and took cover behind a large shock. Several other troopers had worked their way to the same field and Pogue gathered them together. The furious din of battle had ceased as the Germans were convinced the trap they had sprung had wiped out the band of American paratroopers.

Pointing toward the distance, Lieutenant Pogue whispered to the little knot of ambush survivors, "See that line of trees about 50 yards off to the side? We'll make a dash for that. It'll be good concealment until we can get the hell out of this area." The trees were in another direction from the site of the ambush.

Pogue crawled several yards forward to survey the woods one final time for any indication of enemy presence there. He saw none. He got to his feet and called out softly to the four others, "Okay, let's go!"

The five troopers had dashed only about 10 yards when machine guns and rifles positioned at the edge of the woods to which they were heading opened fire. The Americans flopped to the ground as bullets hissed and sang over their heads and thudded into the earth around them. Each man wiggled behind nearby corn shocks for protection against the murderous fire. They had escaped from one ambush only to stumble into another one.

Minutes later firing from the edge of the woods ceased. The Germans apparently believed that they had killed all of the parachutists. After lying motionless and silent for 20 minutes, Lieutenant Pogue called out in a whisper, "We can't stay here or we've had it. Let's head for that other clump of woods over there." He pointed to another line of trees. By now the moon had left the sky and Pogue felt that he and his men could safely reach the woods under the cover of darkness.

Getting to their feet, the little band of paratroopers had stealthily moved a short distance when the silence was again brutally shattered. The enemy force along the edge of the woods had detected movement and began pouring automatic weapons and rifle fire into Lieutenant Pogue and his comrades. One trooper, caught in the open by the first bursts, was carrying a Hawkins mine strapped to his waist. A bullet struck the mine, knocked the trooper to the ground, dazed but otherwise uninjured.

The trooper staggered to his feet and once more began moving out of the line of intense fire. One of the thousands of bullets spitting out of the enemy machine guns struck the detonators the parachutist was carrying in his pants pocket, causing an explosion which brutally ripped off a leg. He writhed in agony on the ground as blood from the stump of his leg poured out onto the ground. His comrades, firing back at the Germans, did not have the means to aid the seriously injured man.

Now other explosions rocked the ground around Lieutenant Pogue and the other troopers as the enemy force began tossing potato-masher grenades. Pogue was firing his carbine in a prone position when a grenade exploded near him and a jagged, white-hot steel fragment tore into his extended elbow, causing him to grimace from the extreme pain. Using only one arm, the lieutenant resumed firing at the machine guns along the edge of the woods.

Pogue and his able-bodied comrades waited for a break in the enemy fire, then began to run in a crouched position to the left, away from the latest ambush. As he ran, the lieutenant held his carbine in his good arm and squeezed off shots at the enemy force. He halted temporarily to take cover behind a shock of corn when a grenade hit right beside him. A blinding orange flash erupted together with an ear-shattering explosion. A hot jagged sliver of metal plunged into his left eyeball, and blood poured in torrents over the front of Pogue's jumpsuit. A split second later he lost consciousness.

Somewhere beyond measure of time, the young officer regained consciousness. He was in agony. His elbow was shattered, his body punctured with grenade fragments, and a steel
sliver was protruding from his left eyeball. He could not see
out of that eye and his vision was minimal in the other optic.
Daylight had arrived and Pogue realized he was lying flat on
the ground in his blood-soaked jumpsuit under a huge tree.

His mind still foggy, the American heard voices around
him—German voices. Slowly turning his head to one side, he
saw that he was next to an enemy machine-gun squad. The
Germans looked at Pogue with casual disinterest. Veterans of
countless battles, they had long grown accustomed to bloody
and mutilated human beings.

Slowly turning his head in the other direction, the American saw a long line of Germans armed with Schmeissers and
rifles. Pogue concluded that these were the same *Wehrmacht*
troops who had shot up his little band of troopers and tossed
the potato-mashers which had wounded him. These enemy
soldiers were positioned just inside the tree line, apparently
waiting in concealment to ambush other unsuspecting paratroopers who might wander into range of their bristling guns.

Pogue wondered how he got to his present position. He
decided that after he had lost consciousness and the firefight
was over, these Germans had dragged him into their positions
to search his pockets for valuable intelligence information.

In his hazy-minded condition, the wounded American had
a curious thought: Was the bottle of Four Roses he had carried into combat to be consumed with his comrades on reaching mainland Italy still in his pocket? Until that moment he
had been too occupied to have the whiskey cache cross his
mind. He felt all of his bulky pockets—no bottle of whiskey
was there. Weak as he was, Pogue became furious. He knew
that the Germans around him had consumed his Four Roses
while he was unconscious.

Suddenly, the quietude was shattered. The German machine gun next to Pogue and Schmeissers along the line of
enemy troops opened an ear-splitting fusillade. A few American paratroopers had wandered past and in seconds a shootout had erupted. Bullets—American bullets—hissed into the

German positions and within inches of the prostrate Pogue's head. His comrades were unaware that a fellow trooper was lying wounded among the Germans.

The firefight was short but intense. Knowing they were up against a much larger enemy force, the Five-O-Niners, unaware that they had almost killed one of their own, withdrew. Silence reigned once more. Due to loss of blood, pain and shock, Jack Pogue again lapsed into unconsciousness.

Earlier in the darkness, Captain Carlos Alden, the battalion surgeon, had crawled away from the German ambush into which the treacherous Italian Roger had led Lieutenant Colonel Doyle Yardley's small band of troopers. Alden had been firing at the enemy with his Garand rifle and two pistols, but knew it was time to escape from the murderous German machine gun bursts and panzer broadsides.

Flat on the ground, his rifle cradled across his arms, Alden began crawling toward the dim outline of a farmhouse some 100 yards to one side of his present position. As he pulled himself along on his elbows, the surgeon's arduous movement was punctuated with machine-gun bullets hissing over his head, hacking off tree branches and leaves which fluttered down on him. Flare after flare was sent aloft by the German force, keeping the sky over the prostrate Alden constantly illuminated. The enemy contingent wanted to make sure that not a single paratrooper escaped the ambush.

Alternately crawling and inching ahead in a low crouch, the captain reached the dark, quiet house. He paused outside. Was it occupied by Germans? That was a chance he would have to take—his alternative would be capture or death. Moving cautiously inside the dark structure, the surgeon became aware another person was inside. He could hear deep, labored breathing. Alden clutched his rifle and edged silently into a tiny room. There, by the muted glow of the moon's rays seeping through a small window he saw an American paratrooper lying motionless on the dirty wooden floor. Alden could detect the crimson blotches on the man's jumpsuit which told him the trooper was seriously wounded.

Alden went to the trooper's side and saw that he was a youth named Private Leroy L. Lauer. Hastily examining his comrade, the surgeon found that Lauer had been shot in the buttocks when caught in the crescendo of German fire. The wound was bleeding profusely. Five or six inches of his rectum was hanging out and he was in excruciating pain, but still conscious.

Recognizing the battalion surgeon stooping over him, Lauer mustered a weak smile and whispered softly, "Christ, it hurts, Doc."

"I know it does, Leroy," Alden replied soothingly. "But I'll give you a grain of morphine to relieve your pain. You'll be as good as new in no time and ready to romance the gals in Naples."

Alden knew that was a benevolent lie. Unless Lauer could be removed to a field hospital where surgery could be conducted, and soon, the young paratrooper was going to die—an agonizing death once the morphine wore off.

The surgeon bandaged the hideous wound as best he could in the dark and dirty farmhouse, then rounded up some straw which he put in a pile under the youth's head. What lamentable conditions in which to die, Alden thought briefly.

Off in the distance the din of gunfire had subsided. Alden had just completed bandaging Lauer when he heard the faint rustle of footsteps approaching the old farmhouse. Germans searching for scattered American survivors of the ambush? The surgeon picked up his rifle and edged silently into the front room. He put the weapon to his shoulder, prepared to shoot the first German who entered the door.

Just outside, Alden heard soft voices—American voices. These had to be other survivors of the ambush, the surgeon knew. Moments later, four paratroopers who, like Alden, were seeking protection from the death-dealing enemy fire, slipped silently into the farmhouse.

Speaking in hushed tones in a room adjoining the one in which Private Lauer was lying, Alden and the other troopers discussed their predicament. A large force of Germans, together with 10 or 12 tanks, was still nearby and would be looking for stray Americans. All agreed they would have to leave the farmhouse promptly, or undoubtedly face sure capture or death.

"Can we take Lauer with us?" a trooper asked of no one in particular. "We can take turns carrying him."

"I'm willing to try," another observed. "But he'll slow us down."

All in the room knew they would have to leave Leroy Lauer behind, probably to die a slow, lonely and agonizing death. "How about it, Doc," a trooper whispered to make sure Lauer in the next room did not hear him, "could Lauer endure it if we carry him along?"

Alden paused momentarily. His compassionate human instincts told him to say yes. But he was being asked for his professional medical opinion.

"Lauer will be dead in 20 minutes if we try to carry him along with us," Alden replied solemnly. "And where are we going to take him? He needs prompt surgery. Our only option is to leave him here and hope the Jerries find him and rush him to a field hospital for attention."

The surgeon's final words trailed off in a whisper. He had seen many soldiers die in battle and had been with scores of them when they perished. But now, although his expert medical opinion had been correct, he somehow felt that he was playing God as to whether youthful Leroy Lauer would live or die. Anguish tugged at his heartstrings.

Moments later the five able-bodied paratroopers in the dark old farmhouse heard the strident shouts of Germans not over 50 yards distant. An intensive search for American survivors of the ambush was underway. The troopers glanced at each other, nearly in tears. It was time to leave—and abandon their wounded comrade Leroy to the vicissitudes of Dame Fate.

"We'd better get the hell out of here or we're goners," a trooper whispered to the others. Despite their personal danger and urgent necessity to depart the farmhouse at once before the searching Germans got close enough to spot the five paratroopers, all went to the open door of Leroy Lauer's room. The youth was still in a mild euphoria from the morphine.

"We gotta take out now, Lauer," one said in a choked voice. "You'll be okay. The Krauts will find you here and take you to a hospital."

"Yeah, you're the lucky bastard, Lauer," added another

softly. "We've got to run all over these mountains and all you've got to do is lay there and wait for the Kraut medics."

"Your war is over, Leroy." "Good luck, Lauer." "You'll make it fine."

Leroy Lauer tried to smile. He uttered several unintelligible words, probably an effort to joke. His comrades would never see him again.

Moving quickly to the front door, the troopers took a quick look outside, then, one by one, slipped through the opening. As they disappeared into the shadows they could hear loud German voices back at the farmhouse.

Elsewhere, over a broad expanse of 200 square miles of rugged Italian landscape, from south of Avellino all the way to Caserta, 40 miles northwest of Salerno, a steady stream of field reports was being sent by *Wehrmacht* commanders to German Tenth Army headquarters at Sant Angelo di Lombardi. Large bands of American parachutists, these reports declared, were marauding about the region, ambushing German patrols and couriers, shooting up truck convoys before vanishing into the night, planting road mines, blowing up bridges and attacking isolated outposts.

These "large bands" of American paratroopers were mainly pairs and tiny groups who, on finding themselves alone and far from the battalion drop zone south of Avellino, went into business for themselves. They struck swiftly and with surprise, then melted into the night to strike again at some other locale. Bold and resourceful by nature and their fighting skills honed through intense training and heavy combat action, the paratroopers were in their element in this hit-and-run Indian warfare.

As the *Wehrmacht* command in Italy analyzed the field reports pouring in from a wide area, the conclusion was reached that at least a division of American parachutists had landed. General Heinrich von Vietinghoff, commander of Tenth Army, reacted swiftly to this serious threat to the rear of his forces around Salerno beachhead. Troops, tanks, flak wagons and armored cars, all badly needed in the death struggle with General Mark Clark's Fifth Army on the bridgehead, were diverted to anti-paratrooper duty.

Even before a cautious autumn sun peeked over the towering Apennines that morning of September 15, heavily armed German battle groups and patrols were scurrying about the countryside in a wide sweep around the mountain town of Avellino.

Meanwhile at dawn that day on the Salerno beachhead, General Fred Walker, commander of the hard-pressed U.S. 36th Infantry Division, had just finished reading field reports which had arrived during the night. As was his custom, he picked up a pen and scribbled an entry in his personal diary:

Last night an American parachute battalion was dropped 20 miles north of Salerno City, around Avellino. Since both ourselves and the British are on the defensive, I don't think the paratroopers will be in action very long. They will be strictly on their own.

10
Raiders
Deep Behind
Enemy Lines

A GRIM *FELDMARSCHALL* Albert Kesselring was earnestly conferring with his subordinate, General Heinrich von Vietinghoff, at the latter's Tenth Army headquarters in the Apennine village of Sant Angelo di Lombardi. It was shortly after dawn on September 15.

Kesselring, on his visit to the front, was explaining to Von Vietinghoff how he still hoped to destroy the Anglo-American beachhead through one more full-blooded assault. But the *Wehrmacht* commander in the Mediterranean inadvertently revealed an inner pessimism as to the success of the attack. He was concerned that his troops had lost their offensive spirit.

"Herr's LXXVI Panzer Korps is reverting to positional warfare," Kesselring complained. "This must not happen."

He added that if attacks on the level plain at the center of the Allied line were impractical due to heavy Allied naval gunfire, then perhaps General Traugott Herr's grenadiers could drive for the sea through the hilly region around the towns of Altavilla and Albanella along the southern sector.

At that moment, Colonel Reuben Tucker's U.S. 504th

Parachute Infantry Regiment, less its 3rd Battalion which was coming in by sea later that day, stood in the way of any German effort to split the Allied beachhead by attacking through Altavilla and Albanella.

While Kesselring and Von Vietinghoff were discussing assorted battle plans to drive Fifth Army into the sea, at his trailer office General Mark Clark was sifting through reports that had arrived overnight. One was a letter from General Bernard Montgomery who had landed virtually unopposed on the toe of Italy on September 3 with his British Eighth Army. Now, 12 days later and even though the German formations to his front had broken contact and were moving northward, Montgomery was slow in pushing up the boot.

Montgomery detailed his progress and said, "Perhaps you could push out a reconnaissance along the road from Agropoli to meet my people. It looks as if you may not be having too good a time and I do hope that all will go well with you. We are on our way to lend a hand and it will be a great day when we actually join hands."

Clark was furious at the tone of the letter, as were other officers, American and British, at Fifth Army headquarters. The implication was that Montgomery, on a white horse and waving a sword, was rushing to the rescue of the Anglo-American force on the beachhead.

General Clark's anger over the British general's patronizing letter was restricted to battle commanders on the beachhead. His reply to Montgomery was polite—yet pointed: "It will be a pleasure to see you again at an early date. Situation here well in hand."

Word of Montgomery's letter to Clark reached Colonel Jim Gavin and his staff at the regimental command post. Gavin's Five-O-Fives had been assigned the mission of defending the extreme southern sector between Colonel Rube Tucker's 504th Regiment near Albanella and the sea at Agropoli. It was through Gavin's regiment that the British Eighth Army would enter the bridgehead.

There was a bitter talk in the CP of the 505th Parachute Infantry. The target: General Bernard Montgomery. Most American officers there believed the British commander was making such slow progress northward because he was "pouting" over having been assigned a secondary role in the invasion of continental Europe. "Monty wants to be wanted," one officer observed.

Gavin had a concern other than Montgomery's lack of progress: What the parachute colonel and his staff considered an indifference at Fifth Army headquarters to the vulnerability of the 505th Regiment, which was strung out over a wide portion of the front.

"Two German panzer divisions, battle-tested and disgruntled over having to retreat, are heading right toward us," Colonel Gavin told his aides. "If we aren't careful, they might push right into the vitals of the bridgehead."

Gavin was not privy to a high level secret: Fifth Army commander Mark Clark had been reading German orders through the interception of enemy messages by *Ultra*, the ingenious British decoding machine, and knew that the two panzer divisions did not intend to smash into the southern sector defended by the 505th parachutists.

Colonel Gavin, whose mission was to "defend" his sector, ordered heavily-armed patrols to push out to the south to provide warning to his regiment of the approach of enemy panzers. The aggressive colonel had not received specific permission to dispatch these patrols, but rationalized that they were part of his "defensive" assignment.

Meanwhile that morning, Fifth Army headquarters in the brush near the shoreline was electrified. Two jeeploads of war correspondents assigned to Montgomery's Eighth Army drove into camp. The group, which included Eric Lloyd Williams of *Reuters*, Alan Moorehead of the London *Daily Express* and Evelyn Montague of the *Manchester Guardian*, had become "fed up" with Eighth Army's slow progress. They set off to drive through "enemy-held" territory toward the beachhead and the morning before, September 14, had left Montgomery's forward patrols behind.

The eight British correspondents presumed, rightly, that the withdrawing Germans would use inland roads. So they secured local guides to show them the back roads and, circumventing blown bridges, drove on into the beachhead at 10:50 A.M.

Some 60 miles behind the enterprising newsmen were forward patrols of Eighth Army.

As the British correspondents were going through a round of handshaking on Salerno beachhead, on a hill far behind German lines, Captain Ralph Whitmore, Lieutenant John Martin and a number of other members of the 509th Parachute Infantry Battalion were holed up waiting for darkness to move out toward the DZ south of Avellino. Suddenly the troopers heard loud explosions in the valley to their front. Unidentified comrades on a ridge a mile away had spotted a force of 60 Germans and a tank moving along a valley road and had dropped several rounds of .60-millimeter mortar shells into the enemy's midst.

Captain Whitmore and his men looked on avidly from their front-row balcony seats as the befuddled Germans, like a prehistoric beast stung by an antogonist it was unable to locate, milled about. Rapidly the enemy force recovered, formed a skirmish line and, preceded by the tank, began moving rapidly up the ridge from which the unseen American paratroopers had fired the mortar.

As the minutes ticked by, not a shot was heard from the opposite ridge. An hour after the mortar rounds had exploded, the German force returned back down the ridge to the road in the valley—empty handed. The parachutists on the ridge, in typical Indian warfare fashion, had struck against a much larger force, then hurriedly vanished to fight again at some other point.

Elsewhere far west of Avellino, Corporal Adolph Fuessel and his ammunition carrier for his machine-gun crew spent much of the day cutting telephone lines and looking for comrades. They were machine gunners without a machine-gun. Fuessel had become separated from his stick in the drop when he frantically slipped his chute to avoid what he thought was a large body of water, and came down on one side of a mountain while his comrades landed on the opposite side.

Discussing what move to make next, "Tex" Fuessel and his ammo carrier, whose nickname was "Moose," were holed up on a ridge, armed with a pistol each and one rifle between them. A German patrol spotted the pair and scrambled up the rugged ridge in a skirmish line. A wild firefight broke out and "Tex" and "Moose" captured two of the Germans and disarmed them. Now the question was: What to do with two enemy soldiers in the predicament in which the Americans found themselves?

There was little time for debate. Behind them the pair of troopers heard a shout in fluent English: "We've got you outnumbered. It's useless. Throw down your guns and give up or you're dead!"

Fuessel and the other trooper peeked around a large boulder. There, only some 30 yards away, was a line of some 15 Germans, all training Schmeisser automatic weapons and rifles at the American fugitives. To resist further would have been committing suicide for no good purpose. Fuessel and his comrade tossed out their pistols and Garand rifle and moved down the ridge with their hands in the air.

South of Avellino, Acting Sergeant Levi W. Carter of the battalion bazooka team was lying in a roadside ditch, trying to make his body as compressed and inconspicuous as possible. During the night he had been one of those caught in the ambush when the treacherous Italian named Roger had led Colonel Yardley's band into the withering fire of a large force of German infantry and armor. He had fought his way free from that ambush, and had spent most of the night exchanging gunfire with enemy patrols seeking paratroopers.

As he huddled in the ditch, several German infantry men came walking along the road, weapons at the ready in the event they would be confronted by marauding American parachutists. Carter did all that he could do as the enemy grenadiers approached—he lay perfectly still hoping they would not see him. His hopes were in vain. He heard shouts of *"kom heraus, schweinehund!"* (come out of there, you son of a bitch!) and peeked out to see several weapons leveled at him.

The Germans forced Sergeant Carter and another paratrooper, Albert Sabat, Colonel Yardley's radio operator, to earn their keep. The two Americans spent the rest of the day burying dead paratrooper comrades.

Sometime that morning Lieutenant Jack Pogue, the battalion communications chief who had been seriously wounded in two firefights during the night, regained consciousness. Blind in one eye and hardly able to see out of the other, his arm aching in extreme pain from grenade fragments, Pogue hazily looked around. He was in the back of a German army ambulance parked in front of an enemy aid station.

The young lieutenant recognized the two other wounded paratroopers in the ambulance—the battalion commander, Colonel Yardley, who had a gaping hole in his buttock, and the trooper who had been in the firefight along side Pogue and had had much of one leg blown off when enemy bullets ignited detonators he was carrying in his jump-suit pocket.

Pogue and Yardley were aware of the shifting of gears and the ambulance began moving down a narrow road. The youth with much of his leg blown off heard nothing—he had died.

The Americans were taken to a German field hospital where Yardley and Pogue were treated. Both were in excruciating pain, but Pogue was the most extremely injured and was relentlessly tortured by the steel fragments protruding from his eyeball. At the hospital, a semiconscious Pogue was vaguely aware of another captured comrade—whom he did not know—edging up to his cot and whispering, "Several other of our wounded guys were just taken out of there by the Krauts. Don't know where they went with them."

Soon two German officers and a few enlisted men appeared at Lieutenant Pogue's cot. "Get up!" one said in English. Pogue was too weak to move. Two of the Germans lifted him to his feet, and he was half-carried, half-dragged outside and placed in the back of an open command car. Three of the Germans got in with him and the driver put the vehicle in gear and moved off down the road.

In a heavily wooded area, the command car halted and Lieutenant Pogue was taken from the vehicle and a short distance into the woods. There an officer rasped at the nearly blind parachute lieutenant, "Kneel down!"

Pogue complied and in his woozy condition was aware that the German officer had pulled his Luger from a belt holster. A clicking sound was heard—the pistol being cocked.

The parachutist felt the muzzle pressing against the side of his head. "All right, start talking, you bastard, or I'm going to blow your goddamned head off!" the enemy officer roared in English.

Pogue said nothing. He concluded his life would end in seconds. "Talk, you bastard," the German shouted. "What's your unit? How many of you jumped last night? What's your mission? Are more paratroopers going to land tonight? Talk!"

One question after the other was hurled at the wounded American. "Go ahead and shoot me, you son of a bitch, and put me out of my misery!" Pogue called out as loudly as his weakened condition permitted. "I won't tell you a goddamned thing!"

Moments later the American felt the gun muzzle leave his head and heard the frustrated German officer mumble, "Stubborn pig!"

Pogue was half-helped, half-thrown back into the command car and returned to the field hospital. Despite his extreme pain the "stubborn pig" felt a deep sense of triumph surge through his aching body.

Shortly after dawn that day, Staff Sergeant Solomon Weber, the hulking battalion communications chief, was wandering around aimlessly. He had landed alone during the night and since then had been desperately searching for comrades. At last his efforts were rewarded: He came across another lone and wandering Five-O-Niner. The two troopers greeted each other enthusiastically, then began poring over Weber's rubberized map to orient themselves.

Sergeant Weber and his companion thought they were near Avellino and set out in search of the railroad tracks that would lead them there. They could not locate the tracks, which were actually many miles from their location. Walking watchfully along a mountain road, weapons ready for action on a moment's notice, the two troopers heard an alarming sound—a vehicle approaching. They leaped behind a large boulder along side the road and awaited developments. Each felt his heart begin to beat at a more rapid pace. Now, after months of arduous training, the two parachutists were about to come face-to-face with The Enemy.

Seconds later a German scout car rounded a curve. Two *Wehrmacht* soldiers were in it, a captain and the driver. The vehicle halted almost directly below the embankment on which the Americans were concealed and the driver dismounted and began walking up the road. Obviously nervous as he knew American paratroopers had dropped during the night, the officer in the car called out, *"Hans! Kommen sie hier!"* (Hans, come back here at once!)

Good soldier that he was, Hans promptly trotted back to the vehicle. Only some 15 yards away, Sergeant Weber poked his rifle around the huge boulder and a loud crack reverberated through the countryside. Hans fell over dead, a bullet in his head. The German captain instinctively reached for his Luger, but a shot from Weber's comrade killed him instantly.

Knowing that the pair of rifle shots would alert Germans in the area, Weber and the other trooper hurriedly leaped to their feet and began dashing through the woods. Only a half-hour previously they had been told by an elderly Italian man that there were many Germans in the area searching for troopers. The native had also pointed toward nearby mountains and indicated that a band of American parachutists had assembled there, so Weber and his comrade headed in that direction.

Jogging through the woods and up one incline and down the other, Sergeant Weber and his companion located the paratrooper band about one hour later. Major William Dudley, the battalion executive officer (second in command), was in charge of about 60 Five-O-Niners.

Soon a difference of opinion on the next course of action emerged. As the 60 troopers were at least 40 miles from the beachhead and had limited ammunition and rations, Major Dudley believed it prudent for the band to remain under cover until Fifth Army pushed forward and relieved them. Dudley expressed the opinion that to try to fight their way back through German troop concentrations for 40 miles, over jagged mountains, would merely result in the parachutists' being wiped out to a man.

Others, including Sergeant Weber, thought otherwise. As battalion communications noncom, Weber felt he should make every effort to inform Fifth Army headquarters of his band's location. He suggested laying out panels in the hope Air Corps pilots would spot the recognition signals and drop much needed food and ammunition. Major Dudley overruled Weber, stating it would be more likely that the Germans would spot the panels than would Allied pilots.

Elsewhere at dawn that day, Privates Edward Pawloski and J.J. O'Brien slipped cautiously out of their hiding place in the woods outside Avellino and set out for the drop zone. Shortly the pair ran onto three more troopers, Private Frank Stanovich, Sergeant Walter Cherry and a man from another company. A hurried conference was held. As Avellino lay directly in the path of their route to the DZ, the men decided to take a risk and move directly through the town in daylight.

Just as the five troopers were approaching the edge of Avellino from the north, weapons at the ready, the relative quietude was angrily shattered. A German machine gun, concealed just inside town, erupted with heavy bursts of fire. Sergeant Cherry was struck in the chest in the initial fusillade, collapsing in a bloody heap. O'Brien was killed by the same burst that had wounded Cherry.

Before Pawloski could hit the ground, he felt a heavy blow strike him on the side of the body—a curious, numbing blow. He instinctively glanced down to where he had been struck and was startled to see smoke pouring from his jacket pocket. With enemy bullets whipping past his head, Pawloski hurriedly opened the pocket and saw that a slug had struck a hand grenade. He reached inside the pocket and rapidly pulled out the smoking lethal object, and tossed it as far away as he could.

Flopping to the ground and unlimbering weapons, the three remaining able-bodied paratroopers began furiously firing back at their tormentors. Pawloski, while so doing, offered up a silent prayer to his protective saint for placing the grenade in the pocket. The grenade had saved Pawloski's life.

Knowing that other Germans in Avellino would be rushing to support the machine-gun crew, the trio of paratroopers, firing as they went, withdrew into the mountains.

The sudden appearance of Pawloski and his four com-

rades, coming from the north, created more panic among
enemy troops in Avellino. They were aware that there were
American parachutists to the south, but now paratroopers
were assaulting the town from the north. The enemy garrison
had no way of knowing that Pawloski and his comrades numbered only five—and two of these were dead or wounded
seriously.

Meanwhile, Sergeant William Sullivan and his two comrades, loaded down with the bazookas and rockets, had been
moving toward what they thought was Avellino and by mid-
morning had hooked up with 18 comrades. The group had
paused on a hillside to contemplate their next action. From
their vantage point, they could view up and down the valley
for long distances.

"We can't sit here on our butts all day," Sullivan told his
companions. "Let's go down into the valley and raise some
hell with the Krauts."

Moments later, Sergeant Sullivan learned that he did not
have to go searching for the enemy; the enemy was coming
to him. A roar of vehicle engines echoed through the valley
below the knot of paratroopers. They looked on in silence
from their front-row balcony seats as five German army trucks
rumbled into view and came to a halt directly in front of the
Americans.

Wehrmacht grenadiers promptly hopped down from the
vehicles, some 60 or 70 soldiers in all, and fanned out into
a skirmish line. Automatic weapons bristling in the sunlight,
the jack-booted, helmet-clad men in field gray uniforms
started across the field—headed directly to where Sullivan
and the others were apprehensively watching.

The sudden appearance of the enemy force caused a curious throught to flow through Sergeant Sullivan's mind. The
fanned-out Germans, heading directly for him and his fellow
parachutists, reminded Sullivan of a rabbit hunt in the corn-
fields of Iowa. This time, it dawned on him, he was the
"rabbit."

Knowing that they were far outnumbered and outgunned,
and that the Germans could send for reinforcements if a firefight broke out, Lieutenant Charles McKinney, the only of-

ficer in the group, after consultation with Sergeant Sullivan
and others, ordered the men to break up into pairs and tiny
groups, drift off into the hills and continue to ambush and
harass the enemy at every opportunity.

When the long line of *Wehrmacht* skirmishers reached the
elevation where they thought they had the band of American
paratroopers trapped, no one was there. The "rabbits" had
escaped the trap.

Elsewhere, Corporal Chris Christonsen found himself
alone after daylight. He was wandering about aimlessly, desperately seeking comrades. Warily moving down a road, he
came suddenly upon a lone German. Whipping up his Tommy
gun, Christonsen shouted, *"Hande hoch!"* (Hands up!) and
took the German prisoner. Now the question for the American was: What to do with his captive?

The pair marched along for several miles until Christonsen
decided it would be best to rid himself of the enemy soldier.
The American simply said to the German, "Okay, Fritz, get
the hell out of here. Take off!"

The young enemy soldier, expecting to be cut down by his
captor with every frenzied stride, was racing at full speed
toward Avellino as he disappeared over a hill.

Dawn of the fifteenth brought renewed hope to Lieutenant
Hugh G. Hogan and Private Donald B. Ellis of the 509th
mortar platoon. Leaping out of the same C-47, Hogan and
Ellis had contacted each other within minutes of landing during the night, and shortly afterward the pair hooked up with
two other troopers.

Ellis had nearly landed directly onto an .88-millimeter gun
and crew in the center of a large field, but dropping from
great heights had sideslipped his parachute to touch down a
hundred yards away behind some trees. Shucking his harness,
Ellis saw Lieutenant Hogan and said matter, of, factly,
"Lieutenant, what do we do now?"

Hogan replied, "Find the enemy and tangle with him."

"Well, that shouldn't be hard to do," the young mortarman observed. "They're all over the place, including an .88
gun crew just the other side of those trees."

As if to underscore Ellis' point, the Germans manning the

anti-aircraft weapon in the adjoining field opened up on several C-47s that had flown over.

Lieutenant Hogan, Ellis and the two other troopers moved away from the .88-millimeter gun crew and walked some distance to a little knoll where they awaited daylight.

Shortly after the arrival of dawn, one of the parachutists with Hogan serving as a lookout called out, "Some Krauts on a motorcycle and sidecar are coming down the road toward us!"

Lieutenant Hogan hurriedly issued instructions and the four paratroopers scrambled into positions along side the road to shoot the Germans on the motorcycle when it reached their position. So involved were the isolated Americans in setting up the ambush that they failed to notice a chilling sight: A company of German infantry was dug in facing Lieutenant Hogan and his three men only 50 yards away. The enemy troops, with the arrival of daylight, quietly watched as the four American paratroopers organized the trap for the oncoming motorcycle and sidecar.

Long before the three-wheeled enemy vehicle and its two occupants reached the site of the American ambush, the nearby grenadiers ceased observing and became active participants. They loosed a withering blast of automatic weapons and rifle fire into the little knot of paratroopers. The four Americans, startled by the heavy gunfire from the undetected infantry company, returned the fire as angry bullets hissed past the troopers' heads.

Above the din of the lopsided firefight, Hogan, Ellis and the others heard the curious fluttering sound of mortar shells descending and seconds later explosives rocked the area around them. The Germans were plastering the Americans with .60-millimeter mortars.

"We're dead if we stay here," one of the troopers called out to his comrades above the sharp blast of exploding mortar shells. "Let's make a run for it."

"I'll go first," Don Ellis shouted. He leaped to his feet and started dashing across a field. He had gone only 15 yards when he felt a sharp pain in one leg as though a white-hot poker had been thrust deep into his flesh. Ellis fell to the ground, his leg bleeding profusely where a bullet had plowed into it.

Seeing Ellis go down in a fusillade of bullets, Hogan and the other two troopers knew it would be suicide to follow in his tracks. So crouching low, they hurried off in the opposite direction. Their efforts were in vain. Later they ran into a heavily-armed German patrol and were taken prisoner.

Ellis lay in the field in agony from the bullet wound, but had the presence of mind to pretend to be dead. Any movement, even a slight one, on his part would have drawn a heavy volley of fire from the Germans less than 50 yards away. His ruse worked. The enemy grenadiers sent no more bullets in his direction.

His head reeling from shock and loss of blood, Ellis lapsed into unconsciousness. When the young bazookaman regained awareness, he was alone. It was daylight. And he was sitting on the ground with his back leaning against a tree. As he remained in that position for several minutes, he struggled to recall how he happened to get to this location and propped up against a tree trunk. He could recall nothing.

As Ellis' inner being slowly become more lucid, he spotted the leg of a man standing behind the low branches of a tree about 40 yards away. Then the other leg came into view. Next Ellis noticed that the two legs were standing beside a machine gun positioned on the ground with the barrel pointing directly at the parachutist.

Moments later two other soldiers in camouflaged smocks and round, bowl-like steel helmets came into Ellis' vision next to the machine gun. It was apparent that none of the machine-gun crew had seen the American propped up against the tree.

The bazookaman was delighted with his discovery. Obviously, he surmised, he was in the British sector and the soldiers in the camouflaged ponchos and round helmets were Red Devils, Britain's parachute troops. Struggling to his feet, Ellis began moving toward the soldiers at the gun, dragging his wounded leg along. "Boy, am I glad to see you!" he called out as he neared the machine-gun position.

A torrent of words he did not understand came from the

soldiers. But Ellis recognized the language—German. He
had mistakenly believed the German paratroopers to be Red
Devils. It was a logical though disastrous error. British
parachute troops in 1940 had adopted virtually identical helmet styles and camouflaged smocks from the Third Reich's
Fallschirmjaeger (parachute soldiers).

Ellis was disarmed and taken into captivity. It may have
been a curious blessing for the paratrooper as he was given
medical treatment for his severe leg wound. Had he remained
alone sitting under a tree, he probably would have bled to
death.

Elsewhere, teenage Private Charles H. Doyle and Private
Edward Peterson were approaching a village. They had been
sent by their company commander to locate a bundle of
.60-millimeter mortar ammunition which had been dropped
separately from a C-47. With weapons at the ready, Doyle
and Peterson began moving through the apparently deserted
hamlet when they heard the rumble of vehicles and the chilling sound of a tank's powerful motor and clanking treads.

Leaping for cover along side a building, the troopers
peeked around a corner of the structure and saw an enemy
panzer, its black-cross insignia of the *Wehrmacht* glistening
in the morning sun, rattling down the narrow street toward
them. Behind the tank were several trucks loaded with German infantrymen. As the last two trucks neared their place
of concealment, Doyle and Peterson sprang into the street,
whirled and began firing bursts from Tommy guns into the
vehicles packed with *Wehrmacht* soldiers.

Panicked by the sudden gunfire into their ranks, the Germans leaped down from the halted trucks, and in seconds
Peterson and Doyle were being raked by withering small arms
volleys. Doyle felt a sharp blow in the pit of his stomach and
was knocked to the ground. Fearful that he had received a
bullet in the abdomen, Doyle rapidly searched his body with
his hands but could find no blood. A bullet had passed through
his ammunition belt and struck his belt buckle, which mini-
mized the impact of the slug and kept it from ripping into his
body.

With the Germans now becoming organized and realizing

they were opposed by only two Americans, a revived Doyle and his comrade Peterson dashed between two buildings and vanished into nearby woods. Left behind were several dead Germans sprawled grotesquely in the street of the nameless hamlet.

As that morning of September 15 wore on, far to the south on the flaming Salerno beachhead Fifth Army commander Mark Clark became increasingly worried over the fate of the 509th Parachute Infantry Battalion, which, under his orders, had bailed out during the night 20 miles or more behind German lines. Not a single radio signal had been received on the bridgehead from the veteran paratroop outfit.

Continual efforts at Fifth Army headquarters to contact Lieutenant Colonel Yardley at the crossroads south of Avellino proved fruitless. No one had any way of knowing that Yardley had been seriously wounded and captured and that his battalion of parachutists had been dropped helter-skelter over 200 square miles of terrain.

Possibly the lofty mountains were responsible for failure to contact Colonel Yardley by radio, Clark's communications men told the general. Clark knew better. So did the communications officers. The angular general hoped for the best, but the worse kept entering his mind. As the minutes ticked by into hours, the army commander and most of his staff began arriving at what seemed a logical conclusion—the 509th Parachute Infantry Battalion had been destroyed.

Late that afternoon, a tired Mediterranean sun was dropping behind the western horizon for a few hours of rest when a tiny flotilla of LCIs edged toward shore along the curving Gulf of Salerno. The nine large landing craft were carrying components of the 82nd Airborne Division, principally the 325th Glider Infantry Regiment and the 3rd Battalion of Colonel Reuben Tucker's 504th Parachute Infantry which had dropped on the beachhead the night of September 13–14.

Colonel Harry Lewis, senior commander on board, saw a destroyer and corvette emerge from the gloom and begin to escort the nine LCIs to their anchorage. Minutes later the craft carrying the airborne men were weaving in and out of masses of gray-silhouetted ships anchored off the beaches.

On land, less than a mile away, an air attack was in progress
and the All Americans began to take cover as best they could.
For many of the men in the glider regiment, these were the
first shots they had ever heard fired in anger.

The destroyer and corvette halted and word was passed to
the LCIs: "A smaller boat will guide you to your anchorage." The minutes dragged by. No boat appeared. Curses
rang out from the LCIs. The airborne men were apprehensive, tired and seasick.

"Another goddamned hurry-up and wait!" a voice echoed
across the water.

Dusk arrived. Inland, where men were locked in lethal
conflict, the glidermen offshore could hear the rattle of automatic weapons and the crash of artillery. Many miles to the
north the 82nd Airborne men could see the muted orange
glow that told them Allied warships were pounding German
targets inland.

The minutes ticked by. The LCIs sat still in the water,
merged in the center of a massive throng of ships. Soon it
became pitch black and the 82nd glidermen could no longer
distinguish one craft from the other. How, Colonel Lewis
conjectured, could the guide boat that was to direct the LCIs
to their anchorage ever locate the nine craft loaded with glidermen in the inky blackness among the mass of ships?

A quick decision was reached by the senior airborne officer and the British naval commander in charge of the LCI
flotilla: They would seek out the task force command ship
for instructions—an almost impossible goal fraught with the
constant probability of colliding with other vessels in the
darkness. The location, or even the appearance, of the command ship was unknown.

The nine LCIs edged cautiously through the water, weaving in and out of the other vessels. Using a loudspeaker, the
British naval officer hailed each one with, "Where is the
command ship?" The reply was invariably "we don't
know"—or silence.

Frustrated in their efforts, Colonel Lewis and his British
colleague were about to abandon their hopeless task when
their LCI nearly collided with a large, bulky vessel the helms-

man had not seen in the darkness. It was the task force command ship they were seeking.

Again asking for instructions by bullhorn, the British commander received a reply that a small American ship would lead the LCIs to the landing beach for the glidermen, two miles to the north. Lewis' LCIs got behind the guide ship when it arrived, and the colonel hoped his other eight vessels were in line. It was too dark to tell.

A cold mist added to the general discomfort of the All Americans aboard the nine LCIs. Eventually, the landing craft reached the designated beach and two ramps were lowered from each vessel. In single file the glidermen and paratroopers moved down the ramps and onto the white sands of Salerno beachhead. Hurriedly forming up into platoons and companies, burdened with heavy combat gear, the airborne reinforcements, grunting and cursing, moved off in the night to assembly areas behind the front lines.

Later that morning, some 300 miles away in the vicinity of Licata, Sicily, two veteran paratroopers of the 509th Parachute Infantry Battalion unexpectedly appeared at the unit's rear headquarters. They were both members of the mortar platoon, Sergeant Cliff Faulkner and Private First Class Joseph E. Bauer. Each was something of a deserter-in-reverse—they had fled the safety of a rear area hospital to reach the scene of the fighting.

Faulkner and Bauer had been in a station hospital in Algeria a week previously for treatment of injured legs. There they heard that the 509th Parachute Infantry Battalion had flown from its base around Kairouan, Tunisia, in North Africa, to Sicily, for an impending jump into Italy. But at that time, the mission behind German lines at Salerno had not yet been visualized or ordered.

Wherever the Five-O-Niners were going to fight, Faulkner and Bauer wanted to go along. But authorities at the station hospital refused to discharge the pair of troopers. So, locating their clothes, the two paratroopers slipped out of the hospital and caught a ride in a rickety old 40 & 8 boxcar. (A crudely lettered sign on this type of rolling stock read, ''40 Men or 8 Horses.'')

After eating and breathing dust for several hundred miles across the North African desert, with the huffing and wheezing ancient locomotive halting countless times, Faulkner and Bauer arrived at Kairouan. There they were put to work washing dishes in a replacement depot. A few hours of ''women's work'' was sufficient for the two combat-tested fighting men, so for the second time in a week they ''deserted'' a rear area facility to rejoin their parachute battalion.

Bauer and Faulkner made their way to a small airport near Kairouan where they accosted a youthful Air Corps pilot who was about to depart for Licata, Sicily, in a C-47, carrying supplies.

''How about a ride to Sicily?'' Bauer asked the pilot.

''Okay, by me,'' the young man with the jaunty cap replied, ''but you've got to earn your way by helping to load those boxes into the C-47.''

Faulkner and Bauer pitched in to shoulder some of the load, and in a short time the troopers were airborne and headed for Licata. There they were disappointed. An officer who had remained at the rear headquarters of the 509th told them that the battalion had jumped behind German lines at Salerno two nights previously—and that not a word had been heard from the parachutists since.

The two paratroopers were crushed. Like many others, they feared their comrades had been wiped out.

On the Salerno beachhead the morning of the sixteenth—D-Day +7—Colonel James Gavin, leader of the 505th Parachute Regiment, which was in the front lines along the southern sector of the curving Allied positions, was conferring with ''Mike'' Dawley, commanding general of the U.S. VI Corps, at Dawley's headquarters. The corps commander was deeply apprehensive that the Germans were building up strength on towering Monte Soprano, almost in the center of his corps sector. Well he might have been concerned—Monte Soprano would furnish *Wehrmacht* observers with an unobstructed view of the entire length of the VI Corps front and furnish an assembly area for launching attacks against American lines.

"I'll look into the situation and report back," Gavin responded.

Probing rugged, altitudinous Monte Soprano, which lay out in front of American lines, normally would have been a job for a combat patrol. Due to General Dawley's considerable concern over the dominating geographical feature, Colonel Gavin decided to take over the task himself.

Taking one trooper armed with a Tommy gun, Gavin traveled in a jeep to the eastern base of Soprano. Dismounting, the colonel located a narrow trail used by natives for decades to ascend the peak. As he and the other parachutist were preparing to start up the side of the mountain, two Italian women with a pile of blankets on top of their heads were preparing to begin the long, arduous climb. Gavin learned that a few enterprising paratroopers had paid the sturdy farm women to carry the blankets to the top of Monte Soprano. The women were in good humor and talking rapidly to each other.

Practicing his limited Italian vocabulary (in fact, they were the only native words he knew) Gavin inquired, *"Dove gli Tedeschi?"* (Where are the Germans?)

The two sturdy women giggled, shrugged their shoulders emphatically to indicate they did not know the answer. With that, the Italian pair started up Monte Soprano with their brown blankets.

Hard on their heels, Gavin and the other trooper began moving up the steep path, which zig-zagged every 10 yards. In minutes the two keenly-conditioned parachutists were perspiring profusely. Twice on the arduous climb to the top they had to rest for a few minutes before resuming their upward trek.

Reaching the top of the mountain, Gavin and the other man, huffing and puffing, came upon the two Italian women who had carried the heavy load of blankets to the peak. The women had deposited their cargo and were starting back down. They laughed boisterously and good-naturedly at the two paratroopers' ineptness at mountain climbing.

As the two women began expertly picking their way down the narrow mountain path, Gavin and his aide noted their

muscular, sun-browned legs, developed in a lifetime of scurrying up and down the rugged peaks along the Gulf of Salerno.

The parachute colonel looked around before moving on
and saw that the mountain was flat on top, a plateau several
miles square. Glad to be back on reasonably level ground,
Gavin and the trooper walked onward, and it was several
hours before they reached the other side of Monte Soprano.
Along the way they had seen numerous indications of a recent
German presence in considerable numbers, but not a single
enemy soldier had been sighted.

Gavin and his aide descended the far side of the mountain
and eventually returned to VI Corps headquarters. "General," Gavin addressed the corps commander, "I've just returned from personally reconnoitering Monte Soprano. We
went up one side and down the far side. There was evidence
the Germans had been there recently, but we did not see
anyone there now."

The young colonel did not tell General Dawley that the
"we" he spoke about consisted of himself and one trooper.

Dawley was greatly relieved to have this one heavy worry
removed from his back. Now he could devote his attention to
a wealth of other battlefield concerns.

While Colonel Gavin was personally probing Monte Soprano, one of the numerous patrols he had sent out from his
505th Regiment was nearing a village 15 miles south of Agropoli. Gavin and his battalion commanders had been concerned that the two German panzer divisions withdrawing
northward in front of the British Eighth Army would smash
into his regimental sector. His patrols were to provide advance warning of the arrival of enemy armor.

It was 2 P.M. when the paratrooper patrols spotted activity
in the village—soldiers and armored cars. Moving forward
cautiously, Gavin's men saw that the troops were British—an
advance patrol of General Montgomery's army which had
been moving slowly up the boot of Italy from the toe for
nearly two weeks. Officially, Mark Clark's U.S. Fifth Army
on Salerno beachhead and Bernard Montgomery's Eighth

Army were linked up. Actually, the main body of Eighth Army was still far to the south.

Early that morning of the sixteenth, two American war correspondents who had arrived on the beachhead by boat a few hours before with the 325th Glider Infantry Regiment and the 3rd Battalion of the 504th Parachute Infantry Regiment were jeeping along a dusty road near the shoreline behind the U.S. 36th and 45th Infantry Divisions. In the vehicle were Richard Tragaskis and Cy Korman. Less than 400 yards from the beach the pair of newsmen came upon a sight that startled them: Two blackened, knocked-out German tanks.

"Good God!" Tregaskis blurted out. "That's how close the Germans came to driving our forces out of Italy!"

11
Hide-and-Seek
with the Enemy

As THE GERMANS continued to launch fierce attacks at many points along the flaming Salerno beachhead, at dawn on the sixteenth, deep behind enemy lines, Lieutenant Lloyd Wilson, Platoon Sergeant George Fontanesi and several comrades of the 509th Parachute Infantry Battalion emerged from their shallow cave on the side of a mountain south of Avellino.

From their vantage point, the troopers could look down onto a main highway over which German convoys were traveling. Most were headed for the Salerno bridgehead.

Down in the valley the parachutists spotted a crew of Germans mining a bridge—a precautionary action in case the Allies would succeed in turning the tables at the bitterly contested beachhead and drive north for Rome. Waiting until the enemy pioneers (engineers) had completed their task and departed, Sergeant Fontanesi and two troopers slipped down the mountainside to the bridge, hurriedly ripped out the charges and threw them into the water, then scrambled back up the side of the elevation.

Using the mountain refuge as a base, the troopers ventured forth that night and marauded about the countryside, planting road mines and engaging in numerous firefights with enemy patrols before retiring to the cave as dawn began to break. As a result of the firefights, the little band of Five-O-Niners was nearly out of ammunition.

Early on the morning of September 17, Lieutenant Wilson, Sergeant Fontanesi and the others were getting edgy—and hungry. They had run out of rations. In the valley to their front, the paratroopers spotted an Italian farmer working in a field, and Fontanesi slipped down to talk with the native. Unsure whether the man could be trusted, but desperate for food, the parachute sergeant asked if the farmer could supply his group with something to eat.

"My wife and I live in that little town over there," the Italian replied, pointed into the distance. "But I don't know if we can get food out here to you or not."

"Well, bring me some civilian clothes and I'll help you get the food here," Fontanesi stated.

Early the following morning, as promised, the farmer returned carrying some bread and moldy bacon, which the starved paratroopers devoured. The Italian also brought along some aging civilian clothes, which Fontanesi tried on. Despite the seriousness of their predicament, the sergeant's comrades guffawed at Fontanesi in the bedraggled garments. The pants were four or five inches too short.

"Your goddamned jump boots stick out like a sore thumb!" a trooper called out.

Fontanesi told his companions that he would go into town dressed in the native garb to seek food. "Like hell you will," Lieutenant Wilson objected adamantly. "If the Krauts catch you in civilian clothes they'll shoot you on the spot."

Wilson added: "And with those boots sticking out like two beacons, the Krauts can hardly miss spotting you!"

An argument erupted. Hunger won out. Fontanesi was given permission to try his luck at obtaining food for the little knot of paratroopers.

The young sergeant of Italian descent wore his regulation dogtags and carried no weapon. If captured, a likely possibility, he would plead that he was an escaped prisoner and not an armed soldier in disguise.

Together with his new-found Italian friend, Fontanesi began the trek into the nearby village. Hardly had the pair reached the valley floor and prepared to cross over a heavily traveled road than a German truck convoy packed with soldiers and accompanied by two tanks approached. They were searching for American paratroopers. As the *Wehrmacht* vehicles rolled past, the Germans waved at the two "Italians" standing along side the road. Fontanesi, his heart thumping furiously and his thoughts directed toward his exposed American paratrooper jump boots, smiled broadly and cheerfully waved back. "Good luck!" he called out to the Germans in fluent Italian.

Fontanesi and his native companion walked on into town and reached a square in which there was a water fountain. The American had not had a drink of water since the previous day, and he began gulping the liquid from the fountain. He heard a roaring sound behind him and, as casually as possible, turned to see what it was. Chills charged up his spinal column—it was a motorcycle and sidecar carrying two German soldiers.

The cycle screeched to a halt near the fountain and the two enemy soldiers walked up along side Fontanesi. "This is it!" the American thought. "How can they miss seeing my jump boots?" He was aware his knees were shaking and his hands quivering slightly. The two Germans and Fontanesi exchanged friendly greetings and talked for several minutes, side by side. Then the enemy soldiers, their jackboots clattering on the cobble-stoned street, went back to their motorcycle and sped away.

Fontanesi and his Italian friend proceeded to the native's modest house where the man's wife loaded the American down with cheese and bread. Feigning a nonchalance he did not feel inside, Fontanesi began walking through town, passing numerous enemy soldiers and patrols, and returned to his comrades on the steep hill outside the town.

On reaching the others, the young Italian-speaking sergeant was accorded a hero's welcome. "We sure as hell never thought we'd see you again, George!" one called out.

Despite the harrowing adventure of walking into a German-infested town in civilian clothes, Fontanesi had lost none of his sense of humor. "I don't know if you guys are happy to see I made it back or because I've got a lot of food with me," he observed.

"A little of both, George," came an honest reply.

For the next six days the wife of the paratroopers' Italian benefactor brought a large pot of food, consisting mainly of thick soup. She toted the heavy container on her head, and Sergeant Fontanesi, dressed in his Italian civilian clothes, went into the valley to help her carry the burden.

Each time Fontanesi ventured forth in daylight to meet the woman halfway to town, he had to cross the busy road. The American always waved and smiled at the enemy soldiers and tank drivers who passed close enough to the "Italian civilian" for him to reach out and touch them. Occasionally he shook hands with a friendly German.

Meanwhile, Sergeant Fontanesi had become something of a one-man intelligence agency. Wearing his tattered civilian clothes, with the trousers five inches too short and his jump boots prominently in view, Fontanesi ventured out each day to prowl the region for some sign of the "missing" 509th Parachute Infantry Battalion that was to have assembled nearby to attack the key crossroads south of Avellino.

Fontanesi never located another paratrooper, but in his daily scouring of the vicinity and numerous talks with Italian civilians, and on occasion *Wehrmacht* soldiers, the platoon sergeant was able to provide Lieutenant Wilson with up-to-the-minute information on what the Germans were doing in the area. Mainly, they were searching for American parachutists.

Almost daily a low-flying German reconnaissance plane zipped in over the shallow cave where the Americans had taken refuge, but always the aircraft's approach was heard in time for the troopers to conceal themselves. Several times German patrols were spotted by the paratroopers coming from the bottom of the mountain up toward the Americans. Lieutenant Wilson and his men, deployed with weapons at the ready, watched the enemy patrols climb upward.

On reaching terraced vineyards halfway to the top, the German patrols found the climb more exhausting as the incline became much steeper and the underbrush much thicker. Each time the enemy detachments would halt, sit on the ground, smoke cigarettes, and then head back down the mountain instead of going on to the top.

"It's good to see that the Kraut army goofs off on occasion just like the American army," a watching paratrooper mused.

One day about noon an American B-25 bomber was brought down by German ack-ack in the valley and crashed on the side of the mountain a short distance from where the paratroopers were based. A few parachutes opened as crew members bailed out and floated to earth.

A short time later enemy infantrymen were swarming all over the mountain where Lieutenant Wilson and his men were holed up. The enemy soldiers were not seeking the paratroopers but rather were trying to capture the B-25 crew members and to grab souvenirs from the downed American medium bomber. Each German was trying to reach the crashed aircraft first before the choice souvenirs were gone, so they paid little attention to anything else they might have seen on the mountain as they rushed by. A piece of American bomber would make an immense impression on a girl friend or wife when mailed back to the Fatherland.

At the time, Lieutenant Wilson in his jump suit and Platoon Sergeant Fontanesi in his Italian clothes were in a little grass-roofed shack near the cave hideout poring over maps of the region and plotting the next move to harass the *Wehrmacht*. The two troopers, glancing out a small window when a movement attracted their eyes, saw a German soldier in full combat gear and carrying a Schmeisser automatic pistol walking directly toward the shack. The man apparently was alone and more inquisitive than his comrades swarming over the mountain in search of souvenirs from an American bomber.

"Let him come on into the shack and we can take care of

him silently with our knives," Lieutenant Wilson whispered to Sergeant Fontanesi.

"No, I've got a better idea," Fontanesi replied softly. "If we knife him, his comrades sooner or later are going to come looking for him."

The parachute sergeant shoved the lieutenant to the wall next to the door and put his finger to his lips to indicate silence. Then Fontanesi opened the door and, with Wilson anxiously peering through a crack, stood casually in the opening. He smiled and greeted the German warmly.

Standing just outside, the enemy grenadier asked in Italian, "What's inside that shack?"

"Oh, nothing much," Fontanesi replied nonchalantly in his native tongue. "Just some tools." He felt the German was staring at his jump boots below his civies.

The German shrugged his shoulders, politely excused himself, and trotted off across the side of the bleak mountain to catch up with his comrades before all the best souvenirs on the crashed American bomber had been picked over.

Meanwhile, Captain Ralph Whitmore, Lieutenant John Martin and four other Five-O-Niners who had dropped many miles to the west of the DZ south of Avellino, were marching through the night toward the battalion's objective. Martin was at the head of the file as it reached a railroad track. The troopers started marching along the track which they thought would take them to Avellino, and a few minutes later Lieutenant Martin heard an ominous sound in the darkness to his front—clump, clump, clump, in a rhythmic pattern. The sound echoed in the night and became louder.

Whoever it was walking along the tracks in the darkness was stepping from tie to tie. The paratroopers leaped for cover on each side of the tracks, and Martin scrambled up a low embankment. Seconds later the lieutenant could discern the dim outline of a figure moving toward him. Then he could make out the distinctive coal-bucket-shape of a German helmet.

As the enemy soldier reached a point directly opposite him, Martin leaped to his feet and aimed his Tommy gun at the intruder. But the trooper was unable to get the safety catch off, lost his footing, and with a loud racket slid down the embankment and came to a halt directly at the startled German's feet.

Aware that he was being accosted by an American soldier, the German tried desperately to remove his rifle, which was slung over a shoulder by the strap. But in his excitement and fear, the enemy grenadier fumbled repeatedly to bring his weapon to bear but was unable to do so.

By now the other Americans had leaped from their concealment and the frightened German threw up his hands in surrender. "Returning from a shack job," was the consensus of the troopers.

"What'll we do with the bastard?" someone called out.

"We can't let him go or he'll spill the beans," said another. "His comrades will be after us with a large force in minutes."

"Knife him!" a voice called out.

"No," replied Captain Whitmore, "There'll be none of that. Get his equipment off him and turn him loose."

After some grumbling, the troopers complied and in seconds the German had disappeared at full speed into the darkness.

In the suddenly vanished German's canteen the Americans discovered hot chocolate—still warm. They eagerly split up the liquid contents and drank it.

Trekking over the broken and rugged terrain at night and holing up during most of the day, Whitmore, Martin and the others ran into an Italian native during daylight hours. Martin did not speak Italian but he tried to converse with the man in broken Spanish. "Do you know where there are other American paratroopers, and can you take us to them?" the lieutenant asked.

The Italian broke out in a grin. "*Si, si,*" he replied and motioned for the parachutists to follow him and he would take them to their comrades. The six Americans fell in line, relieved to have located a guide to link them with other paratroopers. They were unaware that the native did not know one nation's uniform from the other and thought his charges were lost Germans seeking fellow soldiers.

With Lieutenant Martin walking right behind the guide, the column went up and down several steep hillsides and into a thick woods. Martin could see that a clearing was looming just to the front. As the guide was about to emerge from the tree line out into the open, the parachute lieutenant reached out and yanked the Italian back into the woods.

What Martin had seen at the last moment was a German supply dump in the clearing, only 100 feet from the edge of the forest, with about 200 enemy soldiers milling about while carrying out their duties. A few more steps out of the concealment of the woods and the Americans would have been in plain view of the enemy troops.

Whitmore, Martin and the four others whirled around and plunged back deeper into the forest. Left behind was a perplexed Italian guide to ponder over the curious antics of the six ''Germans'' he was leading to their comrades at the supply dump.

Elsewhere that night, far to the west of the DZ outside Avellino, many of the 60 paratroopers under Major William Dudley were getting restless. They wanted action. Sergeant Solomon Weber, the 509th Battalion's communications noncom, thought it important that Fifth Army headquarters on the beachhead knew of his group's location, so that it could parachute in critically needed ammunition and supplies.

That night Weber, Private Theodore J. Fina and three other troopers slipped over into an adjoining valley and built large signal fires, hoping the flames would be spotted by American or British pilots. This procedure continued for several succeeding nights—all in vain.

Despite the failure of the innovative fiery communications procedure, troopers with Major Dudley were not discouraged. Even though they were 40 miles behind enemy lines and with limited ammunition, rations and supplies, the parachutists were eager to strike at the enemy with the means at their disposal.

While foraging about the countryside for food in recent days, the troopers had spotted a bridge about a mile away over which *Wehrmacht* convoys were rolling toward the Sa-

lerno bridgehead with troops and supplies. Twenty of the Five-
O-Nines decided to blow up the bridge.

Captain Edmund J. Tomasik, the battalion supply officer,
Lieutenant Justin T. McCarthy, a rifle platoon leader, Ser-
geant Weber and 17 other troopers loaded themselves down
with all available explosives and stole off into the night.
Reaching the bridge site, a small group of riflemen under
Lieutenant William Sherman scrambled up onto a knoll over-
looking the span. Sherman's orders to his men were simple:
"Shoot any damned Kraut that tries to cross that bridge!"

Sergeant Weber, a communications chief without the
means to communicate, took another three or four riflemen
under the bridge. His intentions were the same as those of
Lieutenant Sherman: Shoot anyone who tried to cross the
span.

Lieutenant McCarthy was overseeing the demolitions men
setting the charges under the bridge supports. The men knew
their business. Within a short period of time the explosives
had been planted.

Just as the job of placing the charges had been completed
and the demolitions men were scrambling up onto the em-
bankments around the bridge, the steady rumble of approaching truck motors was heard from the north. Minutes later a
German army truck, its narrow-slitted cat's eyes lights tiny
white dots in the night, rounded a bend and headed for the
bridge. Several other trucks followed, all loaded with *Wehrmacht* infantry.

As the first unsuspecting driver wheeled his bulky truck
onto the bridge, Lieutenant Sherman's riflemen on the knoll
began sending wicked bursts of fire pouring into the troop-
laden vehicles. Down below, Sergeant Weber's men also
opened fire, shooting upwards. Bullets from Sherman's men
were thudding into the ground all around Weber and his
troopers in the ravine below the bridge.

In the meantime, a demolitions man had lighted a fuse to
the charges and as the first German truck neared the center
of the bridge, the explosives detonated with a noise that rolled
like thunder across the bleak terrain. One of the charges blew
a large hole in the center of the bridge and the first German

truck plunged a front wheel into the opening. The bridge was effectively blocked, and as the confused Germans scrambled off the trucks and dashed for cover, the paratroopers continued to pour rifle and Tommy gun fire into the enemy ranks.

Knowing that they were far outnumbered and their advantage of surprise eroded, a parachute officer called out above the din of battle, "Let's haul ass!" and the little band of paratroopers, tired but triumphant, disappeared into the darkness, leaving behind dead German bodies strewn along the bridge and the road behind it.

A quick head count a few hundred yards from the bridge revealed that not a single trooper had been killed, although several were wounded. The raucous sound the parachute raiders heard while they were a half-mile from the blown bridge was music to their ears: The rattle of small arms fire told the troopers that the confused Germans, ambushed while far behind their own lines, were madly firing at each other.

Elsewhere deep behind German lines in the days ahead, Lieutenant Jack Pogue, who had been taken off jump status— grounded—by his battalion commander just before the 509th mission but had come along anyhow, was being kept prisoner on the third floor of an old schoolhouse. Pogue had been told by others with him that he was in a schoolhouse. He was blind. The sliver from a German grenade still protruded from one eyeball and later he had lost the vision in the other optic. The lieutenant was in extreme pain, and his shattered elbow and grenade fragments elsewhere in his body made it difficult to move. But the parachute officer had lost none of his steel spirit.

Two of his prisoner colleagues were British soldiers. Pogue overheard the pair making plans to escape. "I'll go with you," the American told the Englishmen.

"Why, my dear fellow, you could never make it," a Tommie replied in astonishment. "You can't even see."

"I can make it," Pogue insisted. "Take me along."

As the schoolhouse was a temporary collection point for Allied POWs and far behind the lines, it was relatively lightly guarded. Waiting until the premises were quiet, the two Tommies, leading the unsighted American by the hand, slipped down the stairway to the ground level and to a latrine just outside the door. Glancing quickly around, the Britishers could see no Germans, so they walked rapidly toward a nearby woods, still holding Lieutenant Pogue by the hand.

The three escaping POWs had been in the forest for only a short time when they heard the strident shouts of Germans back near the schoolhouse. The flight had been discovered. Spurred on by the knowledge enemy guards would soon be on their trail, the Tommies tried to move at a faster pace, but were slowed down by their blind comrade.

"Sorry, old fellow," one of the Englishmen told Pogue in an apologetic tone. "But if we don't hurry on, they'll nab all three of us." With that, the two Tommies abandoned the parachute lieutenant, who could hear the rustling of dry leaves as his recent companions raced on through the woods.

Behind him Pogue could hear the calls of German soldiers on the trail of the three escapees. He was determined to press ahead, to make good his escape. He started shuffling along, away from the sound of German voices, and ran into a tree, backed off and collided with another tree, knocking him to the ground. He struggled to his feet, his grenade-shattered elbow bleeding once again from the force of the fall, and continued onward. A tangle of heavy roots caught his jump boots, and once more he crashed heavily to the ground.

The sound of German voices was now very close. Pogue knew his escape bid was over. Sitting on the leaf-covered ground where he had fallen the final time, the lieutenant resignedly waited for the arrival of the enemy guards. Tears of frustration and anger poured down his cheeks.

Meanwhile, in the hamlet of Sirico, 20 miles north of Salerno and not far from Avellino, *Signora* Margherita Ciccone and teenage daughter Anna were going about their evening chores. Sirico was so insignificant in the greater scheme of things that Italian maps did not have it listed. In the village's little square there was a pipe and spigot—the only source of water for washing and cooking and which served as the meeting place for exchanging gossip and war news. Misery and endless struggle had been a way of life for the citizens of the farming settlement. The average yearly income was $200.

Still *Signora* Ciccone and Anna were happy with their lot. They worked hard and raised their own food so they had enough to eat.

Now the Italian matron had put some of that food into a large bowl and, as dusk approached, headed out the back door of the house toward the stable. Reaching the structure, she glanced hurriedly in each direction, then stepped inside. There she was greeted with warm smiles by five young men clad in ankle-length jump boots and trousers with large bulging pockets—American paratroopers of the 509th.

One had been slightly wounded and another had seriously injured his leg in jumping and could not navigate. *Signora* Ciccone handed the young fighting men the large bowl of piping hot food and looked on with pleasure as they gulped it down. By furnishing shelter and food for the paratroopers, the Italian woman was engaged in a perilous task. She stood the chance of being summarily shot by the Germans if her harboring of American soldiers was discovered.

"How is your leg this evening, Jew-en?" the lady inquired of the seriously injured Five-O-Niner named John. "Just fine," John replied. He was in extreme pain.

That night the three able-bodied troopers and the slightly wounded one moved out of the stable and headed for Avellino where they presumed the rest of the parachute battalion had gathered. They regretted leaving John behind, but knew he was reasonably safe, would receive plenty to eat, and have the tender, loving care of Signora Ciccone and her beautiful daughter Anna.

Elsewhere, since bailing out with his stick almost directly upon a German headquarters, Lieutenant Dan DeLeo had collected 12 troopers and in pairs and tiny groups the men had been marauding the vicinity at night to harass the Germans. On one of these nocturnal ventures DeLeo met up with an Italian native who said he would act as a guide or do whatever he could to fight Germans. His name was Steve DiFeo. He had emigrated to America with his parents as an infant, joined the American army in World War I, rose to first sergeant in an infantry division, and later returned to his native Italy.

"I never liked the Germans, I fought them in the last war, and I'm anxious to fight them again," DiFeo told DeLeo.

Five days after the 509th drop, Sergeant Miller's leg, struck by a dum-dum bullet in a savage firefight shortly after he touched ground, had become swollen and was turning purple and black. The young sergeant was in intense pain. Bone was exposed in his buttocks and leg and his boot was overflowing with blood. Comrades were unable to remove the boot due to the swelling of the leg.

Lieutenant DeLeo, along with his other concerns, felt Miller would die if he was not treated soon. "Sergeant, you're going to need medical help," DeLeo told the wounded man. "I think we should carry you out to a main road and lay you along the side of the road so the Krauts will find you and take you to a hospital for medical attention."

"No! No!" Miller pleaded through teeth gritted with pain. "I don't want to be a prisoner."

DiFeo, the native Italian and World War I American doughboy, spoke up. "There's a doctor in a nearby town," the guide observed. "He's a staunch Fascist, but maybe you can 'persuade' him to come here and treat Sergeant Miller."

DeLeo agreed with the proposal, but knew he would be detected and shot or apprehended in minutes in the German-held town—unless he could go in disguise.

DiFeo departed and returned with some civilian clothes. Waiting until dark, Lieutenant DeLeo doffed his jump suit and equipment and put on the tattered native suit. A wide-brimmed hat, dusty and battered, was pulled down over his eyes. Before departing for the nearby town, DeLeo slipped his .45 Colt pistol into his belt.

Patting the handle of the weapon, the lieutenant said, "This might persuade the doctor that making house calls is good business."

As a final touch at authenticity, DeLeo picked up a long staff of the type used by many rural Italians and set out through the night. On reaching the town, DeLeo immediately started passing German soldiers and rolling stock moving about the community, and except for an occasional nod at the "Italian shepherd" the enemy paid no attention to him. The

American, each time a German approached, was fearful that the pounding of his heart would be heard by the enemy and give away his true identity.

On reaching the doctor's house (which had been previously identified by the Italian guide DiFeo), the lieutenant knocked on the door. The physician himself responded to the pounding and DeLeo promptly stuck the muzzle of his .45 Colt into the doctor's face.

"I'm an American paratrooper," DeLeo hurriedly told the startled physician. "I've got a badly wounded man nearby who needs treatment. You're going to come along with me and furnish that treatment. And no funny stuff."

"I'll get my medical bag and coat," the physician responded with no undue show of concern over the sudden appearance at his door of a disguised American parachutist once the Italian had recovered from his initial surprise.

The doctor's wife began sobbing hysterically and begging DeLeo not to harm her husband. "If he does as he's told and keeps his mouth shut, we won't harm him," the officer assured the woman.

Arriving at the cave hideout of Lieutenant DeLeo and his men about a half-hour later, the Italian physician promptly began treating Sergeant Miller. He opened the wounded parachutist's leg from knee to foot with a scalpel, and with medical scissors trimmed away the black and decaying flesh. Pus was running from the wound which created a putrid stench in the cave.

After the hideous wound was sewn up and bandaged, the doctor stood up, replaced his medical instruments in a little black bag, and faced Lieutenant DeLeo as if to say, "What now?" The Italian betrayed no concern as to his fate now that the patient had been treated and he was alone in a cave with a desperate group of American paratroopers. As with other Italians, he had heard tales that American parachutists were ex-convicts, murderers and rapists, who had been released from prison to join the airborne service.

"Well, thanks, doctor," DeLeo stated. He told the physician that if he promised to say nothing of the paratroopers' hideaway he could return home. "I promise," was the reply,

and the Italian left the cave and disappeared into the darkness
in the direction of his home.

Not only did the native doctor keep his word about main-
taining silence, but he went to a German medical facility in
his town and through a ruse obtained bandages and medicine
needed for treating Sergeant Miller. He returned to the cave
the following night, unescorted this time, to treat the injured
trooper and came back on several succeeding nights.

The troopers were grateful to the physician who had been
branded a staunch Fascist and therefore a potential source of
treachery. Each time he surreptitiously visited the cave on the
mountain side, the doctor was risking his life. Aiding the
enemy was a capital offense to the *Wehrmacht*.

Some distance away from the refuge of Lieutenant DeLeo
and his men, Captain Archie Birkner, a company commander, had collected 15 Five-O-Niners after landing alone
and lost on the night of the mass drop. Birkner and his troopers had been quite successful in a new-type of guerilla warfare tactic adopted out of expedience. Instead of marauding
aimlessly about the countryside searching for the enemy, they
waited in one location for the enemy to come to them.

For several days, Captain Birkner and his men had been
positioned along a secondary road periodically used by the
Germans. While the men occupied themselves in idle activities through the day, lookouts posted at high points near the
road signaled the approach of enemy vehicles. Birkner and
his men then concealed themselves in ditches and behind trees
and large boulders, and when the unsuspecting *Wehrmacht*
vehicle and its occupants reached the ambush the paratroopers opened fire.

Captain Birkner's troopers disposed of the staff cars, motorcycles and trucks of the unlucky Germans. The corpses
were dragged just inside a nearby woods where they were
buried in shallow graves. Soon there were 14 tell-tale mounds
of earth.

Despite the success of the tactic, the mysterious disap-
pearance of numerous Germans along this secondary road
resulted in focusing enemy attention on the locale. Birkner's
days as a free man were numbered.

The parachute company commander was seated on a hillside one sunny afternoon with Sergeant Ray Cagle, Corporal Porter and Lieutenant DeLury. Birkner was scanning the landscape with binoculars. Intent on locating signs of enemy activity, the four paratroopers were startled to hear a strident shout behind them: *"Hande hoch!"* (hands up!). The four Americans lifted their arms overhead and slowly turned around to see nine Germans aiming automatic weapons at them.

In the meantime, Captain Carlos "Doc" Alden, the 509th battalion surgeon, was prowling about the countryside alone. Following the ambush into which the treacherous Italian, Roger, had led the battalion commander and a small band of troopers, Alden had hooked up with a few comrades at the old farmhouse in which the grievously wounded Private Leroy Lauer had taken refuge. The surgeon and his companions had then become engaged in another firefight in which Alden became separated from the others. He had used up all of his grenades and most of his ammunition and had lost one of his two pistols.

Now, searching for other Five-O-Niners, Doc Alden came upon an elderly Italian man. Speaking in broken English and gesturing, the native indicated that a seriously wounded American paratrooper and two other soldiers were in a house in a nearby village.

"One of your comrades has a badly injured arm and our Italian doctor there says he's going to cut it off today," the elderly man told Alden.

"Take me to them," Alden told the native. The surgeon was far from trusting the native with the memory of Roger's treachery so fresh in mind. But, the captain assured himself, if this Italian betrayed him the native would "die suddenly of lead poisoning."

True to his word, the elderly man guided the parachute surgeon to the house in the village of San Michele where two of Alden's medics, Royal D. Maynard and Andrew J. Floyd, were holed up and tending to two wounded comrades. The three paratroopers greeted each other warmly. Maynard and Floyd shook hands with the elderly Italian whom they con-

sidered an old friend—even though they had known him but
a few hours.

Maynard told Captain Alden how the two medics had arrived at their current place of refuge. When Maynard had
bailed out of his C-47 he was the last man in his stick. The
trooper just in front of the medic, in his anxiety to leap out,
had stumbled, causing a delay of several seconds before Maynard could jump.

As a result of the brief holdup, Maynard floated to earth
alone. Far off in the distance, the bright moonlight permitted
him to glimpse the white outlines of parachutes of others in
his stick. He estimated his C-47 comrades would touch down
at least a mile away.

Reaching ground, Maynard began walking across the
rough terrain and came to railroad tracks. He started along
the tracks, hoping they would take him to Avellino and the
drop zone. At the time, he had no way of knowing that others
in his C-47 stick would soon locate the same tracks, walk in
the opposite direction as that taken by Maynard, and be taken
prisoner after running into a large force of Germans.

Alone and aware that he was totally lost and that German
patrols were combing the vicinity, Maynard climbed a low
hill and stayed there for two days. Down below him on the
second day, an enemy contingent had set up a temporary
camp. The trooper, concealed behind bushes, felt that he
could almost reach out and touch the Germans in the valley.

Fearful of being discovered, Maynard stealthily moved off
the hill and ran into a 70-year-old Italian man—the same individual who, hours later, would serve as a guide for Doc
Alden. The native told of the two wounded Americans in a
house in San Michele, one with a mangled arm, and led the
medical aid man there.

The elderly man departed and in two hours he returned
with Maynard's fellow medic, Andrew Floyd. Leaving again,
the Italian arrived back at the house once more with Captain
Alden, the battalion surgeon, in tow.

The 33-year-old Alden, wearing his distinctive red beret
of the British parachute forces, treated the trooper with the
serious gunshot wound in one arm as best he could. He had

no medicine, bandages or medical tools. His supply bundle had been dropped separately from his C-47.

Turning to the elderly Italian, the parachute surgeon exclaimed, "This boy's arm is badly injured, but it doesn't have to be amputated. Tell your local doctor that, under no circumstances, is he to amputate the arm."

Having been given a shot of morphine to temporarily relieve his suffering, the trooper with the mangled arm recognized Doc Alden—everyone in the 509th knew and admired the surgeon—and murmured softly, "Thanks, Doc."

"Oh, hell, don't thank me," Alden replied. "This is what the army pays me $138 a month to do."

The badly wounded trooper smiled weakly. Doc was always kidding, even in predicaments like this, he thought.

Alden took Maynard and Floyd into an adjoining room. "The boy needs some medicine badly," the surgeon confided. "You two stay here. I'm going to scour the countryside for my medical supply bundle."

His task was akin to locating a particular grain of sand in the Sahara Desert. But knowing his finding the bundle could result in saving the lives or limbs of wounded comrades, Doc Alden was determined to make the effort.

After prowling the area for hours, periodically having to evade German patrols, the surgeon returned to San Michele. He could not locate the medical bundle. "It might have landed anywhere in Italy or in the sea," a realistic Alden told himself.

Moments after entering the village Alden was approached by an excited native, who was waving his arms wildly, chattering and gesturing up the street. The American concluded the man was telling him Germans were approaching.

While Alden pondered this latest danger signal, he looked up the street and saw a German army truck with a large canvas cover over the bed moving directly toward him. A driver and a passenger were seated in front. The surgeon quickly raised his rifle to fire at the pair of enemy soldiers in the vehicle when suddenly the truck ground to a screeching halt and 12 or 14 Germans hopped down from under the canvas cover.

Realizing that one man with a rifle and out in the open was no match for a dozen German soldiers, many armed with automatic weapons, Captain Alden dashed between two houses and beat a path out of town as fast as his legs would carry him. As he ran, angry bullets hissed past his head. After bolting for about a hundred yards, Alden plunged into a large cornfield which offered concealment. Lungs bursting from the exertion, he plodded on into the field and wearily sat down to await developments.

As the minutes ticked by, Alden began to congratulate himself on his latest near-miss and good fortune. Only silence reigned. He could hear none of the customary strident shouts of German officers directing their men in search of a quarry. It was just a normal, pleasant autumn afternoon in a field of corn.

Some 15 minutes later the battalion surgeon heard a gentle rustling among the nearby cornstalks. Suddenly, as though appearing out of thin air, four Germans with Schmeissers aimed at the American stood in front of him and called out, *"Hande hoch!"* Alden glanced to his left where two more Germans had weapons pointed at him. To his right and behind him were other enemy soldiers. His situation hopeless, Doc Alden raised his arms and slowly got to his feet.

Sergeant Robert Akers and the five troopers with him, all of whom had been forced to depart hastily from inside darkened Avellino on the night of the jump when they heard German tanks clanking toward them, had been roaming the countryside for two nights seeking other Five-O-Niners. Heading up a mountain, Akers and his little band ran into other parachutists and then there were 15 of them.

The next day, high overhead in the clear Mediterranean sky, Akers and the others heard the hum of airplane motors and the muted chatter of machine-gun fire. The troopers gazed skyward in fascination to view a dog-fight taking place between an American P-51 and a *Luftwaffe* fighter plane. The cheering was definitely one-sided: The P-51 was everyone's favorite.

Directly above them the troopers saw a figure depart from the German plane followed by a blossoming parachute. The

Luftwaffe craft plunged earthward. The American P-51 pilot had won this encounter in the bright blue Mediterranean skies.

Nearing the ground under his billowing canopy, the *Luftwaffe* pilot spotted the knot of American paratroopers and, knowing he was far behind the lines, took them to be German soldiers. He waved cheerily at the parachutists and seconds later touched ground. As the troopers neared the pilot to take him prisoner, a look of deep astonishment spread across the pilot's face as he saw these were not fellow Germans but rather American soldiers.

Keeping a close eye on their *Luftwaffe* captive, Akers and the other troopers began the long and perilous trek back toward Allied lines on the beachhead, in accordance with their instructions to hold out for several days and then infiltrate back. At first the troopers guarded the prisoner diligently, but soon relaxed when he showed no inclination to escape. They called him Herman. And Herman was quite pleasant and comradely.

Each morning the Americans would awaken drowsily to find Herman busily engaged taking calisthenics. The German would mockingly scold the paratroopers and ask why they didn't take morning exercises also.

"Hell, Herman," a trooper responded, referring to months of the most rugged training, "we've been taking unending calisthenics since Hitler was a paperhanger."

Herman was also choosy as to his ultimate locale as a prisoner of war. "I want to go to New York City," he told the troopers. "I've always wanted to go to New York." He added emphatically: "I sure as hell don't want to go to London."

Each night on the slow and tortured trek toward the beachhead, a couple of troopers were left behind to guard Herman—who promptly went to sleep—and the others stole off into the darkness to raise havoc with the *Wehrmacht*.

One night Sergeant Akers and four other troopers planted several English-made mines along a dark road and took up positions to either side. An hour later the sound of an approaching vehicle reached their ears and a German truck, filled with infantrymen, struck a mine. An orange flame

leaped into the air and the explosion echoed across the landscape. Those enemy soldiers still alive scrambled from the
vehicle as the concealed Americans raked them with small
arms fire.

Hard on the heels of the first truck, another one drove up.
Forewarned of danger by the land-mine explosion, the second
vehicle halted and Germans leaped from the bed and took up
firing positions along side the road. An intense firefight
erupted and white tracers from the enemy weapons laced the
paratroopers' positions. A third truck carrying German grenadiers drove up. Vastly outnumbered, Sergeant Akers and his
comrades withdrew.

As the days crept by, the little band of parachutists grew
increasingly hungry—and weaker. The three to five days' rations carried into battle had been consumed. It was harvest
time in Italy, so Akers and the others gorged themselves with
figs, grapes and olives as they pushed on toward American
lines on the Salerno beachhead.

Mostly they ate figs. Figs morning, noon and night. As a
result, the column halted repeatedly and, as one man stood
lookout, the others scattered into the woods to heed the call
of nature. Then the Americans and Herman the *Luftwaffe*
pilot resumed their arduous trek.

12
"Retreat, Hell! We're Keeping This Hill!"

WHILE TINY BANDS of raiders of the 109th Parachute Infantry Battalion were marauding about the German rear areas disrupting communications, ambushing patrols, shooting up truck convoys and creating general havoc, bitter fighting continued relentlessly on Salerno beachhead. General Mike Dawley, commander of the U.S. VI Corps along the southern half of the Allied line, on the morning of September 16 ordered Fred Walker's 36th Infantry Division to seize and hold the commanding heights around the town of Altavilla, which provided enemy observation over the entire 15-mile sweep of the VI Corps sector.

Generals Dawley and Walker were unaware that the American attackers would be sent into a devil's cauldron. The area in the Altavilla region had been a firing range for German artillery, and nearly every foot of ground had been zeroed in by mortars and field pieces. It was across this German artillery-practice impact area that American infantrymen would have to advance to assault the heights around Altavilla.

General Walker selected Colonel Reuben Tucker's attached 504th Parachute Infantry Regiment, less the 3rd Battalion which had landed by boat the night before, and one company of the 636th Tank Destroyer Battalion to seize and hold the crucial high ground. Three days before, a battalion of the green 36th Infantry Division had been driven out of Altavilla and the heights around it, suffering heavy casualties. Altavilla was a typical Italian mountain town, a collection of light-colored houses and buildings. At its center was a three-and-one-half story house, imposing for that impoverished region, which was the home of the mayor. The first floor housed domestic animals—two cows, a horse, a pig and a flock of chickens—and the second level was for servants and relatives. On the third floor the mayor and his family lived. The mayor's level was luxuriously appointed and furnished with chrome and walnut furniture and paneled walls.

Now that war had come to the Gulf of Salerno and American forces were arrayed on the flatlands down below, the mayor of Altavilla had additional guests in his palatial home— German artillery observers. From the mayor's luxurious bedroom, *Wehrmacht* officers could view every approach to Altavilla and surrounding heights.

Perched on another elevation was the town of Albanella. For Colonel Rube Tucker's 504th Parachute Infantry Regiment to attack the high ground around Altavilla it would have to make an approach march through Albanella and then press on to the objective. Tucker's 1st and 2nd Battalions had been in position near Albanella since the Five-O-Fours bailed out on the beachhead the night of September 13–14.

Elements of the 504th Parachute Infantry had been in Albanella since the night of September 14. Just before dusk that day, some 14 hours after the regiment had jumped onto the bridgehead, Lieutenant G. W. Jaubert, a rifle platoon-leader, was ordered to take his men and probe Albanella and surrounding heights. The area to be reconnoitered was thought to be occupied by Germans, as the town furnished excellent observation of a wide expanse of the coastline.

With the hot Mediterranean sun in the act of disappearing into the western horizon that night of the fourteenth, Lieutenant Jaubert and his platoon set out for the arduous six-mile march to Albanella. Walking at a fast pace, the troopers scrambled up the sides of rugged mountains and down into valleys, through orchards and vineyards, across cold mountain streams. Chests nearly bursting from the strenuous cross-country trek, Jaubert and his men reached a large plateau on which sat Albanella. Due to the protective blanket of night, the parachute platoon reached its objective without being fired upon by German artillery.

Lieutenant Jaubert halted his men short of the town and ordered them to fan out by squads to probe the surrounding area in search of the enemy. A few hours later, with dawn nearly at hand, Jaubert's squads returned to the assembly area on the Albanella plateau. None had seen a single German. The lieutenant established a defensive position on a gentle slope facing Albanella and awaited developments.

Shortly after daybreak an Italian farmer happened by and Jaubert inquired of him, *"Dove gli Tedeschi?"* (Where are the Germans?) The native indicated that two or three enemy soldiers were hiding in Albanella. Jaubert concluded that the Germans in the town were artillery observers.

Jaubert gathered a few men and moved off into Albanella in search of the enemy observers. In a short time, the lieutenant abandoned the effort as hopeless—there were too many houses and buildings in which the two or three Germans could be hiding. Jaubert summoned the rest of his platoon to join him in the town and for the rest of the day a contingent of American paratroopers and a handful of *Wehrmacht* artillery observers coexisted in the community. Not a shot was fired, not an artillery round fell in the town. The citizens had long since departed. Albanella on that beautiful autumn day in the Mediterranean was a Ghost Town.

Later that afternoon a messenger arrived in town and told Lieutenant Jaubert that his platoon was to return to the assembly area of the 504th Regiment immediately and as rapidly as possible. Amid curses from the troopers that turned the already azure sky a deeper shade of blue, gear was gathered and the platoon began its arduous six-mile trek back to the area it had left some 24 hours previously. On the return trip, the platoon was heavily shelled by long-range guns, but kept on marching as the projectiles were landing a hundred yards to the left.

On arriving at the regimental assembly area, Jaubert and his men were near exhaustion from the long forced march across rugged mountain terrain and throats were parched from thirst. Canteen water had been consumed many hours previously. The lieutenant approached his company commander who told him, "Better get your men ready to move out, Jaubert. The battalion is marching to Albanella to jump off for Altavilla."

Lieutenant Jaubert was speechless with anger. He could not recall having been so furious. His tired men had just completed an arduous forced march of six miles over some of the world's most rugged terrain to return to the regimental assembly area and now would have to turn around and retrace their steps. Jaubert cursed and ranted. His company commander shrugged his shoulders in resignation and walked off.

On the morning of September 16, with a rosy sun beaming down from high in the heavens, Colonel Tucker's Five-O-Fours, less the 3rd Battalion, moved out of their assembly area and began the exhausting six-mile march to Albanella. The going was rough. Up one mountainside, down the other. Through a vineyard. Down into a valley. Up a mountain. Down a mountain. Men slipping and falling on the rocky, uneven terrain. Water soon gone. Throats parched. Curses ringing out. Chests burning. Shells screaming overhead.

Eventually Rube Tucker's paratroopers reached Albanella, the Ghost Town Lieutenant Jaubert and his men had occupied earlier. There Colonel Tucker called for Lieutenant Colonel Warren Williams, the 1st Battalion commander, and Major Dan Danielson, leader of the 2nd Battalion. Tucker gave them their battle orders.

Williams' battalion had the toughest nut to crack—the main objective, Altavilla and Hill 424 which commanded a view of the town. "Take the goddamned place and hold it!" Colonel Tucker admonished Williams in customary tone.

Dan Danielson's battalion would seize another key hill nearby—Hill 415. Each battalion would have a tough fight as the Germans could be expected to react with their usual tenacity and would be dug in on commanding heights, requiring the paratroopers to attack uphill to root them out.

Curiously, an eerie quiet had settled over the region. It was the calm before the storm. As Tucker finished giving orders to Colonel Williams and Major Danielson, the roar of airplane engines was heard overhead and Rube Tucker casually looked into the cloudless blue sky to see a flight of *Luftwaffe* fighter planes streak past and dive into an adjoining valley, strafing and bombing.

"Nasty little bastards, aren't they?" Tucker spit out.

The 504th command post was set up on a hillside at Albanella. Colonel Tucker left Major Julian Cook in temporary charge and, together with his 1st and 2nd battalions, moved on toward the objective—the high ground adjacent to Altavilla.

It was not long after Tucker had left on the approach march from Albanella that Major Cook at the CP became disturbed. He could not reach the regimental commander by telephone or radio. It appeared that matters had already become confused.

Lieutenant Colonel Williams' 1st Battalion was marching through the twilight toward Hill 424, Major Danielson's 2nd Battalion was laboriously picking its way in the direction of adjoining Hill 415, and Colonel Tucker and forward elements of his headquarters company were moving ahead somewhere between the two assault battalions of infantry.

Suddenly in the gloaming an American light observation plane swooped low over the 1st Battalion. An observer in the craft leaned out the window and dropped a wrench with a note attached to it. Taken promptly to Colonel Williams, the note warned that the Germans were dug in in strength on the hills about a mile to the front. Even closer, the message stated, enemy machine-gun nests were waiting in ambush for the approaching Americans.

Acting immediately to continue his advance, Williams sent out troops to flank the machine guns and after a short fight the parachutists wiped out the enemy automatic weapons with rifles, Tommy guns and grenades.

Any hope the paratroopers held for a surprise attack on

Hill 424 vanished into the Mediterranean air. The Germans knew the Americans were advancing.

As the 1st Battalion moved out of a valley and into some woods, a trooper with Colonel Williams spotted a low wire across their route. The wire marked an enemy minefield. Williams started gingerly picking his way around the area when his radio operator decided to join the battalion commander instead of waiting for Williams to call him.

The radio operator unknowingly walked into the minefield. Williams called out, "Stop! Go back!" just as the trooper hit a trip wire. A loud blast followed as a Teller mine exploded. There was no shrapnel but the force of the detonation knocked both the battalion commander and the radio operator to the ground. Each was dazed but otherwise uninjured. Regaining their feet, they carefully backed away from the area and took a wide detour.

As Colonel Williams' paratroopers pushed closer to Hill 424, German artillery fire steadily increased. Spread out in single file, the men listened intently for the tell-tale sound of incoming artillery rounds, and peered through the darkness ahead for any indication that they were about to stumble into enemy machine-gun ambushes. A number of abandoned German positions were encountered. One German was captured who admitted he was an artillery observer.

A dim, stark mass loomed ahead which Colonel Williams thought was his objective—Hill 424. Artillery fire from the beachhead was pounding the elevation near the top. The battalion commander halted his force and conferred with the other officers in an attempt to clarify the situation. He had not been advised that American artillery would be directed onto his objective.

Williams was mildly concerned. He had lost contact with Major Danielson's 2nd Battalion, with Colonel Tucker's command group, and with regimental headquarters back on the hillside at Albanella. But with the coming of daylight, he was confident that communications would be restored before his battalion jumped off to assault the objective to his front.

While Colonel Rube Tucker and his command group were advancing by a route thought to be between the 1st and 2nd

Battalions, they came under heavy artillery fire and took cover in a drainage ditch. The moon by now was hanging high in the heavens, so Tucker and his troopers were visible to German artillery observers in the hills. The first salvo to explode around the regimental commander and his group had been to zero in. The worst was yet to come.

As Colonel Tucker and his men flattened out on the bottom of the drainage ditch, jagged white flashes lighted the sky to the rear of the stark outlines of mountains to the front of the paratroopers. German gun batteries, perhaps a battalion, were seeking out the parachutists in the ditch. Moments later there was the frightening sound of many shells rustling through the dark sky. The rustling turned into angry hisses as the projectiles neared and crashed into the ground around the headquarters company men. Explosions rocked the prostrate troopers and seemed to lift them a short distance off the ground. The acrid smell of cordite wafted through the air and was picked up by the sensitive noses of the Americans.

Now the Germans had the range. Soon more shells—closer this time—were exploding on the huddled men in the ditch. Troopers tried to pull themselves far into their helmets and they cursed the buttons on their shirts for not permitting them to press closer to the earth.

There was a brief respite from the shelling. The men cornered in the drainage ditch knew that the pause was ominous in its significance. The battalion of *Wehrmacht* artillery had found the range and was now ready to fire for effect—to pour relentless salvos onto Colonel Tucker and his men. Minutes later, the sky again broke out in flashes of light on the other side of the mountain silhouettes. Then the screeching of shells and loud concussions all around the ditch. White-hot, jagged steel fragments hissed and sang as they flew over the troopers. Tree branches were hacked off by the shell splinters, and leaves and pieces of trees showered down on the Americans. Masses of dirt gushered into the air, then plunged back down on top of the men in the ditch. Each trooper tried to get lower. And lower.

Above the crashing of shells a booming voice rang out which all recognized as that of Colonel Tucker: "We'd better get the hell out of here. They've got our range." His tone was matter-of-fact. There was no trace of panic.

Tucker got to his feet and started trotting forward, as the others in the command group leaped up and followed the regimental commander across the field and up a steep hillside. Having covered several hundred yards at a sprint while burdened with heavy combat gear, Tucker and his men jumped into another ditch. There they lay, panting and exhausted.

Wherever the German artillery observers were posted, they had a clear view in the bright moonlight of Tucker's sprinting troopers. Hardly had the last headquarters company man scrambled into the depression in the ground than the enemy batteries behind the mountains began pounding the new place of refuge. The *Wehrmacht* observers and the American parachutists were playing a cat-and-mouse game; in this instance, the paratroopers were the mouse.

Again a pause. The Five-O-Fours in the advanced trench saw two shadowy figures dashing across the ground leading from the first ditch and Lieutenant Colonel Leslie G. Freeman, XO (executive officer, or second in command) of the regiment and Major Don B. Dunham scrambled into the forward ditch. They had remained at the first trench to care for Captain Thomas Wright, who had been hit by a shell fragment just as the headquarters men were preparing to dash forward out of the impact area. Captain Wright died in their arms.

After the troopers in the ditch had regained their breath, Colonel Tucker motioned the men forward. They moved off into the night, stumbling over rocks and furrowed fields, cursing and falling. Now the terrain became a panorama of sameness—the silhouette of one hill looked much like that of another.

Moving along a valley dotted with olive groves and vineyards, the troopers spotted the outline of a steep hill looming to their front. "That's it," Colonel Tucker called out in a stage whisper. "That's our main objective—Hill 424." He waved his men onward.

The parachutists picked their way up the lower slopes of

the incline and heard a low-voiced challenge: "Red River!" It was the American password for the night. Came back the countersign: "Valley!" Tucker and his men had run onto a patrol sent out to probe Hill 424.

Tucker talked briefly with members of the patrol. Voices were hushed. The enemy could be nearby. The colonel turned to aides and said softly, "No one's showed up yet. We are the point!"

Instead of being in the customary position to direct a battle—behind advancing rifle companies—Rube Tucker and his command group formed the leading combat element in the assault on Hill 424.

Now the nighttime air was pierced by the booming roar of cannon being fired. The Germans had opened up again. Only this time the enemy guns were firing at the beachhead from *behind* Tucker and his command group. Unknowingly the troopers had infiltrated behind enemy lines. A confused situation in the dark had become even more chaotic. Tucker, to compound his quandary of being the "point" and behind enemy formations, was out of contact with both of his assault battalions and his regimental CP back at Albanella.

On a small knoll on the lower slopes of Hill 424, the colonel set up his command post and deployed his men into defensive positions to await the arrival of daylight. Sentries were placed on all sides of the knoll, much in the manner of wagon-train pioneers of the Old West, for the Germans could assault the little command group from any direction—including the rear.

A patrol of two troopers, all that could be spared, was sent out to contact the 1st and 2nd battalions and request reinforcements for Tucker's isolated group. Minutes ticked on into hours and the two-man patrol did not return. Neither man was heard from again. The pair had been swallowed up by the night.

As Colonel Tucker tried to establish radio contact with his units, the angry sound of Schmeisser machine-pistol bursts erupted to the rear of the CP. White tracer bullets laced the sky just over the head of Tucker's group. Above the noise of the enemy automatic weapons could be heard the slower-paced reports of American Tommy guns. A German force had worked its way behind Rube Tucker's CP and grenadiers were charging up the rear slope of the knoll. After an intense firefight of 20 minutes, during which some Germans had advanced as far as the paratroopers' foxholes guarding the rear of the CP, the enemy force broke off the engagement and withdrew down the hill.

Knowing reinforcements were needed or the command post would be overrun and the regiment left without central direction, Lieutenant Colonel Freeman, the 504th executive officer, and Lieutenant Forrest Richter moved out into the valley to the east in search of either Colonel Williams' 1st Battalion or Major Danielson's 2nd Battalion. Both units were to be advancing through the inky blackness toward their hill objectives.

As the parachute officers were stealing softly across a vineyard, the shriek of Schmeisser fire echoed across the landscape and streams of white tracers hissed past the Americans. Each was hit by a bullet.

Freeman and Richter, bleeding profusely, fell to the ground. With enemy automatic weapons bursts searching them out repeatedly, the two officers arduously crawled and scrambled back over the route they had just traveled and returned to Colonel Tucker's command post.

Meanwhile, Major Don Dunham had been prowling around the dark slopes of the knoll, Tommy gun in hand and crouched low for immediate action. He was a self-appointed one-man patrol seeking a sniper or two who had been firing into the CP at irregular intervals. Later he returned to the others on the little knoll. His stalking had been in vain.

Now it was obvious to all among the besieged troopers at Colonel Tucker's CP on the dark crown of the knoll: There were Germans on four sides and enemy artillery had the hill zeroed in. The group was isolated.

A grim-faced Major Dunham approached Tucker and told him he would try to get through the encircling enemy troops and go for help. He would try to succeed where others had failed.

Dunham, who only a few nights before back in Sicily had

jokingly told his comrades, "I hope I get killed first in Italy," picked out a sergeant to go with him. Knowing his chances for returning were minimal, the young major handed several of his personal belongings, including a German Luger, to those on the knoll. "Keep these until I get back," Dunham said matter of factly, much in the manner of a tennis player back home in saner times about to take to the court for an important match.

The major solemnly shook hands with a number of close friends and, together with the sergeant, disappeared into the darkness down the rear slope of the knoll.

Despite their own extreme peril, every man's thoughts on the hill were with Major Dunham and his sergeant. Minutes later those at the CP heard the angry chatter of Schmeisser fire pierce the darkness in the direction Dunham and the other trooper had taken. Then there was silence.

A short time later a shadow figure emerged out of the shadows of the wooded slope to the rear of the CP. A shaken sergeant, the one who had accompanied Major Dunham, scrambled onto the crown of the knoll. He told of running into a band of Germans at the bottom of the hill who opened fire on the two paratroopers.

"The major went down and I couldn't get over to him," the ashen-faced noncom blurted out.

Breathing heavily and with the customary haunted look of a man who had just escaped sure death through the inscrutable whim of Dame Fate, he added in a low voice, "I could hear the death rattle in his throat."

Only one able-bodied officer now was left in the regimental command group—Colonel Tucker. Major Dunham was dead. Lieutenant Colonel Freeman and Lieutenant Richter were painfully wounded but able to hobble about. As daylight of the seventeenth broke out over central Italy, German shells continued to scream into the small knoll.

As dawn approached, Lieutenant Colonel Warren Williams, commander of the 1st Battalion which was to assault the primary objective, Hill 424, made an alarming discovery: His battalion was on the lower slopes of Hill 415, which was the objective of Major Dan Danielson's 2nd Battalion, and

Danielson's troopers were elsewhere. Approaching in the
darkness over heavily-wooded and mountainous terrain laced
with deep ravines and under unrelenting artillery fire, neither
504th assault battalion had reached its correct objective.

Taking prompt action, Colonel Williams summoned his A
Company commander, Captain Willard Harrison. ''Willard,'' the battalion commander said, ''take your company
and get the hell over to Hill 424 and hold on. We're on the
wrong goddamned hill. I'll bring the rest of the battalion as
soon as I can.''

Captain Harrison's troopers hurried across the wooded and
boulder-strewn saddle that connected Hill 415 with Hill 424
and at the bottom of Hill 424 Harrison ran onto the command
group of Colonel Rube Tucker.

''Get the hell up to the top of 424 and hold it!'' the regimental commander rasped to Harrison.

Scrambling and pulling their way up the steep, dark slope
of Hill 424, scouts of Harrison's company had just crossed
the top of the elevation when bursts of German automatic
weapons fire began to rake them. The enemy was coming up
the other side of the hill from the direction of Altavilla.

Captain Harrison's men behind the scouts reacted swiftly.
They stormed the German positions over the crest and after
a brief but fierce shootout sent those enemy soldiers who
were not dead or wounded fleeing back down the reverse
slope.

In the meantime, Colonel Williams, the 1st Battalion
leader, had contacted Major Danielson of the 2nd Battalion
and informed him that both units were on the wrong hills.
Danielson promptly began marching his battalion toward its
true objective, Hill 415, in order to permit Williams' remaining units to reinforce Captain Harrison's company on Hill
424.

Harrison's men barely had time to regain their breath from
the physical and emotional exertion of the fight to reach and
hold the top of Hill 424 when they detected the telltale rustle
of shells headed toward their positions, followed by eerie
hissing sounds just before the projectiles crashed and exploded. The troopers hugged the bottom of their shallow slit

trenches. Above the din of artillery shells exploding around them, the parachutists heard the weird fluttering noise of mortar rounds falling through space, then detonating with ground-shaking blasts.

Presently the thunderous barrage lifted. Peering out of their slit trenches the men of A Company saw gray-clad German grenadiers, armed with Schmeissers and bolt-action rifles, again working their way up the wooded slope of Hill 424. Most of A Company's machine guns had not arrived and there was no contact with American artillery batteries to call for supporting fire.

Putting down their entrenching tools and grabbing rifles and Tommy guns, the paratroopers opened fire, pouring lethal volleys into the ranks of the attackers. Germans to their front were dashing from boulder to boulder, from tree to tree, as they scrambled up the hill. Strident shouts of enemy officers and noncoms, urging their grenadiers to press onward, rang out above the din of battle. Soon German corpses were strewn about the slopes. Pitiful cries of enemy soldiers writhing on the ground with agonizing wounds drifted over the landscape.

It was a one-sided battle. The Americans calmly lay in their slit trenches and squeezed off shots at the advancing *Wehrmacht* grenadiers. German automatic weapons and rifle fire hissed past the dug-in parachutists, but few enemy bullets found their mark. Flat in their slit trenches, the Americans were small targets.

The assaulting grenadiers, with dead and wounded piling up under the smoking guns of the sharp-shooting Americans, wavered, halted and, with paratrooper bullets nipping at their heels every step of the way, broke and fled back down the hill. The fierce shootout on Hill 424 was over—for the time being.

As they rested in slit trenches from their labors, the troopers were certain of one thing: The Germans would be back. Hill 424 was too crucial to both sides for the *Wehrmacht* to give up after only two efforts to seize the commanding elevation.

While Captain Harrison's company was fighting on Hill

424, the remainder of Lieutenant Colonel Williams' 1st Battalion, still on the wrong hill, was hit with heavy artillery and mortar barrages followed by infantry assaults. But, as had Harrison's men, the Five-O-Fours lay in their slit trenches and picked off the charging grenadiers. The Germans withdrew back down Hill 415, leaving the slope littered with dead and wounded.

As in all savage battles, a temporary lull had settled over the disputed peaks overlooking Salerno beachhead. American paratroopers held Hill 424 and Hill 415, but each was earmarked for capture by *Wehrmacht* commanders.

It was an eerie atmosphere on the two elevations. Only minutes before there had been the crashing of artillery and mortar shells, the sharp detonation of grenades, the angry chatter of machine guns and the crack of rifles, the shouts of leaders giving orders and the pitiful shrieks of men being mutilated by bullets and shell fragments. Now, only silence. A few crickets chirped. Even a bird shrilled a cry off in the distance. That was all.

Awaiting the next German onslaught, troopers on beleaguered Hill 424 were growing uncomfortable from the elements. The Mediterranean sun had risen high into the cloudless heavens and was blistering mortals below with its torrid rays. Clothes saturated with perspiration, the parachutists had emptied canteens. Throats were parched. There was no way to bring up water from the rear to the isolated paratroopers.

That morning Lieutenant Colonel Williams was crossing the top of Hill 424 to check his battalion which was busily digging in just over the crown on four sides of the embattled elevation. He was greeted by a ghastly sight. Strewn about the landscape were the bodies of many American soldiers. Shoulder patches identified them as Texans of the 36th Infantry Division whose battalion had been driven out of Altavilla four days previously. Since that time the cadavers had become bloated and turned black from hours of exposure to the fireball Mediterranean sun.

Some corpses had burst open from the heat, Williams noted, spilling intestines over the bodies. Sun-seared eyeballs had swollen and popped from sockets, dangling by thin cords on faces and necks. The white of the dangling eyeballs was in sharp contrast to the black faces of the dead Thirty-Sixers. Swarms of flies hovered over the bodies and feasted on puss oozing from hideous wounds.

Many of these dead men, only a few days before, had been among the seaborne assault troops who so joyously celebrated the surrender of Italy, believing it meant they would not have to fight for a foothold on continental Europe.

A putrid stench from the scores of decaying bodies permeated Hill 424. The sight and smell sickened the nearby paratroopers. Some Five-O-Fours leaned out of their holes and vomited.

Now German medics, waving the white flags and with red cross arm bands prominently displayed, moved up the hill and began tending to wounded comrades, gunned down by the fierce fire of Colonel Williams' men. Many of the enemy wounded lay motionless, indistinguishable from dead comrades. In their holes, the troopers looked on impassively as the enemy aidmen scurried from body to body in search of those still alive.

Minutes after the German medics withdrew down the hill, enemy artillery and mortars began to pound American positions. The paratroopers hugged the bottom of their holes and awaited the charge of enemy grenadiers as soon as the barrage lifted. The charge was not long in coming. It resulted in another bloody repulsion for the attackers, who again fled back down the hill, leaving behind scores of dead and wounded. Despite the success of Colonel Williams' paratroopers on Hill 424 in picking off attacking *Wehrmacht* soldiers, much like shooting fish in a barrel, casualties among the Five-O-Fours were being brought to the battalion aid station in mounting numbers. Most were victims of the intense German artillery and mortar barrages.

Captain Charles Pack, surgeon of the 1st Battalion, was running short of medical supplies by the end of the first day on Hill 424. His aid station was located in a clump of olive trees only a stone's throw behind front-line foxholes. The facility had been shelled regularly by enemy guns which were blanketing all parts of the hill.

Captain Pack, at 34 years of age the oldest member of the battalion, had performed two amputations that day with limited equipment and medical supplies. Now he was desperate. His supplies were nearly exhausted and he knew more casualties would be streaming into his makeshift facility.

Much of that day on the shell-swept hill, Pack had been periodically contacting the battalion commander, Colonel Williams. "We urgently need blood up here," Captain Pack stressed. "And we need litter teams. I've got a lot of seriously wounded. They're laying on the ground all around my aid station."

"I'll do all I can," Williams replied. His agonizing problem was that he was out of contact with the rear area. In effect, his battalion was isolated on the rugged, wooded terrain of Hill 424.

Captain Pack, a native of Tennessee, had not volunteered for the paratroopers, but had been assigned to the fledgling parachute service in the fall of 1942. "This is just a temporary assignment until a jump-qualified doctor can be located," Pack was told.

The weeks and months flew by and the 82nd Airborne Division moved to the port of embarkation in New York. There Captain Pack thought he would be replaced. But he was not. He sailed for North Africa, expecting to be reassigned there. Still no qualified replacement had been found.

By the spring of 1943, Captain Pack had grown fond of his comrades and his regiment. Led by Colonel Williams, several Five-O-Four officers persuaded Pack to attend jump school and qualify as a parachutist. Days later the doctor returned from jump school—still not a parachutist. He had sprained his ankle leaping off a four-foot platform.

As the 82nd Airborne Division prepared to jump into Sicily, in July, Doc Pack approached his battalion commander. "Colonel," he said earnestly to Warren Williams, "our fellows are going into Sicily and you don't have a doctor. I'd like to go along."

"Okay, Doc," Williams replied. "We'll get you a parachute and strap you in it. You'll be between two experienced jumpers so when you get to the C-47 door just follow the man in front of you. The man behind will see that you don't stop there."

"I'll go out the door all right," replied Captain Pack. "I'm not going to let my friends go into combat without a doctor."

Captain Pack flew to Sicily the night of July 11–12 in the C-47 carrying Colonel Williams. The surgeon bailed out in a parachute for the first time in his life, and made a routine landing on rocky terrain 15 miles from the designated drop zone. Williams spotted the uninjured surgeon minutes later and breathed a deep sigh of relief.

Still without formal training, Doc Park jumped with his comrades the second time on the Salerno beachhead and moved up onto Hill 424 with them.

Later on that afternoon of September 17, Colonel Williams was able to establish radio contact with the regimental rear. His first order of business was to request medical supplies for Doc Pack and small arms ammunition for his rifle companies. He had no way of knowing at the time that his call would be intercepted by monitors at Fifth Army headquarters near the shoreline or that he would be reprimanded after the battle action for "breach of security" for ordering desperately needed medical supplies and ammo over the radio, his only means of communication.

As the day of intense fighting wore on, the situation around Hill 424, Hill 415 and Altavilla became entangled and confused—for both American and German commanders. There was no continuous front line in the mountainous terrain and packets of American paratroopers and *Wehrmacht* soldiers often found themselves prowling about to the rear of larger enemy forces.

Lieutenant Colonel Williams' CP was located in a draw on the back slope of Hill 424 when three members of his headquarters staff were sent on a mission. They were Staff Sergeant Sam De Crenzo, the battalion draftsman, Staff Sergeant Edgar Lauritsen, and Private Richard B. Hill.

Completing their mission, the three troopers were returning to the CP when one man glanced to the side and saw four German helmets pop up from behind a mound. "Krauts!" he called out, as the trio of troopers leaped into a draw and began blazing away at the Germans, who were several hundred yards behind American forward positions.

Minutes after the shootout began the four enemy soldiers leaped from cover and dashed across a field, shooting back at the Americans as they ran.

One enemy bullet passed through Private Hill's helmet, the impact knocking him to the ground. Hill was dazed and frightened by the projectile zipping through his steel headgear less than one inch from his brain. As he lay there, Hill called out to DeCrenzo and Lauritsen, "I'm dead! I'm dead!"

The two sergeants looked at the helmet lying on the ground nearby, saw the neat hole where the bullet had entered and one where it had left, and examined Hill's head for some sign of blood or other injury. They saw none.

"You're okay, the bullet just went through your helmet," DeCrenzo assured the ashen-faced Hill. The two troopers got Hill to his feet, picked up his helmet and moved on the short distance to the battalion CP. There Colonel Williams noted Hill's still wobbly condition and inquired matter of factly to DeCrenzo, "What in the hell happened to him?"

"Oh, nothing much, colonel," DeCrenzo replied with a straight face. "Hill was only shot through the head."

After dawn on September 17, Colonel Rube Tucker, 504th commander, was ready to depart from his shell-swept CP on the little knoll at the base of Hill 424. "We're moving over to another ridge," Tucker told his men. "Williams' battalion should be over there."

The command group formed in single file with Colonel Tucker in the lead and moved off toward the rear of the knoll. Lieutenant Colonel Freeman and Lieutenant Richter, both of whom had been shot during the night while on a two-man patrol, hobbled painfully along. Swathed in blood-stained bandages, Freeman and Richter clutched .45 Colts in their hands.

Less than 40 yards to the rear of Tucker's CP the column of parachutists came upon the bodies of several Germans sprawled grotesquely along the narrow path and in adjoining vegetation. They were part of the enemy force that had charged up the rear slope during the night and had been driven off by the paratroopers.

As Colonel Tucker and his headquarters staff picked their way down the steep and rock-strewn path, off in the distance, in what should have been the rear area of the 504th Parachute Infantry Regiment, a German .88-millimeter gun barked several times.

"What's the bastard doing back there?" a perspiring trooper called out.

"Why doesn't someone get him?" another inquired aloud.

Tucker and his men soon reached the CP of Warren Williams' 1st Battalion, a complex of foxholes. "Better keep your eyes open," one of Williams' men cautioned the new arrivals. "There's been a sniper or two peppering us all day."

Tucker agreed, after a discussion with Williams, that Captain Harrison's company could probably hold Hill 424 until the rest of the 1st Battalion joined it there, and that Hill 415 should be held by elements of Williams' battalion until units of Dan Danielson's 2nd Battalion arrived to take over its objective—Hill 415. Tucker decided to set up his regimental command group between Hills 424 and 415, and to give priority to establishing telephone communications and a protected supply line with the beachhead.

Before marching off to set up his new command post, Tucker said to Lieutenant Colonel Freeman and Lieutenant Richter, "You two go on back to the rear and get patched up." He added: "Tell them to get some ammo, food and water to hell up here."

Colt pistols in hand, Freeman and Richter hobbled off. They halted at an aid station a short distance away to collect more of the walking wounded. Just as the column of troopers wearing bloody bandages and splints started to leave the field aid facility, enemy artillery shells came screaming in, exploding with great violence all around the Americans.

As the wounded Five-O-Fours flattened themselves to the ground, bursts of Schmeisser fire from thick vegetation on an adjoining hill whistled into their ranks. An enemy force had infiltrated far behind paratrooper foxholes on Hills 424 and 415. Other Americans opened fire in the direction of the concealed Germans and after a firefight of 10 minutes' duration a lull settled over the embattled aid station.

Taking advantage of the respite, Lieutenant Colonel Freeman, his blood-stained white bandages now a dirty brown, struggled to his feet. Brandishing his .45 Colt, he shouted to the other walking wounded, "Let's go!" He hobbled off down the rocky ridge with the other injured troopers in single file behind him. Every few yards the little group had to flop to the ground as incoming artillery shells sought them out. The German salvos followed the column for more than a mile.

The first night on a heavily-shelled Hill 424, Lieutenant Colonel Williams was lying on his back in a slit trench. A tree burst exploded nearby and the battalion commander felt a hard blow in the pit of his stomach. Unable to rise due to the nearby barrage, Williams ran his hands over the front of his body, certain that he had been wounded. He could find no blood. His hand touched a piece of hot metal on the bottom of the slit trench, and he instinctively recoiled from the pain. Next to the jagged shell fragment was his heavy belt buckle, which prevented the flying metal from penetrating his body.

Dame Fortune did not smile as benignly on Lieutenant Ned Walls, who was in a slit trench near Colonel Williams. He was hit and killed by a shell fragment in the same barrage.

Late on the second day of the bitter struggle for the commanding heights around Altavilla, the paratroopers received artillery support, and machine-guns and .81-millimeter mortars were brought forward. Now the parachutists would not have to rely solely on their marksmanship with rifles and Tommy guns to repel enemy assaults.

German artillery and mortars continued to pound the Five-O-Fours. An American artillery forward observer and his radio operator, in an exposed position, took a direct hit from an .88-millimeter gun and were killed instantly. Their deaths resulted in the artillery "eyes" of the 1st Battalion being blinded.

Sergeant Howard Jones, platoon sergeant of a machine-gun platoon, and Sergeant Milton "Fuzzy" Knight, who landed as a pathfinder the night of September 13, crawled out to the observation post where the crumpled bodies of the two artillery men lay. The troopers found that the radio was in good working order.

Jones and Knight had not reached the OP a minute too soon. Down in the valley they spotted several German tanks and an infantry column crossing a bridge. Although neither was trained as an artillery observer, they managed to contact the artillery fire direction center, pointed out the bridge site, and within minutes American shells were exploding among the Germans at the river span.

Minutes later the Germans began plastering the observation post with flat-trajectory .88-millimeter guns. Knight and Jones, their self-appointed mission a success, withdrew and rejoined their comrades.

Throughout September 17, the fighting at close quarters remained savage—and confusing for the 504th Parachute Infantry Regiment. It was not only confusing to the American paratrooper and German grenadier struggling face to face on the craggy mountains, but to higher level commanders on both sides as well. Back at headquarters of the U.S. VI Corps near the shoreline, General Mike Dawley, the corps commander, and General Matt Ridgway, leader of the 82nd Airborne Division but recently appointed to the additional post of deputy corps commander, were intently discussing the situation around Altavilla. From the vantage point of a corps headquarters, far removed from the front lines, it appeared that Colonel Rube Tucker's paratroopers were extremely hard pressed.

Knowing that the parachutists had been pounded by artillery incessantly, were under repeated ground attack and that an undetermined number of Germans had infiltrated behind the two 504th battalions perched on the key high ground overlooking the beachhead, General Dawley contacted Colonel Tucker by radio and suggested that the parachute regiment withdraw to more secure positions to the rear.

The proposal to withdraw infuriated the fighting heart of Rube Tucker. "Retreat, hell!" he shouted at the corps commander. ''We've taken this goddamned hill and we're keeping it! Send me my other battalion!''

Word of Colonel Tucker's vocal defiance to pulling back the regiment swept through the foxholes of the Five-O-Fours on the heights around Altavilla like a brush fire across a dry prairie. Paratrooper morale, already high, sky-rocketed. ''Retreat, hell!'' the men called gleefully to each other from their holes.

General Dawley and General Ridgway agreed to accept Colonel Tucker's forceful recommendation. The 3rd Battalion of the 504th Regiment, which had come in by sea in landing craft, was sent overland from the vicinity of the beach to the Albanella area to serve as backup for the 1st and 2nd Battalions. Now, with all three of his battalions in position as a cohesive unit, Rube Tucker was convinced the Germans would never dislodge his fighting men.

Late on the afternoon of the seventeenth, evidence that the death struggle along the Gulf of Salerno was tilting almost imperceptibly toward Mark Clark's Fifth Army appeared on the sandy white beaches. His four stars glistening in the rays of a setting Mediterranean sun, General Dwight D. Eisenhower, Supreme Commander of Allied Forces, stepped ashore from a landing craft.

The self-styled Kansas farm boy only three days before had been racked with deep concern over the fate of Fifth Army and its slender toehold on continental Europe. He had been aware of the whispers of ''an American Dunkirk'' in dark corners of his North African headquarters. Now, on the embattled beachhead itself, General Eisenhower was beaming broadly with the smile that had become world renowned.

Early on the morning of the eighteenth—D-Day + 9— Allied reconnaissance planes reported heavy German traffic moving northward from the beachhead. A patrol from the 1st Battalion of the 504th Parachute Infantry Regiment pushed far forward and reported finding no Germans, and paratroopers occupied Altavilla unopposed.

The *Wehrmacht* was also pulling back from the British right flank and English armor and Tommies entered the bitterly-contested road center of Battipaglia without firing a shot. General Troy Middleton's 45th and General Fred Walker's 36th Infantry Divisions pushed forward for several miles against minimal resistance and by nightfall had lost contact with the enemy.

Even as Colonel Reuben Tucker's parachutists were pushing on into Altavilla that September 18, more than 175,000 soldiers of the retreating German Tenth Army were reading a printed message from their commander, *General der Panzer Truppen* Heinrich von Vietinghoff. Amounting to a victory proclamation, the statement concluded:

> Success has been ours. Once again German soldiers
> have proved their superiority over the enemy.

On September 20 a regiment of the U.S. 36th Infantry Division relieved surviving American paratroopers on the heights around Altavilla, the once peaceful and insignificant little Italian mountain town. Grim-faced, bone-weary and hungry after several days of existing on ripe olives, Colonel Reuben Tucker's men climbed out of their foxholes, shouldered weapons and began the downhill trek to the rear and a brief respite from the horrors of war.

There was no sign of heady triumph on these tired, unshaven and once youthful faces. Too much had been seen. Too much had been endured. Too many close friends had been cut down in the prime of their lives. These fighting men with the bulky jump-suit pockets and ankle-high boots had viewed closeup the ghastly specter of the Black Angel of Death who had hovered over the heights around Altavilla, always reaching out to clasp Americans and Germans alike to her bosom.

The savage struggle for Salerno beachhead was over. The bloody confrontation for Adolph Hitler's *Festung Europa* was about to commence.

Epilogue

SHORTLY AFTER DAWN on September 23, Fifth Army artillery on Salerno beachhead unleashed a thunderous barrage on German positions along the Gulf of Salerno. Spearheaded by the British X Corps, General Mark Clark's forces struck northward for the primary objective of *Operation Avalanche*, the major city of Naples, 30 miles away.

Fighting over some of Europe's most rugged terrain and battling cold rains, enemy demolitions and a masterful rear guard action, the attack soon bogged down. General Clark rushed in the U.S. 82nd Airborne Division, and on the evening of September 29 patrols of Colonel James M. Gavin's 505th Parachute Infantry Regiment and the British 23rd Armored Brigade fought into the southern outskirts of Naples.

By October 1 the entire 82nd Airborne had moved into the port, and General Clark and General Matthew Ridgway made a triumphant entry into the first major European city to be captured by the Allies.

Meanwhile, individually, in pairs and small bands the men of the 509th Parachute Infantry Battalion infiltrated back toward the advancing Fifth Army from deep behind enemy lines. It would be three weeks from their mass jump the night of September 14–15 over 200 square miles of the Avellino region before all Five-O-Nines were accounted for.

Many of the returning paratroopers had severe diarrhea, some had wounds, most had cuts and bruises, all were weak from hunger, lack of sleep, and long days and nights of fighting and physical exertion. Only their steel spirits remained intact. In the final accounting, of the 641 men of the 509th Parachute Infantry Battalion who jumped in the perilous mission 532 made it back. Others survived the war in German prisoner of war camps.

To what extent did the parachute battalion accomplish its mission? Writing years later, James M. Gavin, who at 37 became commander of the 82nd Airborne Division and the youngest army major general since the Civil War, declared:

> The battalion accomplished what General Clark had in mind. Despite the handicap of being widely scattered, the men disrupted German communications and partly blocked enemy supplies and reserves.

> They also caused the Germans to keep anti-parachute missions that otherwise could have been used at the point of the German main effort at Salerno (beachhead).

Also writing in his memoirs six years after the war, General Mark Clark, later a four-star officer, who ordered the Avellino mission, said:

> The outfit did a wonderful job. They made many raids that seriously disrupted German communications . . . The mission of the 509th paid off in big dividends.

Lieutenant Colonel William P. Yarborough, Mark Clark's airborne advisor who recommended the three parachute missions to relieve the pressure on Fifth Army at Salerno, was appointed commander of the 509th Parachute Infantry Bat-

talion on September 30 when it was confirmed the unit's leader
had been wounded and captured near Avellino.

The jump by the two parachute regiments of the 82nd
Airborne Division to reinforce the hard-pressed ground forces
created a spectacular psychological boost to all ranks on the
embattled beachhead far in excess of the relatively modest
number of paratroopers involved. Sky warriors of the 504th
and 505th Parachute Infantry Regiments filled gaps in the
Allied lines denuded to stop German assaults elsewhere.

When victory or defeat hung in the balance in the death
struggle at Salerno, the three American ''crash'' parachute
missions helped tip the scales in favor of the Allies.

Principal Interviews
and Contacts

FIFTH ARMY HEADQUARTERS:

General Mark W. Clark (Ret.), Lieutenant General William P. Yarborough (Ret.)

82nd AIRBORNE DIVISION:

Colonel Mark J. Alexander (Ret.), Edward J. Bisso, Buffalo Boy Canoe, Sam DeCrenzo, Lieutenant General James M. Gavin (Ret.), Colonel Alfred W. Ireland (Ret.), Lieutenant Colonel G. Wilfred Jaubert (Ret.), Milton V. Knight, Lieutenant Colonel Walter B. Kroener (Ret.), Charles Sammon, Otis L. Sampson, Thomas Shockley, Lou Varrone, Colonel Warren R. Williams (Ret.), Ivan Woods.

509th PARACHUTE INFANTRY BATTALION:

Dr. Robert Akers, Colonel Carlos C. Alden (Ret.), Joseph Bauer, Lieutenant Colonel Archie Birkner (Ret.), Levi Carter, Dan A. DeLeo, Donald Ellis, Jack Faulkner, George Fontanesi, Adolph Fuessel, Stanley Gerk, Leon Maenhout, Royal Maynard, Lieutenant Colonel John R. Martin (Ret.), Edward W. Pawloski, Jack Pogue, Carl Salisbury, Ernest R. Siegel, William W. Sullivan, Dolphus R. Walker, Solomon Weber, Lloyd Wilson, Otto Weer.

Bibliography

BOOKS

Ambrose, Stephen E., *The Supreme Commander: The War Years of General Dwight D. Eisenhower*, New York, Doubleday, 1970.

Bauer, Eddy, *Encyclopedia of World War II*, New York, Marshall Cavendish Corp., 1970.

Bekker, Cajus, *The Luftwaffe War Diaries*, New York, Doubleday, 1969.

Blumenson, Martin, *Salerno to Cassino*, Washington, D.C., United States Army, 1969.

Bokum, Branco, *Spy in the Vatican*, New York, Praeger Publishers, 1973.

Brown, Anthony Cave, *Bodyguard of Lies*, New York, Harper & Row, 1975.

Butcher, Harry C., *My Three Years with Eisenhower*, New York, Simon & Schuster, 1946.

Churchill, Winston S., *Closing the Ring*, Boston, Houghton Mifflin, 1951.

Clark, Mark W., *Calculated Risk*, New York, Harper & Row, 1951.

Dawson, W. Forrest, *Saga of the All American*, Privately Printed, 1946.

Devlin, Gerard, M., *Paratrooper!*, New York, St. Martin's Press, 1979.

Eisenhower, Dwight D., *Crusade in Europe*, New York, Doubleday, 1948.

Foley, Charles, *Commando Extraordinary*, New York, Ballantine Books, 1955.

Garland, Albert N., *Sicily and the Surrender of Italy*, Washington, D.C., United States Army, 1965.

Gavin, James M., *On to Berlin: Battles of an Airborne Commander*, New York, Viking, 1978.

Gregory, Barry, and Batchelor, John, *Airborne Warfare*, London, Phoebus, 1979.

Keitel, Field Marshal Wilhelm, *The Memoirs of Field Marshal Keitel*, New York, Stein & Day, 1965.

Kesselring, Field Marshal Albert, *A Soldier's Record*, New York, William Morrow Co., 1954.

Killen, John, *A History of the Luftwaffe*, New York, Doubleday, 1968.

Lewin, Ronald, *Ultra Goes to War*, New York, McGraw-Hill, 1978.

Liddell Hart, B.H., *History of the Second World War*, New York, Putnam's Sons, 1971.

Montgomery, Field Marshal Bernard, *Memoirs*, London, Collins, 1958.

Morison, Samuel Elliott, *Sicily and Salerno*, Boston, Little, Brown & Co., 1954.

Pond, Hugh, *Salerno*, Boston, Little, Brown & Co., 1961.

Ridgway, Matthew B., *Soldier: The Memoirs of Matthew B. Ridgway*, New York, Harper, 1956.

Senger und Etterlin, General Fridolin von, *Neither Fear Nor Hope*, New York, Putnam's, 1964.

Shirer, William L., *The Rise and Fall of the Third Reich*, New York, Simon & Schuster, 1960.

Skorzeny, Otto, *Skorzeny's Secret Missions*, New York, E.P. Dutton, 1950.

Speer, Albert, *Inside the Third Reich*, New York, Macmillan Co., 1970.

Summersby, Kay, *Eisenhower Was My Boss*, New York, Prentice-Hall, 1948.

Taylor, Maxwell D., *Swords and Plowshares*, New York, W.W. Norton & Co., 1972.

Toland, John, *Adolf Hitler*, New York, Ballantine Books, 1972.

Tregaskis, Richard, *Invasion Diary*, New York, Random House, 1944.

Walker, General Fred L., *From Texas to Rome*, Taylor Publishing Co., Dallas, 1969.

Winterbotham, F.W., *The Ultra Secret*, New York, Harper & Row, 1974.

Yarborough, William P., *Bailout over North Africa*, Williamstown, N.J., Phillips Publications, 1979.

PERSONAL COMBAT DIARIES

Colonel Carlos C. Alden (Ret.), 509th Parachute Infantry Battalion.

Sam DeCrenzo, 504th Parachute Infantry, 82nd Airborne Division.

Major General Ralph Eaton (Ret.), Wartime Chief of Staff, 82nd Airborne Division.

Lieutenant Colonel John R. Martin (Ret.), 509th Parachute Infantry Battalion.

BOOKLETS

Andrews, John C., *Airborne Album*, Williamstown, N.J., Phillips Publications, 1982.

Davies, Howard, *British Parachute Forces*, New York, Arco, 1974.

Davis, Brian L., *German Parachute Forces*, New York, Arco, 1974.

Warren, Dr. John C., *Airborne Missions in the Mediterranean*, Department of the Air Force, 1955.

NEWSPAPER FILES

Chicago *Tribune*

St. Louis Globe-Democrat

MAGAZINES

Life

Men's Magazine

Saturday Evening Post

Time

MISCELLANEOUS

Allied Forces Headquarters Intelligence Summary, September 1-20, 1943

Index